The Great Illusion

A Study of the Relation of Military
Power to National Advantage

The Great Illusion

A Study of the Relation of Military
Power to National Advantage

By

Norman Angell

First Edition

Printed in the United States of America and Australia.

Bottom of the Hill Publishing
Memphis, TN
www.BottomoftheHillPublishing.com

ISBN: 9781483798646

PREFACE TO THE FOURTH AMERICAN EDITION

If this, the fourth American edition, is bulkier than its predecessors, it is chiefly because the events of the last two years throw an interesting light upon the bearing of the book's main thesis on actual world problems. I have, therefore, added an appendix dealing with certain criticisms based upon the nature of the first Balkan War, in the course of which I attempt to show just how the principles elaborated here have been working out in European politics.

That American interest in the problems here discussed is hardly less vital than that of Europe I am even more persuaded than when the first American edition of this book was issued in 1910. It is certain that opinion in America will not be equipped for dealing with her own problems arising out of her relations with the Spanish American states, with Japan, with the Philippines, unless it has some fair understanding of the principles with which this book deals. Its general interest even goes farther than this: no great community like that of modern America can remain indifferent to the drift of general opinion throughout the world on matters wrapped up with issues so important as those of war and peace.

That the tangible commercial and business interests of America are involved in these European events is obvious from the very factors of financial and commercial interdependence which form the basis of the argument.

That the interests of Americans are inextricably, if indirectly, bound up with those of Europe, has become increasingly clear as can be proved by the barest investigation of the trend of political thought in this country.

The thesis on its economic side is discussed in terms of the gravest problem which now faces European statesmanship, but these terms are also the living symbols of a principle of universal application, as true with reference to American conditions as to European. If I have not "localized" the discussion by using illustrations drawn from purely American cases, it is because these problems have not at present, in the United States, reached the acute stage that they have in Europe, and illustrations drawn from the conditions of an actual and pressing problem give to any discussion a reality which to some extent it might lose if discussed on the basis of more supposititious cases.

It so happens, however, that in the more abstract section of the discussion embraced in the second part, which I have termed the "Human Nature of the Case," I have gone mainly to American authors for the statement of cases based on those illusions with which the book deals.

For this edition I have thought it worthwhile thoroughly to revise the whole of the book and to re-write the chapter on the payment of the French Indemnity, in order to clear up a misunderstanding to which in its first form it gave rise. Part III has also been re-written, in order to meet the changed form of criticism which has resulted from the discussion of this subject during the last year or two.

It is with very great regret that I have seen this book grow in bulk; but as it constitutes the statement of a thesis still revolutionary, it has to cover the whole ground of the discussion, sometimes in great detail. I have, however, adopted an arrangement and method of presentation by which, I trust, the increase in bulk will not render it less clear. The general arrangement is as follows:

The Synopsis is a very brief indication of the scope of the whole argument, which is not that war is impossible, but that it is futile--useless, even when completely victorious, as a means of securing those moral or material ends which represent the needs of modern civilized peoples; and that on a general realization of this truth depends the solution of the problem of armaments and warfare.

The general economic argument is summarized in Chapter III, Part I.

The moral, psychological, and biological argument is summarized in Chapter II, Part II.

The practical outcome--what should be our policy with reference to defense, why progress depends upon the improvement of public opinion and the best general methods of securing that--is discussed in Part III.

This method of treatment has involved some small repetition of fact and illustration, but the repetition is trifling in bulk--it does not amount in all to the value of more than three or four pages--and I have been more concerned to make the matter in hand clear to the reader than to observe all the literary canons. I may add that, apart from this, the process of condensation has been carried to its extreme limit for the character of data dealt with, and that those who desire to understand thoroughly the significance of the thesis with which the book deals--it is worth understanding--had really better read every line of it!

One personal word may perhaps be excused as explaining certain phraseology, which would seem to indicate that the author is of English nationality. He happens to be of English birth, but to have passed his youth and early manhood in the United States, having acquired American citizenship there. This I hope entitles him to use the collective "we" on both sides of the Atlantic. I may add that the last fifteen years have been passed mainly in Europe studying at first hand the problems here dealt with.

N. A. LONDON, October, 1913.

PREFACE

The present volume is the outcome of a large pamphlet published in Europe at the end of last year entitled *Europe's Optical Illusion*. The interest that the pamphlet created and the character of the discussion provoked throughout Europe persuaded me that its subject-matter was worth fuller and more detailed treatment than then given it. Herewith the result of that conviction. The thesis on its economic side is discussed in the terms of the gravest problem which now faces European statesmanship, but these terms are also the living symbols of a principle of universal application, as true with reference to American conditions as to European. If I have not "localized" the discussion by using illustrations drawn from purely American cases, it is because these problems have not at present in the United States reached the acute stage that they have in Europe, and illustrations drawn from the conditions of an actual and pressing problem give to any discussion a reality which to some extent it might lose if discussed on the basis of more suppositious cases.

It so happens, however, that in the more abstract section of the discussion embraced in the second part, which I have termed the "Human Nature of the Case," I have gone mainly to American authors for the statement of cases based on those illusions with which the book deals.

N. A. PARIS, August, 1910.

SYNOPSIS

What are the fundamental motives that explain the present rivalry of armaments in Europe, notably the Anglo-German? Each nation pleads the need for defense; but this implies that someone is likely to attack, and has therefore a presumed interest in so doing. What are the motives which each State thus fears its neighbors may obey?

They are based on the universal assumption that a nation, in order to find outlets for expanding population and increasing industry, or simply to ensure the best conditions possible for its people, is necessarily pushed to territorial expansion and the exercise of political force against others (German naval competition is assumed to be the expression of the growing need of an expanding population for a larger place in the world, a need which will find a realization in the conquest of English Colonies or trade, unless these are defended); it is assumed, therefore, that a nation's relative prosperity is broadly determined by its political power; that nations being competing units, advantage, in the last resort, goes to the possessor of preponderant military force, the weaker going to the wall, as in the other forms of the struggle for life.

The author challenges this whole doctrine. He attempts to show that it belongs to a stage of development out of which we have passed; that the commerce and industry of a people no longer depend upon the expansion of its political frontiers; that a nation's political and economic frontiers do not now necessarily coincide; that military power is socially and economically futile, and can have no relation to the prosperity of the people exercising it; that it is impossible for one nation to seize by force the wealth or trade of another--to enrich itself by subjugating, or imposing its will by force on another; that, in short, war, even when victorious, can no longer achieve those aims for which peoples strive.

He establishes this apparent paradox, in so far as the economic problem is concerned, by showing that wealth in the economically civilized world is founded upon credit and commercial contract (these being the outgrowth of an economic interdependence due to the increasing division of labor and greatly developed communication). If credit and commercial contract are tampered with in an attempt at confiscation, the credit-dependent wealth is undermined, and its collapse involves that of the conqueror; so that if conquest is not to be self-injurious it must respect the enemy's property, in which case it becomes economically futile. Thus the wealth of conquered territory remains in the hands of the population of such territory. When Germany annexed Alsatia, no individual German secured a single mark's worth of Alsatian property as the spoils of war. Conquest in the modern world is a process of multiplying by x, and then obtaining the original figure by dividing by x. For a modern nation to add to its territory no more adds to the wealth of the people of such nation than it would add to the wealth of Londoners if the City of London were to annex the county of Hertford.

The author also shows that international finance has become so inter-dependent and so interwoven with trade and industry that the intangi-bility of an enemy's property extends to his trade. It results that political and military power can in reality do nothing for trade; the individual merchants and manufacturers of small nations, exercising no such power, compete successfully with those of the great. Swiss and Belgian merchants drive English from the British Colonial market; Norway has, relatively to population, a greater mercantile marine than Great Britain; the public credit (as a rough-and-ready indication, among others, of se-curity and wealth) of small States possessing no political power often stands higher than that of the Great Powers of Europe, Belgian Three per Cents. standing at 96, and German at 82; Norwegian Three and a Half per Cents. at 102, and Russian Three and a Half per Cent at 81.

The forces which have brought about the economic futility of military power have also rendered it futile as a means of enforcing a nation's moral ideals or imposing social institutions upon a conquered people. Germany could not turn Canada or Australia into German colonies--*i.e.*, stamp out their language, law, literature, traditions, etc.--by "capturing" them. The necessary security in their material possessions enjoyed by the inhabitants of such conquered provinces, quick inter-communica-tion by a cheap press, widely-read literature, enable even small commu-nities to become articulate and effectively to defend their special social or moral possessions, even when military conquest has been complete. The fight for ideals can no longer take the form of fight between nations, because the lines of division on moral questions are within the nations themselves and intersect the political frontiers. There is no modern State which is completely Catholic or Protestant, or liberal or autocratic, or aristocratic or democratic, or socialist or individualist; the moral and spiritual struggles of the modern world go on between citizens of the same State in unconscious intellectual co-operation with corresponding groups in other States, not between the public powers of rival States.

This classification by strata involves necessarily a redirection of human pugnacity, based rather on the rivalry of classes and interests than on State divisions. War has no longer the justification that it makes for the survival of the fittest; it involves the survival of the less fit. The idea that the struggle between nations is a part of the evolutionary law of man's advance involves a profound misreading of the biological analogy.

The warlike nations do not inherit the earth; they represent the decay-ing human element. The diminishing rôle of physical force in all spheres of human activity carries with it profound psychological modifications.

These tendencies, mainly the outcome of purely modern conditions (*e.g.* rapidity of communication), have rendered the problems of modern international politics profoundly and essentially different from the ancient; yet our ideas are still dominated by the principles and axioms, images and terminology of the bygone days.

The author urges that these little-recognized facts may be utilized for the solution of the armament difficulty on at present untried lines--by such modification of opinion in Europe that much of the present motive to aggression will cease to be operative, and by thus diminishing the risk of attack, diminishing to the same extent the need for defense. He shows how such a political reformation is within the scope of practical politics, and the methods which should be employed to bring it about.

CONTENTS

England--German trade dependent upon English credit--Confiscation of an enemy's property an economic impossibility under modern conditions--Intangibility of a community's wealth.

The non-economic motives of war--Moral and psychological-
-The importance of these pleas--English, German, and American exponents--The biological plea.

THE PSYCHOLOGICAL CASE FOR PEACE
The shifting ground of pro-war arguments--The narrowing
gulf between the material and moral ideals--The non-rational
causes of war--False biological analogies--The real law of man's
struggles: struggle with Nature, not with other men--Outline
sketch of man's advance and main operating factor therein-
-The progress towards elimination of physical force--Co-oper-
ation across frontiers and its psychological result--Impossible
to fix limits of community--Such limits irresistibly expanding-
-Break-up of State homogeneity--State limits no longer coinciding with real conflicts between men.

UNCHANGING HUMAN NATURE
The progress from cannibalism to Herbert Spencer--The disappearance of religious oppression by Government--Disappear-
ance of the duel--The Crusaders and the Holy Sepulcher--The
wail of militarist writers at man's drift away from militancy.

DO THE WARLIKE NATIONS INHERIT THE EARTH?
The confident dogmatism of militarist writers on this subject-
-The facts--The lessons of Spanish America--How conquest
makes for the survival of the unfit--Spanish method and Eng-
lish method in the New World--The virtues of military training-
-The Dreyfus case--The threatened Germanization of England-
"The war which made Germany great and Germans small."

THE DIMINISHING FACTOR OF PHYSICAL FORCE: PSYCHO-
LOGICAL RESULTS
Diminishing factor of physical force--Though diminishing,
physical force has always had an important rôle in human af-
fairs--What is underlying principle, determining advantageous
and disadvantageous use of physical force?--Force that aids
co-operation in accord with law of man's advance: force that
is exercised for parasitism in conflict with such law and disadvantageous for both parties--Historical process of the abandonment of physical force--The Khan and the London tradesman-
-Ancient Rome and modern Britain--The sentimental defense of
war as the purifier of human life--The facts--The redirection of
human pugnacity.

PART I

THE ECONOMICS OF THE CASE

CHAPTER I

STATEMENT OF THE ECONOMIC CASE FOR WAR

Where can the Anglo-German rivalry of armaments end?--Why peace advocacy fails--Why it deserves to fail--The attitude of the peace advocate--The presumption that the prosperity of nations depends upon their political power, and consequent necessity of protection against aggression of other nations who would diminish our power to their advantage--These the universal axioms of international politics.

It is generally admitted that the present rivalry in armaments in Europe--notably such as that now in progress between England and Germany--cannot go on in its present form indefinitely. The net result of each side meeting the efforts of the other with similar efforts is that at the end of a given period the relative position of each is what it was originally, and the enormous sacrifices of both have gone for nothing. If as between England and Germany it is claimed that England is in a position to maintain the lead because she has the money, Germany can retort that she is in a position to maintain the lead because she has the population, which must, in the case of a highly organized European nation, in the end mean money. Meanwhile, neither side can yield to the other, as the one so doing would, it is felt, be placed at the mercy of the other, a situation which neither will accept.

There are two current solutions which are offered as a means of egress from this *impasse*. There is that of the smaller party, regarded in both countries for the most part as one of dreamers and doctrinaires, who hope to solve the problem by a resort to general disarmament, or, at least, a limitation of armament by agreement. And there is that of the larger, which is esteemed the more practical party, of those who are persuaded that the present state of rivalry and recurrent irritation is bound to culminate in an armed conflict, which, by definitely reducing one or other of the parties to a position of manifest inferiority, will settle the thing for at least some time, until after a longer or shorter period a state of relative equilibrium is established, and the whole process will be recommenced *da capo*.

This second solution is, on the whole, accepted as one of the laws of life: one of the hard facts of existence which men of ordinary courage take as all in the day's work. And in every country those favoring the other solution are looked upon either as people who fail to realize the hard facts of the world in which they live, or as people less concerned with the security of their country than with upholding a somewhat emasculate ideal; ready to weaken the defenses of their own country on no better assurance than that the prospective enemy will not be so wicked as to attack them.

To this the virile man is apt to oppose the law of conflict. Most of what the nineteenth century has taught us of the evolution of life on the planet is pressed into the service of this struggle-for-life philosophy. We are reminded of the survival of the fittest, that the weakest go to the wall, and that all life, sentient and non-sentient, is but a life of battle. The sacrifice involved in armament is the price which nations pay for their safety and for their political power. The power of England has been the main condition of her past industrial success; her trade has been extensive and her merchants rich, because she has been able to make her political and military force felt, and to exercise her influence among all the nations of the world. If she has dominated the commerce of the world, it is because her unconquered navy has dominated, and continues to dominate, all the avenues of commerce. This is the currently accepted argument.

The fact that Germany has of late come to the front as an industrial nation, making giant strides in general prosperity and well-being, is deemed also to be the result of *her* military successes and the increasing political power which she is coming to exercise in Continental Europe. These things, alike in England and in Germany, are accepted as the axioms of the problem, as the citations given in the next chapter sufficiently prove. I am not aware that a single authority of note, at least in the world of workaday politics, has ever challenged or disputed them. Even those who have occupied prominent positions in the propaganda of peace are at one with the veriest fire-eaters on this point. Mr. W. T. Stead was one of the leaders of the big navy party in England. Mr. Frederic Harrison, who all his life had been known as the philosopher protagonist of peace, declared recently that, if England allowed Germany to get ahead of her in the race for armaments, "famine, social anarchy, incalculable chaos in the industrial and financial world, would be the inevitable result. Britain may live on ... but before she began to live freely again she would have to lose half her population, which she could not feed, and all her overseas Empire, which she could not defend.... How idle are fine words about retrenchment, peace, and brotherhood, whilst we lie open to the risk of unutterable ruin, to a deadly fight for national existence, to war in its most destructive and cruel form." On the other side we have friendly critics of England, like Professor von Schulze-Gaevernitz, writing: "We want our [*i.e.* Germany's] navy in order to confine the commercial rivalry of England within innocuous limits, and to deter the sober sense of the English people from the extremely threatening thought of attack upon

us.... The German navy is a condition of our bare existence and independence, like the daily bread on which we depend not only for ourselves,
but for our children."

Confronted by a situation of this sort, one is bound to feel that the ordinary argument of the pacifist entirely breaks down; and it breaks down
for a very simple reason. He himself accepts the premise which has just
been indicated--viz., that the victorious party in the struggle for political
predominance gains some material advantage over the party which is
conquered. The proposition even to the pacifist seems so self-evident that
he makes no effort to combat it. He pleads his case otherwise. "It cannot be denied, of course," says one peace advocate, "that the thief *does*
secure some material advantage by his theft. What we plead is that if the
two parties were to devote to honest labor the time and energy devoted
to preying upon each other, the permanent gain would more than offset
the occasional booty."

Some pacifists go further, and take the ground that there is a conflict
between the natural law and the moral law, and that we must choose the
moral even to our hurt. Thus Mr. Edward Grubb writes:

Self-preservation is not the final law for nations any more than for
individuals.... The progress of humanity may demand the extinction (in
this world) of the individual, and it may demand also the example and
the inspiration of a martyr nation. So long as the Divine providence has
need of us, Christian faith requires that we shall trust for our safety to
the unseen but real forces of right dealing, truthfulness, and love; but,
should the will of God demand it, we must be prepared, as Jeremiah
taught his nation long ago, to give up even our national life for furthering
those great ends "to which the whole creation moves."

This may be "fanaticism," but, if so, it is the fanaticism of Christ and
of the prophets, and we are willing to take our places along with them.[1]

The foregoing is really the keynote of much pacifist propaganda. In our
own day, Count Tolstoi has even expressed anger at the suggestion that
any reaction against militarism, on other than moral grounds, can be
efficacious.

The peace advocate pleads for "altruism" in international relationships, and in so doing admits that successful war may be to the interest,
though the immoral interest, of the victorious party. That is why the "inhumanity" of war bulks so largely in his propaganda, and why he dwells
so much upon its horrors and cruelties.

It thus results that the workaday world and those engaged in the rough
and tumble of practical politics have come to look upon the peace ideal
as a counsel of perfection, which may one day be attained when human
nature, as the common phrase is, has been improved out of existence,
but not while human nature remains what it is. While it remains possible
to seize a tangible advantage by a man's strong right arm the advantage
will be seized, and woe betide the man who cannot defend himself.

Nor is this philosophy of force either as conscienceless, as brutal, or as ruthless as its common statement would make it appear. We know that in the world as it exists to-day, in spheres other than those of international rivalry, the race is to the strong, and the weak get scant consideration. Industrialism and commercialism are as full of cruelties as war itself--cruelties, indeed, that are longer drawn out, more refined, though less apparent, and, it may be, appealing less to the common imagination than those of war. With whatever reticence we may put the philosophy into words, we all feel that conflict of interests in this world is inevitable, and that what is an incident of our daily lives should not be shirked as a condition of those occasional titanic conflicts which mould the history of the world.

The virile man doubts whether he ought to be moved by the plea of the "inhumanity" of war. The masculine mind accepts suffering, death itself, as a risk which we are all prepared to run even in the most unheroic forms of money-making; none of us refuses to use the railway train because of the occasional smash, to travel because of the occasional shipwreck, and so on. Indeed, peaceful industry demands a heavier toll even in blood than does a war, fact which the casualty statistics in railroading, fishing, mining and seamanship, eloquently attest; while such peaceful industries as fishing and shipping are the cause of as much brutality.[2] The peaceful administration of the tropics takes as heavy a toll in the health and lives of good men, and much of it, as in the West of Africa, involves, unhappily, a moral deterioration of human character as great as that which can be put to the account of war.

Beside these peace sacrifices the "price of war" is trivial, and it is felt that the trustees of a nation's interests ought not to shrink from paying that price should the efficient protection of those interests demand it. If the common man is prepared, as we know he is, to risk his life in a dozen dangerous trades and professions for no object higher than that of improving his position or increasing his income, why should the statesman shrink from such sacrifices as the average war demands, if thereby the great interests which have been confided to him can be advanced? If it be true, as even the pacifist admits that it may be true, that the tangible material interests of a nation can be advanced by warfare; if, in other words, warfare can play some large part in the protection of the interests of humanity, the rulers of a courageous people are justified in disregarding the suffering and the sacrifice that it may involve.

Of course, the pacifist falls back upon the moral plea: we have no right to take by force. But here again the common sense of ordinary humanity does not follow the peace advocate. If the individual manufacturer is entitled to use all the advantages which great financial and industrial resources may give him against a less powerful competitor, if he is entitled, as under our present industrial scheme he is entitled, to overcome competition by a costly and perfected organization of manufacture, of advertisement, of salesmanship, in a trade in which poorer men gain their livelihood, why should not the nation be entitled to overcome the rivalry of other nations by utilizing the force of its public services? It is a commonplace of industrial competition that the "big man" takes advantage of *all* the weaknesses of the small man--his narrow means, his ill-health even--to undermine and to undersell. If it were true that industrial competition were always merciful, and national or political competition always cruel, the plea of the peace man might be unanswerable; but we know, as a matter of fact, that this is not the case, and, returning to our starting-point, the common man feels that he is obliged to accept the world as he finds it, that struggle and warfare, in one form or another, are among the conditions of life, conditions which he did not make. Moreover he is not at all sure that the warfare of arms is necessarily either the hardest or the most cruel form of that struggle which exists throughout the universe. In any case, he is willing to take the risks, because he feels that military predominance gives him a real and tangible advantage, a material advantage translatable into terms of general social well-being, by enlarged commercial opportunities, wider markets, protection against the aggression of commercial rivals, and so on. He faces the risk of war in the same spirit as that in which a sailor or a fisherman faces the risk of drowning, or a miner that of the choke damp, or a doctor that of a fatal disease, because he would rather take the supreme risk than accept for himself and his dependents a lower situation, a narrower and meaner existence, with complete safety. He also asks whether the lower path is altogether free from risks. If he knows much of life he knows that in very many circumstances the bolder way is the safer way.

That is why it is that the peace propaganda has so signally failed, and why the public opinion of the countries of Europe, far from restraining the tendency of their Governments to increase armaments, is pushing them into still greater expenditure. It is universally assumed that national power means national wealth, national advantage; that expanding territory means increased opportunity for industry; that the strong nation can guarantee opportunities for its citizens that the weak nation cannot. The Englishman, for instance, believes that his wealth is largely the result of his political power, of his political domination, mainly of his sea power; that Germany with her expanding population must feel cramped; that she must fight for elbow-room; and that if he does not defend himself he will illustrate that universal law which makes of every stomach a graveyard. He has a natural preference for being the diner rather than the dinner. As it is universally admitted that wealth and prosperity and well-being go with strength and power and national greatness, he intends, so long as he is able, to maintain that strength and power and greatness, and not to yield it even in the name of altruism. And he will not yield it, because should he do so it would be simply to replace British power and greatness by the power and greatness of some other nation, which he feels sure would do no more for the well-being of civilization as a whole than he is prepared to do. He is persuaded that he can no more yield in the competition of armaments, than as a business man or as a manufacturer he could yield in commercial competition to his rival; that he must fight out his salvation under conditions as he finds them, since he did not make them, and since he cannot change them.

Admitting his premises--and these premises are the universally accepted axioms of international politics the world over--who shall say that he is wrong?

CHAPTER II

THE AXIOMS OF MODERN STATECRAFT

Are the foregoing axioms unchallengeable?--Some typical statements of them--German dreams of conquest--Mr. Frederic Harrison on results of defeat of British arms and invasion of England--Forty millions starving.

Are the axioms set out in the last chapter unchallengeable?

Is it true that the wealth, prosperity and well-being of a nation depend upon its military power, or have necessarily anything whatever to do therewith?

Can one civilized nation gain moral or material advantage by the military conquest of another?

Does conquered territory add to the wealth of the conquering nation?

Is it possible for a nation to "own" the territory of another in the way that a person or corporation would "own" an estate?

Could Germany "take" English trade and Colonies by military force?

Could she turn English Colonies into German ones, and win an overseas empire by the sword, as England won hers in the past?

Does a modern nation need to expand its political boundaries in order to provide for increasing population?

If England could conquer Germany to-morrow, completely conquer her, reduce her nationality to so much dust, would the ordinary British subject be the better for it?

If Germany could conquer England, would any ordinary German subject be the better for it?

The fact that all these questions have to be answered in the negative, and that a negative answer seems to outrage common sense, shows how much our political axioms are in need of revision.

The literature on the subject leaves no doubt whatever that I have correctly stated the premises of the matter in the foregoing chapter. Those whose special vocation is the philosophy of statecraft in the international field, from Aristotle and Plato, passing by Machiavelli and Clausewitz down to Mr. Roosevelt and the German Emperor, have left us in no doubt whatever on the point. The whole view has been admirably summarized by two notable writers--Admiral Mahan, on the Anglo-Saxon side, and Baron Karl von Stengel (second German delegate to the First Hague Conference) on the German. Admiral Mahan says:

The old predatory instinct that he should take who has the power survives ... and moral force is not sufficient to determine issues unless supported by physical. Governments are corporations, and corporations have no souls; governments, moreover, are trustees, and as such must put first the lawful interests of their wards--their own people.... More and more Germany needs the assured importation of raw materials, and, where possible, control of regions productive of such materials. More and more she requires assured markets and security as to the importation of food, since less and less comparatively is produced within her own borders by her rapidly increasing population. This all means security at sea.... Yet the supremacy of Great Britain in European seas means a perpetually latent control of German commerce.... The world has long been accustomed to the idea of a predominant naval power, coupling it with the name of Great Britain, and it has been noted that such power, when achieved, is commonly often associated with commercial and industrial predominance, the struggle for which is now in progress between Great Britain and Germany. Such predominance forces a nation to seek markets, and, where possible, to control them to its own advantage by preponderant force, the ultimate expression of which is possession.... From this flow two results: the attempt to possess and the organization of force by which to maintain possession already achieved.... This statement is simply a specific formulation of the general necessity stated; it is an inevitable link in the chain of logical sequences--industrial markets, control, navy bases....[3]

But in order to show that this is no special view, and that this philosophy does indeed represent the general public opinion of Europe, the opinion of the great mass which prompts the actions of Governments and explains their respective policies, I take the following from the current newspapers and reviews ready to my hand:

It is the prowess of our navy ... our dominant position at sea ... which has built up the British Empire and its commerce.--London *Times* leading article.

Because her commerce is infinitely vulnerable, and because her people are dependent upon that commerce for food and the wages with which to buy it.... Britain wants a powerful fleet, a perfect organization behind the fleet, and an army of defense. Until they are provided this country will exist under perpetual menace from the growing fleet of German *Dreadnoughts*, which have made the North Sea their parade-ground. All security will disappear, and British commerce and industry, when no man knows what the morrow will bring forth, must rapidly decline, thus accentuating British national degeneracy and decadence.--H. W. Wilson in the *National Review*, May, 1909.

Sea-power is the last fact which stands between Germany and the supreme position in international commerce. At present Germany sends only some fifty million pounds worth, or about a seventh, of her total domestic produce to the markets of the world outside Europe and the United States.... Does any man who understands the subject think there is any power in Germany, or, indeed, any power in the world, which can prevent Germany, she having thus accomplished the first stage of her work, from now closing with Great Britain for her ultimate share of this

240 millions of overseas trade? Here it is that we unmask the shadow which looms like a real presence behind all the moves of present-day diplomacy, and behind all the colossal armaments that indicate the present preparations for a new struggle for sea-power.--Mr. Benjamin Kidd in the *Fortnightly Review*, April 1, 1910.

It is idle to talk of "limitation of armaments" unless the nations of the earth will unanimously consent to lay aside all selfish ambitions.... Nations, like individuals, concern themselves chiefly with their own interests, and when these clash with those of others, quarrels are apt to follow. If the aggrieved party is the weaker he usually goes to the wall, though "right" be never so much on his side; and the stronger, whether he be the aggressor or not, usually has his own way. In international politics charity begins at home, and quite properly; the duty of a statesman is to think first of the interests of his own country.--*United Service Magazine*, May, 1909.

Why should Germany attack Britain? Because Germany and Britain are commercial and political rivals; because Germany covets the trade, the colonies, and the Empire which Britain now possesses.--Robert Blatchford, "Germany and England," p. 4.

Great Britain, with her present population, exists by virtue of her foreign trade and her control of the carrying trade of the world; defeat in war would mean the transference of both to other hands and consequent starvation for a large percentage of the wage-earners.--T.G. Martin in the London *World*.

We offer an enormously rich prize if we are not able to defend our shores; we may be perfectly certain that the prize which we offer will go into the mouth of somebody powerful enough to overcome our resistance and to swallow a considerable portion of us up.--The Speaker of the House of Commons in a speech at Greystoke, reported by the London *Times*.

What is good for the beehive is good for the bee. Whatever brings rich lands, new ports, or wealthy industrial areas to a State enriches its treasury, and therefore the nation at large, and therefore the individual.--Mr. Douglas Owen in a letter to the *Economist*, May 28, 1910.

Do not forget that in war there is no such thing as international law, and that undefended wealth will be seized wherever it is exposed, whether through the broken pane of a jeweler's window or owing to the obsession of a humanitarian Celt.--London *Referee*, November 14, 1909.

We appear to have forgotten the fundamental truth--confirmed by all history--that the warlike races inherit the earth, and that Nature decrees the survival of the fittest in the never-ending struggle for existence.... Our yearning for disarmament, our respect for the tender plant of Nonconformist conscience, and the parrot-like repetition of the misleading formula that the "greatest of all British interests is peace" ... must inevitably give to any people who covet our wealth and our possessions ... the ambition to strike a swift and deadly blow at the heart of the Empire-

-undefended London.--*Blackwood's Magazine*, May, 1909.

These are taken from English sources, but there is not a straw to choose between them and other European opinion on the subject.

Admiral Mahan and the other Anglo-Saxons of his school have their counterpart in every European country, but more especially in Germany. Even so "Liberal" a statesman as Baron Karl von Stengel, the German delegate to the First Hague Peace Conference, lays it down in his book that--

Every great Power must employ its efforts towards exercising the largest influence possible, not only in European but in world politics, and this mainly because economic power depends in the last resort on political power, and because the largest participation possible in the trade of the world is a vital question for every nation.

The writings of such classic authorities as Clausewitz give full confirmation of this view, while it is the resounding note of most popular German political literature that deals with "Weltpolitik." Grand Admiral von Koster, President of the Navy League, writes:

The steady increase of our population compels us to devote special attention to the growth of our overseas interests. Nothing but the strong fulfillment of our naval program can create for us that importance upon the free-world-sea which it is incumbent upon us to demand. The steady increase of our population compels us to set ourselves new goals and to grow from a Continental into a world power. Our mighty industry must aspire to new overseas conquests. Our world trade--which has more than doubled in twenty years, which has increased from 2500 million dollars to 4000 million dollars during the ten years in which our naval program was fixed, and 3000 million dollars of which is sea-borne commerce--only can flourish if we continue honorably to bear the burdens of our armaments on land and sea alike. Unless our children are to accuse us of short-sightedness, it is now our duty to secure our world power and position among other nations. We can do that only under the protection of a strong German fleet, a fleet which shall guarantee us peace with honor for the distant future.

One popular German writer sees the possibility of "overthrowing the British Empire" and "wiping it from the map of the world in less than twenty-four hours." (I quote his actual words, and I have heard a parallel utterance from the mouth of a serious English public man.) The author in question, in order to show how the thing could come about, deals with the matter prophetically. Writing from the standpoint of 1911,[4] he admits that--

At the beginning of the twentieth century Great Britain was a free, a rich, and a happy country, in which every citizen, from the Prime Minister to the dock-laborer, was proud to be a member of the world-ruling nation. At the head of the State were men possessing a general mandate to carry out their program of government, whose actions were subject to the criticism of public opinion, represented by an independent Press.

Educated for centuries in self-government, a race had grown up which seemed born to rule. The highest triumphs attended England's skill in the art of government, in her handling of subject peoples.... And this immense Empire, which stretched from the Cape to Cairo, over the southern half of Asia, over half of North America and the fifth continent, could be wiped from the map of the world in less than twenty-four hours! This apparently inexplicable fact will be intelligible if we keep in sight the circumstances which rendered possible the building up of England's colonial power. The true basis of her world supremacy was not her own strength, but the maritime weakness of all the other European nations. Their almost complete lack of naval preparations had given the English a position of monopoly which was used by them for the annexation of all those dominions which seemed of value. Had it been in England's power to keep the rest of the world as it was in the nineteenth century, the British Empire might have continued for an unlimited time. The awakening of the Continental States to their national possibilities and to political independence introduced quite new factors into Weltpolitik, and it was only a question of time as to how long England could maintain her position in the face of the changed circumstances.

And the writer tells how the trick was done, thanks to a fog, efficient espionage, the bursting of the English war balloon, and the success of the German one in dropping shells at the correct tactical moment on to the British ships in the North Sea:

This war, which was decided by a naval battle lasting a single hour, was of only three weeks' duration--hunger forced England into peace. In her conditions Germany showed a wise moderation. In addition to a war indemnity in accordance with the wealth of the two conquered States, she contented herself with the acquisition of the African Colonies, with the exception of the southern States, which had proclaimed their independence, and these possessions were divided with the other two powers of the Triple Alliance. Nevertheless, this war was the end of England. A lost battle had sufficed to manifest to the world at large the feet of clay on which the dreaded Colossus had stood. In a night the British Empire had crumbled altogether; the pillars which English diplomacy had erected after years of labour had failed at the first test.

A glance at any average Pan-Germanist organ will reveal immediately how very nearly the foregoing corresponds to a somewhat prevalent type of political aspiration in Germany. One Pan-Germanist writer says:

"The future of Germany demands the absorption of Austria-Hungary, the Balkan States, and Turkey, with the North Sea ports. Her realms will stretch towards the east from Berlin to Bagdad, and to Antwerp on the west."

For the moment we are assured there is no immediate intention of seizing the countries in question, nor is Germany's hand actually ready yet to catch Belgium and Holland within the net of the Federated Empire.

"But," he says, "all these changes will happen within our epoch," and he fixes the time when the map of Europe will thus be rearranged as from twenty to thirty years hence.

Germany, according to the writer, means to fight while she has a penny left and a man to carry arms, for she is, he says, "face to face with a crisis which is more serious than even that of Jena."

And, recognizing the position, she is only waiting for the moment she judges the right one to break in pieces those of her neighbors who work against her.

France will be her first victim, and she will not wait to be attacked. She is, indeed, preparing for the moment when the allied Powers attempt to dictate to her.

Germany, it would seem, has already decided to annex the Grand Duchy of Luxemburg, and Belgium, incidentally with, of course, Antwerp, and will add all the northern provinces of France to her possessions, so as to secure Boulogne and Calais.

All this is to come like a thunderbolt, and Russia, Spain, and the rest of the Powers friendly to England will not dare to move a finger to aid her. The possession of the coasts of France and Belgium will dispose of England's supremacy forever.

In a book on South Africa entitled "Reisen Erlebnisse und Beobachtungen," by Dr. F. Bachmar, occurs the passage:

"My second object in writing this book is that it may happen to our children's children to possess that beautiful and unhappy land of whose final absorption (*gewinnung*) by our Anglo-Saxon cousins I have not the least belief. It may be our lot to unite this land with the German Fatherland, to be equally a blessing to Germany and South Africa."

The necessity for armament is put in other than fictional form by so serious a writer as Dr. Gaevernitz, Pro-Rector of the University of Freiburg. Dr. Schulze-Gaevernitz is not unknown in England, nor is he imbued with inimical feelings towards her. But he takes the view that the commercial prosperity of Germany depends upon her political domination.[5]

After having described in an impressive way the astonishing growth of Germany's trade and commerce, and shown how dangerous a competitor Germany has become for England, he returns to the old question, and asks what might happen if England, unable to keep down the inconvenient upstart by economic means, should, at the eleventh hour, try to knock him down. Quotations from the *National Review*, the *Observer*, the *Outlook*, the *Saturday Review*, etc., facilitate the professor's thesis that this presumption is more than a mere abstract speculation. Granted that they voice only the sentiments of a small minority, they are, according to our author, dangerous for Germany in this--that they point to a feasible and consequently enticing solution. The old peaceful Free Trade, he says, shows signs of senility. A new and rising Imperialism is everywhere inclined to throw the weapons of political warfare into the arena of economic rivalry.

How deeply the danger is felt even by those who sincerely desire peace

and can in no sense be considered Jingoes may be judged by the following from the pen of Mr. Frederic Harrison. I make no apology for giving
the quotations at some length. In a letter to the London *Times* he says:

Whenever our Empire and maritime ascendancy are challenged it will
be by such an invasion in force as was once designed by Philip and
Parma, and again by Napoleon. It is this certainty which compels me to
modify the anti-militarist policy which I have consistently maintained
for forty years past.... To me now it is no question of loss of prestige--no
question of the shrinkage of the Empire; it is our existence as a foremost
European Power, and even as a thriving nation.... If ever our naval defense were broken through, our Navy overwhelmed or even dispersed for
a season, and a military occupation of our arsenals, docks, and capital
were effected, the ruin would be such as modern history cannot parallel.
It would not be the Empire, but Britain, that would be destroyed.... The
occupation by a foreign invader of our arsenals, docks, cities, and capital
would be to the Empire what the bursting of the boilers would be to a
Dreadnought. Capital would disappear with the destruction of credit....
A catastrophe so appalling cannot be left to chance, even if the prob-
abilities against its occurring were 50 to 1. But the odds are not 50 to
1. No high authority ventures to assert that a successful invasion of our
country is absolutely impossible if it were assisted by extraordinary conditions. And a successful invasion would mean to us the total collapse of
our Empire, our trade, and, with trade, the means of feeding forty millions in these islands. If it is asked, "Why does invasion threaten more
terrible consequences to us than it does to our neighbors?" the answer
is that the British Empire is an anomalous structure, without any real
parallel in modern history, except in the history of Portugal, Venice, and
Holland, and in ancient history Athens and Carthage. Our Empire presents special conditions both for attack and for destruction. And its destruction by an enemy seated on the Thames would have consequences
so awful to contemplate that it cannot be left to be safeguarded by one
sole line of defense, however good, and for the present hour however adequate.... For more than forty years I have raised my voice against every
form of aggression, of Imperial expansion, and Continental militarism.
Few men have more earnestly protested against postponing social reforms and the well-being of the people to Imperial conquests and Asiatic
and African adventures. I do not go back on a word that I have uttered
thereon. But how hollow is all talk about industrial reorganization until
we have secured our country against a catastrophe that would involve
untold destitution and misery on the people in the mass--which would
paralyze industry and raise food to famine prices, whilst closing our factories and our yards!

CHAPTER III

THE GREAT ILLUSION

These views founded on a gross and dangerous misconception--What a German victory could and could not accomplish--What an English victory could and could not accomplish--The optical illusion of conquest--There can be no transfer of wealth--The prosperity of the little States in Europe--German Three per Cents. at 82 and Belgian at 96--Russian Three and a Half per Cents. at 81, Norwegian at 102--What this really means--If Germany annexed Holland, would any German benefit or any Hollander?--The "cash value" of Alsace-Lorraine.

I think it will be admitted that there is not much chance of misunderstanding the general idea embodied in the passage quoted at the end of the last chapter. Mr. Harrison is especially definite. At the risk of "damnable iteration" I would again recall the fact that he is merely expressing one of the universally accepted axioms of European politics, namely, that a nation's financial and industrial stability, its security in commercial activity--in short, its prosperity and wellbeing depend, upon its being able to defend itself against the aggression of other nations, who will, if they are able, be tempted to commit such aggression because in so doing they will increase their power, prosperity and well-being, at the cost of the weaker and vanquished.

I have quoted, it is true, largely journalistic authorities because I desired to indicate real public opinion, not merely scholarly opinion. But Mr. Harrison has the support of other scholars of all sorts. Thus Mr. Spenser Wilkinson, Chichele Professor of Military History at Oxford, and a deservedly respected authority on the subject, confirms in almost every point in his various writings the opinions that I have quoted, and gives emphatic confirmation to all that Mr. Frederic Harrison has expressed. In his book, "Britain at Bay," Professor Wilkinson says: "No one thought when in 1888 the American observer, Captain Mahan, published his volume on the influence of sea-power upon history, that other nations beside the British read from that book the lesson that victory at sea carried with it a prosperity and influence and a greatness obtainable by no other means."

Well, it is the object of these pages to show that this all but universal idea, of which Mr. Harrison's letter is a particularly vivid expression, is a gross and desperately dangerous misconception, partaking at times of the nature of an optical illusion, at times of the nature of a superstition--a misconception not only gross and universal, but so profoundly mischievous as to misdirect an immense part of the energies of mankind, and to misdirect them to such degree that unless we liberate ourselves from this superstition civilization itself will be threatened.

And one of the most extraordinary features of this whole question is that the absolute demonstration of the falsity of this idea, the complete exposure of the illusion which gives it birth, is neither abstruse nor difficult. This demonstration does not repose upon any elaborately constructed theorem, but upon the simple exposition of the political facts of Europe as they exist to-day. These facts, which are incontrovertible, and which I shall elaborate presently, may be summed up in a few simple propositions stated thus:

1. An extent of devastation, even approximating to that which Mr. Harrison foreshadows as the result of the conquest of Great Britain, could only be inflicted by an invader as a means of punishment costly to himself, or as the result of an unselfish and expensive desire to inflict misery for the mere joy of inflicting it. Since trade depends upon the existence of natural wealth and a population capable of working it, an invader cannot "utterly destroy it," except by destroying the population, which is not practicable. If he could destroy the population he would thereby destroy his own market, actual or potential, which would be commercially suicidal.[6]

2. If an invasion of Great Britain by Germany did involve, as Mr. Harrison and those who think with him say it would, the "total collapse of the Empire, our trade, and the means of feeding forty millions in these islands ... the disturbance of capital and destruction of credit," German capital would also be disturbed, because of the internationalization and delicate interdependence of our credit-built finance and industry, and German credit would also collapse, and the only means of restoring it would be for Germany to put an end to the chaos in England by putting an end to the condition which had produced it. Moreover, because of this delicate interdependence of our credit-built finance, the confiscation by an invader of private property, whether stocks, shares, ships, mines, or anything more valuable than jewelry or furniture--anything, in short, which is bound up with the economic life of the people--would so react upon the finance of the invader's country as to make the damage to the invader resulting from the confiscation exceed in value the property confiscated. So that Germany's success in conquest would be a demonstration of the complete economic futility of conquest.

3. For allied reasons, in our day the exaction of tribute from a conquered people has become an economic impossibility; the exaction of a large indemnity so costly directly and indirectly as to be an extremely disadvantageous financial operation.

4. It is a physical and economic impossibility to capture the external or carrying trade of another nation by military conquest. Large navies are impotent to create trade for the nations owning them, and can do nothing to "confine the commercial rivalry" of other nations. Nor can a conqueror destroy the competition of a conquered nation by annexation;

his competitors would still compete with him--*i.e.*, if Germany conquered Holland, German merchants would still have to meet the competition of Dutch merchants, and on keener terms than originally, because the Dutch merchants would then be within the German's customs lines; the notion that the trade competition of rivals can be disposed of by conquering those rivals being one of the illustrations of the curious optical illusion which lies behind the misconception dominating this subject.

5. The wealth, prosperity, and well-being of a nation depend in no way upon its political power; otherwise we should find the commercial prosperity and social well-being of the smaller nations, which exercise no political power, manifestly below that of the great nations which control Europe, whereas this is not the case. The populations of States like Switzerland, Holland, Belgium, Denmark, Sweden, are in every way as prosperous as the citizens of States like Germany, Russia, Austria, and France. The wealth *per capita* of the small nations is in many cases in excess of that of the great nations. Not only the question of the security of small States, which, it might be urged, is due to treaties of neutrality, is here involved, but the question of whether political power can be turned in a positive sense to economic advantage.

6. No other nation could gain any advantage by the conquest of the British Colonies, and Great Britain could not suffer material damage by their loss, however much such loss would be regretted on sentimental grounds, and as rendering less easy a certain useful social co-operation between kindred peoples. The use, indeed, of the word "loss" is misleading. Great Britain does not "own" her Colonies. They are, in fact, independent nations in alliance with the Mother Country, to whom they are no source of tribute or economic profit (except as foreign nations are a source of profit), their economic relations being settled, not by the Mother Country, but by the Colonies. Economically, England would gain by their formal separation, since she would be relieved of the cost of their defense. Their "loss" involving, therefore, no change in economic fact (beyond saving the Mother Country the cost of their defense), could not involve the ruin of the Empire, and the starvation of the Mother Country, as those who commonly treat of such a contingency are apt to aver. As England is not able to exact tribute or economic advantage, it is inconceivable that any other country, necessarily less experienced in colonial management, would be able to succeed where England had failed, especially in view of the past history of the Spanish, Portuguese, French, and British Colonial Empires. This history also demonstrates that the position of British Crown Colonies, in the respect which we are considering, is not sensibly different from that of the self-governing ones. It is *not* to be presumed, therefore, that any European nation, realizing the facts, would attempt the desperately expensive business of the conquest of England for the purpose of making an experiment which all colonial history shows to be doomed to failure.

The foregoing propositions traverse sufficiently the ground covered in the series of those typical statements of policy, both English and German, from which I have quoted. The simple statement of these propositions, based as they are upon the self-evident facts of present-day European politics, sufficiently exposes the nature of those political axioms which I have quoted. But as men even of the caliber of Mr. Harrison normally disregard these self-evident facts, it is necessary to elaborate them at somewhat greater length.

For the purpose of presenting a due parallel to the statement of policy embodied in the quotations made from the London *Times* and Mr. Harrison and others, I have divided the propositions which I desire to demonstrate into seven clauses, but such a division is quite arbitrary, and made only in order to bring about the parallel in question. The whole seven can be put into one, as follows: That as the only possible policy in our day for a conqueror to pursue is to leave the wealth of a territory in the complete possession of the individuals inhabiting that territory, it is a logical fallacy and an optical illusion to regard a nation as increasing its wealth when it increases its territory; because when a province or State is annexed, the population, who are the real and only owners of the wealth therein, are also annexed, and the conqueror gets nothing. The facts of modern history abundantly demonstrate this. When Germany annexed Schleswig-Holstein and Alsatia not a single ordinary German citizen was one *pfennig* the richer. Although England "owns" Canada, the English merchant is driven out of the Canadian markets by the merchant of Switzerland, who does not "own" Canada. Even where territory is not formally annexed, the conqueror is unable to take the wealth of a conquered territory, owing to the delicate interdependence of the financial world (an outcome of our credit and banking systems), which makes the financial and industrial security of the victor dependent upon financial and industrial security in all considerable civilized centers; so that widespread confiscation or destruction of trade and commerce in a conquered territory would react disastrously upon the conqueror. The conqueror is thus reduced to economic impotence, which means that political and military power is economically futile--that is to say, can do nothing for the trade and well-being of the individuals exercising such power. Conversely, armies and navies cannot destroy the trade of rivals, nor can they capture it. The great nations of Europe do not destroy the trade of the small nations for their own benefit, because they cannot; and the Dutch citizen, whose Government possesses no military power, is just as well off as the German citizen, whose Government possesses an army of two million men, and a great deal better off than the Russian, whose Government possesses an army of something like four million. Thus, as a rough-and-ready though incomplete indication of the relative wealth and security of the respective States, the Three per Cents. of powerless Belgium are quoted at 96, and the Three per Cents. of powerful Germany at 82; the Three and a Half per Cents. of the Russian Empire, with its hundred and twenty million souls and its four million army, are quoted at 81, while the Three and a Half per Cents. of Norway, which has not an army at all (or any that need be considered in this discussion), are quoted at 102. All of which carries with it the paradox that the more a nation's wealth is militarily protected the less secure does it become.[7]

The late Lord Salisbury, speaking to a delegation of business men, made this notable observation: The conduct of men of affairs acting individually in their business capacity differs radically in its principles and application from the conduct of the same men when they act collectively in political affairs. And one of the most astonishing things in politics is the little trouble business men take to bring their political creed into keeping with their daily behavior; how little, indeed, they realize the political implication of their daily work. It is a case, indeed, of the forest and the trees.

But for some such phenomenon we certainly should not see the contradiction between the daily practice of the business world and the prevailing political philosophy, which the security of property in, and the high prosperity of, the smaller States involves. We are told by all the political experts that great navies and great armies are necessary to protect our wealth against the aggression of powerful neighbors, whose cupidity and voracity can be controlled by force alone; that treaties avail nothing, and that in international politics might makes right, that military and commercial security are identical, that armaments are justified by the necessity of commercial security; that our navy is an "insurance," and that a country without military power with which their diplomats can "bargain" in the Council of Europe is at a hopeless disadvantage economically. Yet when the investor, studying the question in its purely financial and material aspect, has to decide between the great States, with all their imposing paraphernalia of colossal armies and fabulously costly navies, and the little States, possessing relatively no military power whatever, he plumps solidly, and with what is in the circumstances a tremendous difference, in favor of the small and helpless. For a difference of twenty points, which we find as between Norwegian and Russian, and fourteen as between Belgian and German securities, is the difference between a safe and a speculative one--the difference between an American railroad bond in time of profound security and in time of widespread panic. And what is true of the Government funds is true, in an only slightly less degree, of the industrial securities in the national comparison just drawn.

Is it a sort of altruism or quixotism which thus impels the capitalists of Europe to conclude that the public funds and investments of powerless Holland and Sweden (any day at the mercy of their big neighbors) are 10 to 20 per cent. safer than those of the greatest Power of Continental Europe. The question is, of course, absurd. The only consideration of the financier is profit and security, and he has decided that the funds of the undefended nation are more secure than the funds of one defended by colossal armaments. How does he arrive at this decision, unless it be through his knowledge as a financier, which, of course, he exercises without reference to the political implication of his decision, that modern wealth requires no defense, because it cannot be confiscated?

If Mr. Harrison is right; if, as he implies, a nation's commerce, its very industrial existence, would disappear if it allowed neighbors who envied it that commerce to become its superiors in armaments, and to exercise political weight in the world, how does he explain the fact that the great Powers of the Continent are flanked by little nations far weaker than themselves having nearly always a commercial development equal to, and in most cases greater than theirs? If the common doctrines be true, the financiers would not invest a dollar in the territories of the undefended nations, and yet, far from that being the case, they consider that a Swiss or a Dutch investment is more secure than a German one; that industrial undertakings in a country like Switzerland defended by an army of a few thousand men, are preferable in point of security to enterprises backed by two millions of the most perfectly trained soldiers in the world. The attitude of European finance in this matter is the absolute condemnation of the view commonly taken by the statesman. If a country's trade were really at the mercy of the first successful invader; if armies and navies were really necessary for the protection and promotion of trade, the small countries would be in a hopelessly inferior position, and could only exist on the sufferance of what we are told are unscrupulous aggressors. And yet Norway has relatively to population a greater carrying trade than Great Britain,[8] and Dutch, Swiss, and Belgian merchants compete in all the markets of the world successfully with those of Germany and France.

The prosperity of the small States is thus a fact which proves a good deal more than that wealth can be secure without armaments. We have seen that the exponents of the orthodox statecraft--notably such authorities as Admiral Mahan--plead that armaments are a necessary part of the industrial struggle, that they are used as a means of exacting economic advantage for a nation which would be impossible without them. "The logical sequence," we are told, is "markets, control, navy, bases." The nation without political and military power is, we are assured, at a hopeless disadvantage economically and industrially.[9]

Well, the relative economic situation of the small States gives the lie to this profound philosophy. It is seen to be just learned nonsense when we realize that all the might of Russia or Germany cannot secure for the individual citizen better general economic conditions than those prevalent in the little States. The citizens of Switzerland, Belgium, or Holland, countries without "control," or navy, or bases, or "weight in the councils of Europe," or the "prestige of a great Power," are just as well off as Germans, and a great deal better off than Austrians or Russians.

Thus, even if it could be argued that the security of the small States is due to the various treaties guaranteeing their neutrality, it cannot be argued that those treaties give them the political power and "control" and "weight in the councils of the nations" which Admiral Mahan and the other exponents of the orthodox statecraft assure us are such necessary factors in national prosperity.

I want, with all possible emphasis, to indicate the limits of the argument that I am trying to enforce. That argument is not that the facts just cited show armaments or the absence of them to be the sole or even the determining factor in national wealth. It does show that the security of wealth is due to other things than armaments; that absence of political and military power is on the one hand no obstacle to, and on the other hand no guarantee of, prosperity; that the mere size of the administrative area has no relation to the wealth of those inhabiting it.

Those who argue that the security of the small States is due to the international treaties protecting their neutrality are precisely those who argue that treaty rights are things that can never give security! Thus one British military writer says:

The principle practically acted on by statesmen, though, of course, not openly admitted, is that frankly enunciated by Machiavelli: "A prudent ruler ought not to keep faith when by so doing it would be against his interests, and when the reasons which made him bind himself no longer exist." Prince Bismarck said practically the same thing, only not quite so nakedly. The European waste-paper basket is the place to which all treaties eventually find their way, and a thing which can any day be placed in a waste-paper basket is a poor thing on which to hang our national safety. Yet there are plenty of people in this country who quote treaties to us as if we could depend on their never being torn up. Very plausible and very dangerous people they are--idealists too good and innocent for a hard, cruel world, where force is the chief law. Yet there are some such innocent people in Parliament even at present. It is to be hoped that we shall see none of them there in future.[10]

Major Murray is right to this extent: the militarist view, the view of those who "believe in war," and defend it even on moral grounds as a thing without which men would be "sordid," supports this philosophy of force, which flourishes in the atmosphere which the militarist regimen engenders.

But the militarist view involves a serious dilemma. If the security of a nation's wealth can only be assured by force, and treaty rights are mere waste paper, how can we explain the evident security of the wealth of States possessing relatively no force? By the mutual jealousies of those guaranteeing their neutrality? Then that mutual jealousy could equally well guarantee the security of any one of the larger States against the rest. Another Englishman, Mr. Farrer, has put the case thus:

If that recent agreement between England, Germany, France, Denmark, and Holland can so effectively relieve Denmark and Holland from the fear of invasion that Denmark can seriously consider the actual abolition of her army and navy, it seems only one further step to go, for all the Powers collectively, great and small, to guarantee the territorial independence of each one of them severally.

In either case, the plea of the militarist stands condemned: national safety can be secured by means other than military force.

But the real truth involves a distinction which is essential to the right understanding of this phenomenon: the political security of the small States is *not* assured; no man would take heavy odds on Holland being able to maintain complete political independence if Germany cared seriously to threaten it. But Holland's economic security *is* assured. Every financier in Europe knows that if Germany conquered Holland or Belgium to-morrow, she would have to leave their wealth untouched; there could be no confiscation. And that is why the stocks of the lesser States, not in reality threatened by confiscation, yet relieved in part at least of the charge of armaments, stand fifteen to twenty points higher than those of the military States. Belgium, politically, might disappear to-morrow; her wealth would remain practically unchanged.

Yet, by one of those curious contradictions we are frequently meeting in the development of ideas, while a fact like this is at least subconsciously recognized by those whom it concerns, the necessary corollary of it--the positive form of the merely negative truth that a community's wealth cannot be stolen--is not recognized. We admit that a people's wealth must remain unaffected by conquest, and yet we are quite prepared to urge that we can enrich ourselves by conquering them! But if we must leave their wealth alone, how can we take it?

I do not speak merely of "loot." It is evident, even on cursory examination, that no real advantage of any kind is achieved for the mass of one people by the conquest of another. Yet that end is set up in European politics as desirable beyond all others. Here, for instance, are the Pan-Germanists of Germany. This party has set before itself the object of grouping into one great Power all the peoples of the Germanic race or language in Europe. Were this aim achieved, Germany would become the dominating Power of the Continent, and might become the dominating Power of the world. And according to the commonly accepted view, such an achievement would, from the point of view of Germany, be worth any sacrifice that Germans could make. It would be an object so great, so desirable, that German citizens should not hesitate for an instant to give everything, life itself, in its accomplishment. Very good. Let us assume that at the cost of great sacrifice, the greatest sacrifice which it is possible to imagine a modern civilized nation making, this has been accomplished, and that Belgium and Holland and Germany, Switzerland and Austria, have all become part of the great German hegemony: *is there one ordinary German citizen who would be able to say that his well-being had been increased by such a change?* Germany would then "own" Holland. *But would a single German citizen be the richer for the ownership?* The Hollander, from having been the citizen of a small and insignificant State, would become the citizen of a very great one. *Would the individual Hollander be any the richer or any the better?* We know that, as a matter of fact, neither the German nor the Hollander would be one whit the better; and we know also, as a matter of fact, that in all probability they would be a great deal the worse. We may, indeed, say that the Hollander would be certainly the worse, in that he would have exchanged the relatively light taxation and light military service of Holland for the much heavier taxation and the much longer military service of the "great" German Empire.

The following, which appeared in the London *Daily Mail* in reply to an article in that paper, throws some further light on the points elaborated in this chapter. The *Daily Mail* critic had placed Alsace-Lorraine as an asset in the German conquest worth $330,000,000 "cash value," and added: "If Alsace-Lorraine had remained French, it would have yielded, at the present rate of French taxation, a revenue of $40,000,000 a year to the State. That revenue is lost to France, and is placed at the disposal of Germany."

To which I replied:

Thus, if we take the interest of the "cash value" at the present price of money in Germany, Alsace-Lorraine should be worth to the Germans about $15,000,000 a year. If we take the other figure, $40,000,000. Suppose we split the difference, and take, say, 20. Now, if the Germans are enriched by 20 millions a year--if Alsace-Lorraine is really worth that income to the German people--how much should the English people draw from their "possessions"? On the basis of population, somewhere in the region of $5,000,000,000; on the basis of area, still more--enough not only to pay all English taxes, wipe out the National Debt, support the army and navy, but give every family in the land a fat income into the bargain. There is evidently something wrong.

Does not my critic really see that this whole notion of national possessions benefiting the individual is founded on mystification, upon an illusion? Germany conquered France and annexed Alsace-Lorraine. The "Germans" consequently "own" it, and enrich themselves with this newly acquired wealth. That is my critic's view, as it is the view of most European statesmen; and it is all false. Alsace-Lorraine is owned by its inhabitants, and nobody else; and Germany, with all her ruthlessness, has not been able to dispossess them, as is proved by the fact that the matricular contribution (*matrikularbeitrag*) of the newly acquired State to the Imperial treasury (which incidentally is neither 15 millions nor 40, but just over five) is fixed on exactly the same scale as that of the other States of the Empire. Prussia, the conqueror, pays *per capita* just as much as and no less than Alsace, the conquered, who, if she were not paying this $5,600,000 to Germany, would be paying it--or, according to my critic, a much larger sum--to France; and if Germany did not "own" Alsace-Lorraine, she would be relieved of charges that amount not to five but many more millions. The change of "ownership" does not therefore of itself change the money position (which is what we are now discussing) of either owner or owned.

In examining, in the last article on this matter, my critic's balance-sheet, I remarked that were his figures as complete as they are absurdly incomplete and misleading, I should still have been unimpressed. We all know that very marvelous results are possible with figures; but one can generally find some simple fact which puts them to the supreme test without undue mathematics. I do not know whether it has ever happened to my critic, as it has happened to me, while watching the gambling in the casino of a Continental watering resort, to have a financial genius present weird columns of figures, which demonstrate conclusively, irre-fragably, that by the system which they embody one can break the bank and win a million. I have never examined these figures, and never shall, for this reason: the genius in question is prepared to sell his wonderful secret for twenty francs. Now, in the face of that fact I am not interested in his figures. If they were worth examination they would not be for sale.

And so in this matter there are certain test facts which upset the adroit-est statistical legerdemain. Though, really, the fallacy which regards an addition of territory as an addition of wealth to the "owning" nation is a very much simpler matter than the fallacies lying behind gambling systems, which are bound up with the laws of chance and the law of averages and much else that philosophers will quarrel about till the end of time. It requires an exceptional mathematical brain to refute those fallacies, whereas the one we are dealing with is due simply to the diffi-culty experienced by most of us in carrying in our heads two facts at the same time. It is so much easier to seize on one fact and forget the oth-er. Thus we realize that when Germany has conquered Alsace-Lorraine she has "captured" a province worth, "cash value," in my critic's phrase, $330,000,000. What we overlook is that Germany has also captured the people who own the property and who continue to own it. We have mul-tiplied by x, it is true, but we have overlooked the fact that we have had to divide by x, and that the result is consequently, so far as the individ-ual is concerned, exactly what it was before. My critic remembered the multiplication all right, but he forgot the division. Let us apply the test fact. If a great country benefits every time it annexes a province, and her people are the richer for the widened territory, the small nations ought to be immeasurably poorer than the great, instead of which, by every test which you like to apply--public credit, amounts in savings banks, standard of living, social progress, general well-being--citizens of small States are, other things being equal, as well off as, or better off than, the citizens of great States. The citizens of countries like Holland, Belgium, Denmark, Sweden, Norway are, by every possible test, just as well off as the citizens of countries like Germany, Austria, or Russia. These are the facts which are so much more potent than any theory. If it is true that a country benefits by the acquisition of territory, and widened territory means general well-being, why do the facts so eternally deny it? There is something wrong with the theory.

In every civilized State, revenues which are drawn from a territory are expended on that territory, and there is no process known to modern government by which wealth may first be drawn from a territory into the treasury and then be redistributed with a profit to the individuals who have contributed it, or to others. It would be just as reasonable to say that the citizens of London are richer than the citizens of Birmingham because London has a richer treasury; or that Londoners would become richer if the London County Council were to annex the county of Hertford; as to say that people's wealth varies according to the size of the administrative area which they inhabit. The whole thing is, as I have called it, an optical illusion, due to the hypnotism of an obsolete terminology. Just as poverty may be greater in the large city than in the small one, and taxation heavier, so the citizens of a great State may be poorer than the citizens of a small one, as they very often are. Modern government is mainly, and tends to become entirely, a matter of administration. A mere jugglery with the administrative entities, the absorption of small States into large ones, or the breaking up of large States into small, is not of itself going to affect the matter one way or the other.

CHAPTER IV

THE IMPOSSIBILITY OF CONFISCATION

Our present terminology of international politics an historical survival-
-Wherein modern conditions differ from ancient--The profound change
effected by Division of Labor--The delicate interdependence of international finance--Attila and the Kaiser--What would happen if a German
invader looted the Bank of England--German trade dependent upon English credit--Confiscation of an enemy's property an economic impossibility under modern conditions--Intangibility of a community's wealth.

During the Victorian Jubilee procession an English beggar was heard
to say:

I own Australia, Canada, New Zealand, India, Burmah, and the Islands
of the Far Pacific; and I am starving for want of a crust of bread. I am a
citizen of the greatest Power of the modern world, and all people should
bow to my greatness. And yesterday I cringed for alms to a negro savage,
who repulsed me with disgust.

What is the meaning of this?

The meaning is that, as very frequently happens in the history of ideas,
our terminology is a survival of conditions no longer existing, and our
mental conceptions follow at the tail of our vocabulary. International
politics are still dominated by terms applicable to conditions which the
processes of modern life have altogether abolished.

In the Roman times--indeed, in all the ancient world--it may have been
true that the conquest of a territory meant a tangible advantage to the
conqueror; it meant the exploitation of the conquered territory by the
conquering State itself, to the advantage of that State and its citizens.
It not infrequently meant the enslavement of the conquered people and
the acquisition of wealth in the form of slaves as a direct result of the
conquering war. In mediæval times a war of conquest meant at least immediate tangible booty in the shape of movable property, actual gold and
silver, land parceled out among the chiefs of the conquering nation, as it
was at the Norman Conquest, and so forth.

At a later period conquest at least involved an advantage to the reign-
ing house of the conquering nation, and it was mainly the squabbles of
rival sovereigns for prestige and power which produced the wars of many
centuries.

At a still later period, civilization, as a whole--not necessarily the conquering nation--gained (sometimes) by the conquest of savage peoples, in
that order was substituted for disorder. In the period of the colonization
of newly-discovered land, the preemption of territory by one particular

nation secured an advantage for the citizens of that nation, in that its overflowing population found homes in conditions preferable socially, or politically, to the conditions imposed by alien nations. *But none of these considerations applies to the problem with which we are dealing.* We are concerned with the case of fully civilized rival nations in fully occupied territory or with civilizations so firmly set that conquest could not sensibly modify their character, and the fact of conquering such territory gives to the conqueror no material advantage which he could not have had without conquest. And in these conditions--the realities of the political world as we find it to-day--"domination," or "predominance of armament," or the "command of the sea," can do nothing for commerce and industry or general well-being: England may build fifty *Dreadnoughts* and not sell so much as a penknife the more in consequence. She might conquer Germany to-morrow, and she would find that she could not make a single Englishman a shilling's worth the richer in consequence, the war indemnity notwithstanding.

How have conditions so changed that terms which were applicable to the ancient world--in one sense at least to the mediæval world, and in another sense still to the world of that political renaissance which gave to Great Britain its Empire--are no longer applicable in *any* sense to the conditions of the world as we find them to-day? How has it become impossible for one nation to take by conquest the wealth of another for the benefit of the people of the conqueror? How is it that we are confronted by the absurdity (which the facts of the British Empire go to prove) of the conquering people being able to exact from conquered territory rather less than more advantage than it was able to do before the conquest took place?

I am not at this stage going to pass in review all the factors that have contributed to this change, because it will suffice for the demonstration upon which I am now engaged to call attention to a phenomenon which is the outcome of all those factors and which is undeniable, and that is, the financial interdependence of the modern world. But I will forecast here what belongs more properly to a later stage of this work, and will give just a hint of the forces which are the result mainly of one great fact--the division of labor intensified by facility of communication.

When the division of labor was so little developed that every homestead produced all that it needed, it mattered nothing if part of the community was cut off from the world for weeks and months at a time. All the neighbors of a village or homestead might be slain or harassed, and no inconvenience resulted. But if to-day an English county is by a general railroad strike cut off for so much as forty-eight hours from the rest of the economic organism, we know that whole sections of its population are threatened with famine. If in the time of the Danes, England could by some magic have killed all foreigners, she would presumably have been the better off. If she could do the same thing to-day, half her population would starve to death. If on one side of the frontier a community is, say, wheat-producing, and on the other coal-producing, each is dependent for its very existence, on the fact of the other being able to carry on its labor. The miner cannot in a week set to and grow a crop of wheat; the farmer must wait for his wheat to grow, and must meantime feed his family and dependents. The exchange involved here must go on, and each party have fair expectation that he will in due course be able to reap the fruits of his labor, or both must starve; and that exchange, that expectation, is merely the expression in its simplest form of commerce and credit; and the interdependence here indicated has, by the countless developments of rapid communication, reached such a condition of complexity that the interference with any given operation affects not merely the parties directly involved, but numberless others having at first sight no connection therewith.

The vital interdependence here indicated, cutting athwart frontiers, is largely the work of the last forty years; and it has, during that time, so developed as to have set up a financial interdependence of the capitals of the world, so complex that disturbance in New York involves financial and commercial disturbance in London, and, if sufficiently grave, compels financiers of London to co-operate with those of New York to put an end to the crisis, not as a matter of altruism, but as a matter of commercial self-protection. The complexity of modern finance makes New York dependent on London, London upon Paris, Paris upon Berlin, to a greater degree than has ever yet been the case in history. This interdependence is the result of the daily use of those contrivances of civilization which date from yesterday--the rapid post, the instantaneous dissemination of financial and commercial information by means of telegraphy, and generally the incredible increase in the rapidity of communication which has put the half-dozen chief capitals of Christendom in closer contact financially, and has rendered them more dependent the one upon the other than were the chief cities of Great Britain less than a hundred years ago.

A well-known French authority, writing recently in a financial publication, makes this reflection:

The very rapid development of industry has given rise to the active intervention therein of finance, which has become its *nervus rerum*, and has come to play a dominating rôle. Under the influence of finance, industry is beginning to lose its exclusively national character to take on a character more and more international. The animosity of rival nationalities seems to be in process of attenuation as the result of this increasing international solidarity. This solidarity was manifested in a striking fashion in the last industrial and monetary crisis. This crisis, which appeared in its most serious form in the United States and Germany, far from being any profit to rival nations, has been injurious to them. The nations competing with America and Germany, such as England and France, have suffered only less than the countries directly affected. It must not be forgotten that, quite apart from the financial interests involved, directly or indirectly, in the industry of other countries, every producing country is at one and the same time, as well as being a competitor and a rival, a client and a market. Financial and commercial solidarity is increasing every day at the expense of commercial and industrial competition. This was certainly one of the principal causes which a year or two ago prevented the outbreak of war between Germany and France *à propos* of Morocco, and which led to the understanding of Algeciras. There can be no doubt, for those who have studied the question, that the influence of this international economic solidarity is increasing despite ourselves. It has not resulted from conscious action on the part of any of us, and it certainly cannot be arrested by any conscious action on our part.[11]

A fiery patriot sent to a London paper the following letter:

When the German army is looting the cellars of the Bank of England, and carrying off the foundations of our whole national fortune, perhaps the twaddlers who are now screaming about the wastefulness of building four more *Dreadnoughts* will understand why sane men are regarding this opposition as treasonable nonsense.

What would be the result of such an action on the part of a German army in London? The first effect, of course, would be that, as the Bank of England is the banker of all other banks, there would be a run on every bank in England, and all would suspend payment. But London being the clearing-house of the world, bills drawn thereon but held by foreigners would not be met; they would be valueless; the loanable value of money in other centers would be enormously raised, and instruments of credit enormously depreciated; prices of all kinds of stocks would fall, and holders would be threatened by ruin and insolvency. German finance would represent a condition as chaotic as that of England. Whatever advantage German credit might gain by holding England's gold it would certainly be more than offset by the fact that it was the ruthless action of the German Government that had produced the general catastrophe. A country that could sack bank reserves would be a good one for foreign investors to avoid: the essential of credit is confidence, and those who repudiate it pay dearly for their action. The German Generalissimo in London might be no more civilized than Attila himself, but he would soon find the difference between himself and Attila. Attila, luckily for him, did not have to worry about a bank rate and such-like complications; but the German General, while trying to sack the Bank of England, would find that his own balance in the Bank of Germany would have vanished into thin air, and the value of even the best of his investments dwindled as though by a miracle; and that for the sake of loot, amounting to a few sovereigns apiece among his soldiery, he would have sacrificed the greater part of his own personal fortune. It is as certain as anything can be that, were the German army guilty of such economic vandalism, there is no considerable institution in Germany that would escape grave damage--a damage in credit and security so serious as to constitute a loss immensely greater[12] than the value of the loot obtained. It is not putting the case too strongly to say that for every pound taken from the Bank of England German trade would pay many times over. The influence of the whole finance of Germany would be brought to bear on the German Government to put an end to a situation ruinous to German trade, and German finance would only be saved from utter collapse by an undertaking on the part of the German Government scrupulously to respect private property, and especially bank reserves. It is true the German Jingoes might wonder what they had made war for, and this elementary lesson in international finance would do more than the greatness of the British navy to cool their blood. For it is a fact in human nature that men will fight more readily than they will pay, and that they will take personal risks much more readily than they will disgorge money, or, for that matter, earn it. "Man," in the language of Bacon, "loves danger better than travail."

Events which are still fresh in the memory of business men show the extraordinary interdependence of the modern financial world. A financial crisis in New York sends up the English bank rate to 7 per cent., thus involving the ruin of many English businesses which might otherwise have weathered a difficult period. It thus happens that one section of the financial world is, against its will, compelled to come to the rescue of any other considerable section which may be in distress.

From a modern and delightfully lucid treatise on international finance,[13] I take the following very suggestive passages:

Banking in all countries hangs together so closely that the strength of the best may easily be that of the weakest if scandal arises owing to the mistakes of the worst.... Just as a man cycling down a crowded street depends for his life not only on his skill, but more on the course of the traffic there.... Banks in Berlin were obliged, from motives of self-protection (on the occasion of the Wall Street crisis), to let some of their gold go to assuage the American craving for it.... If the crisis became so severe that London had to restrict its facilities in this respect, other centers, which habitually keep balances in London which they regard as so much gold, because a draft on London is as good as gold, would find themselves very seriously inconvenienced; and it thus follows that it is to the interest of all other centers which trade on those facilities which London alone gives to take care that London's task is not made too difficult. This is especially so in the case of foreigners, who keep a balance in London which is borrowed. In fact, London drew in the gold required for New York from seventeen other countries....

Incidentally it may be mentioned in this connection that German commerce is in a special sense interested in the maintenance of English credit. The authority just quoted says:

It is even contended that the rapid expansion of German trade, which pushed itself largely by its elasticity and adaptability to the wishes of its customers, could never have been achieved if it had not been assisted by the large credit furnished in London.... No one can quarrel with the Germans for making use of the credit we offered for the expansion of the German trade, although their over-extension of credit facilities has had results which fall on others besides themselves....

Let us hope that our German friends are duly grateful, and let us avoid the mistake of supposing that we have done ourselves any permanent harm by giving this assistance. It is to the economic interests of humanity at large that production should be stimulated, and the economic interest of humanity at large is the interest of England, with its mighty world-wide trade. Germany has quickened production with the help of English credit, and so has every other economically civilized country in the world. It is a fact that all of them, including our own colonies, develop their resources with the help of British capital and credit, and then do their utmost to keep out our productions by means of tariffs, which make it appear to superficial observers that England provides capital for the destruction of its own business. But in practice the system works quite otherwise, for all these countries that develop their resources with our money aim at developing an export trade and selling goods to us, and as they have not yet reached the point of economic altruism at which they are prepared to sell goods for nothing, the increase in their production means an increasing demand for our commodities and our services. And in the meantime the interest on our capital and credit, and the profits of working the machinery of exchange, are a comfortable addition to our national income.

But what is a further corollary of this situation? It is that Germany is to-day in a larger sense than she ever was before England's debtor, and that her industrial success is bound up with English financial security.

What would be the situation in Britain, therefore, on the morrow of a conflict in which that country was successful?

I have seen mentioned the possibility of the conquest and annexation of the free port of Hamburg by a victorious British fleet. Let us assume that the British Government has done this, and is proceeding to turn the annexed and confiscated property to account.

Now, the property was originally of two kinds: part was private property, and part was German Government, or rather Hamburg Government, property. The income of the latter was earmarked for the payment of interest of certain Government stock, and the action of the British Government, therefore, renders the stock all but valueless, and in the case of the shares of the private companies entirely so. The paper becomes unsaleable. But it is held in various forms--as collateral and otherwise--by many important banking concerns, insurance companies, and so on, and this sudden collapse of value shatters their solvency. Their collapse not only involves many credit institutions in Germany, but, as these in their turn are considerable debtors of London, English institutions are also involved. London is also involved in another way. As explained previously, many foreign concerns keep balances in London, and the action of the British Government having precipitated a monetary crisis in Germany, there is a run on London to withdraw all balances. In a double sense London is feeling the pinch, and it would be a miracle if already at

this point the whole influence of British finance were not thrown against
the action of the British Government. Assume, however, that the Government, making the best of a bad job, continues its administration of the
property, and proceeds to arrange for loans for the purpose of putting it
once more in good condition after the ravages of war. The banks, however, finding that the original titles have through the action of the British
Government become waste paper, and British financiers having already
burned their fingers with that particular class of property, withhold support, and money is only procurable at extortionate rates of interest--so
extortionate that it becomes quite evident that as a Governmental enterprise the thing could not be made to pay. An attempt is made to sell
the property to British and German concerns. But the same paralyzing
sense of insecurity hangs over the whole business. Neither German nor
British financiers can forget that the bonds and shares of this property
have already been turned into waste paper by the action of the British
Government. The British Government finds, in fact, that it can do nothing with the financial world unless first it confirms the title of the original
owners to the property, and gives an assurance that titles to all property
throughout the conquered territory shall be respected. In other words,
confiscation has been a failure.

It would really be interesting to know how those who talk as though
confiscation were still an economic possibility would proceed to effect it.
As material property in the form of that booty which used to constitute
the spoils of victory in ancient times, the gold and silver goblets, etc.,
would be quite inconsiderable, and as Britain cannot carry away sections
of Berlin and Hamburg, she could only annex the paper tokens of wealth-
-the shares and bonds. But the value of those tokens depends upon the
reliance which can be placed upon the execution of the contracts which
they embody. The act of military confiscation upsets all contracts, and
the courts of the country from which contracts derive their force would
be paralyzed if judicial decisions were thrust aside by the sword. The
value of the stocks and shares would collapse, and the credit of all those
persons and institutions interested in such property would also be shak-
en or shattered, and the whole credit system, being thus at the mercy
of alien governors only concerned to exact tribute, would collapse like a
house of cards. German finance and industry would show a condition
of panic and disorder beside which the worst crises of Wall Street would
pale into insignificance. Again, what would be the inevitable result? The
financial influence of London itself would be thrown into the scale to
prevent a panic in which London financiers would be involved. In other
words, British financiers would exert their influence upon the British
Government to stop the process of confiscation.

But the intangibility of wealth can be shown in yet another fashion.
I once asked an English chartered accountant, very subject to attacks
of Germanophobia, how he supposed the Germans would profit by the
invasion of England, and he had a very simple program. Admitting the

impossibility of sacking the Bank of England, they would reduce the British population to practical slavery, and make them work for their foreign taskmasters, as he put it, under the rifle and lash. He had it all worked out in figures as to what the profit would be to the conqueror. Very well, let us follow the process. The population of Great Britain are not allowed to spend their income, or at least are only allowed to spend a portion of it, on themselves. Their dietary is reduced more or less to a slave dietary, and the bulk of what they earn is to be taken by their "owners." But how is this income, which so tempts the Germans, created--these dividends on the railroad shares, the profits of the mills and mines and provision companies and amusement concerns? The dividends are due to the fact that the population eat heartily, clothe themselves well, travel on railroads, and go to theatres and music-halls. If they are not allowed to do these things, if, in other words, they cannot spend their money on these things, the dividends disappear. If the German taskmasters are to take these dividends, they must allow them to be earned. If they allow them to be earned, they must let the population live as it lived before--spending their income on themselves; but if they spend their income on themselves, what is there, therefore, for the taskmasters? In other words, consumption is a necessary factor of the whole thing. Cut out consumption, and you cut out the profits. This glittering wealth, which so tempted the invader, has disappeared. If this is not intangibility, the word has no meaning. Speaking broadly and generally, the conqueror in our day has before him two alternatives: to leave things alone, and in order to do that he need not have left his shores; or to interfere by confiscation in some form, in which case he dries up the source of the profit which tempted him.

The economist may object that this does not cover the case of such profit as "economic rent," and that dividends or profits being part of exchange, a robber who obtains wealth without exchange can afford to disregard them; or that the increased consumption of the dispossessed English community would be made up by the increased consumption of the "owning" Germans.

If the political control of economic operations were as simple a matter as in our minds we generally make it, these objections would be sound. As it is, none of them would in practice invalidate the general proposition I have laid down. The division of labor in the modern world is so complex--the simplest operation of foreign trade involving not two nations merely, but many--that the mere military control of one party to an operation where many are concerned could ensure neither shifting of the consumption nor the monopolization of the profit within the limits of the conquering group.

Here is a German manufacturer selling cinematograph machines to a Glasgow suburb (which, incidentally, lives by selling tools to Argentine ranchers, who live by selling wheat to Newcastle boiler-makers). Assuming even that Germany could transfer the surplus spent in cinemato-

graph shows to Germany, what assurance has the German manufacturer in question that the enriched Germans will want cinematograph
films? They may insist upon champagne and cigars, coffee and Cognac,
and the French, Cubans, and Brazilians, to whom this "loot" eventually goes, may not buy their machinery from Germany at all, much less
from the particular German manufacturer, but in the United States or
Switzerland. The redistribution of the industrial rôles might leave German industry in the lurch, because at best the military power would
only be controlling one section of a complex operation, one party to it out
of many. When wealth was corn or cattle, the transference by political
or military force of the possessions of one community to another may
have been possible, although even then, or in a slightly more developed
period, we saw the Roman peasantry ruined by the slave exploitation of
foreign territory. How far this complexity of the international division of
labor tends to render futile the other contrivances of conquest such as
exclusive markets, tribute, money indemnity, etc., succeeding chapters
may help to show.

CHAPTER V

FOREIGN TRADE AND MILITARY POWER

Why trade cannot be destroyed or captured by a military Power--What the processes of trade really are, and how a navy affects them--*Dreadnoughts* and business--While *Dreadnoughts* protect British trade from hypothetical German warships, the real German merchant is carrying it off, or the Swiss or the Belgian--The "commercial aggression" of Switzerland--What lies at the bottom of the futility of military conquest--Government brigandage becomes as profitless as private brigandage--The real basis of commercial honesty on the part of Government.

Just as Mr. Harrison has declared that a "successful invasion would mean to the English the total eclipse of their commerce and trade, and with that trade the means of feeding forty millions in their islands," so I have seen it stated in a leading English paper that "if Germany were extinguished to-morrow, the day after to-morrow there is not an Englishman in the world who would not be the richer. Nations have fought for years over a city or right of succession. Must they not fight for 1250 million dollars of yearly commerce?"

What does the "extinction" of Germany mean? Does it mean that Britain shall slay in cold blood sixty or seventy millions of men, women, and children? Otherwise, even though the fleet and army were annihilated the country's sixty millions of workers would still remain,--all the more industrious, as they would have undergone great suffering and privation--prepared to exploit their mines and workshops with as much thoroughness and thrift and industry as ever, and consequently just as much trade rivals as ever, army or no army, navy or no navy.

Even if the British could annihilate Germany, they would annihilate such an important section of their debtors as to create hopeless panic in London, and that panic would so react on their own trade that it would be in no sort of condition to take the place which Germany had previously occupied in neutral markets, leaving aside the question that by the act of annihilation a market equal to that of Canada and South Africa combined would be destroyed.

What does this sort of thing mean? Am I wrong in saying that the whole subject is overlaid and dominated by a jargon which may have had some relation to facts at one time, but from which in our day all meaning has departed?

The English patriot may say that he does not mean permanent destruction, but only temporary "annihilation." (And this, of course, on the other side, would mean not permanent, but only temporary acquisition of that

1250 millions of trade.)

He might, like Mr. Harrison, put the case conversely--that if Germany could get command of the sea she could cut England off from its customers and intercept its trade for her benefit. This notion is as absurd as the other. It has already been shown that the "utter destruction of credit" and "incalculable chaos in the financial world," which Mr. Harrison foresees as the result of Germany's invasion, could not possibly leave German finance unaffected. It is a very open question whether her chaos would not be as great as the English. In any case, it would be so great as thoroughly to disorganize her industry, and in that disorganized condition it would be out of the question for her to secure the markets left unsupplied by England's isolation. Moreover, those markets would also be disorganized, because they depend upon England's ability to buy, which Germany would be doing her best to destroy. From the chaos which she herself had created, Germany could derive no possible benefit, and she could only terminate financial disorder, fatal to her own trade, by bringing to an end the condition which had produced it--that is, by bringing to an end the isolation of Great Britain.

With reference to this section of the subject we can with absolute certainty say two things: (1) That Germany can only destroy British trade by destroying British population; and (2) that if she could destroy that population, which she could not, she would destroy one of her most valuable markets, as at the present time she sells to it more than it sells to her. The whole point of view involves a fundamental misconception of the real nature of commerce and industry.

Commerce is simply and purely the exchange of one product for another. If the British manufacturer can make cloth, or cutlery, or machinery, or pottery, or ships cheaper or better than his rivals, he will obtain the trade; if he cannot, if his goods are inferior or dearer, or appeal less to his customers, his rivals will secure the trade, and the possession of *Dreadnoughts* will make not a whit of difference. Switzerland, without a single *Dreadnought*, will drive him out of the market even of his own colonies, as, indeed, she is driving him out.[14] The factors which really constitute prosperity have not the remotest connection with military or naval power, all our political jargon notwithstanding. To destroy the commerce of forty million people Germany would have to destroy Britain's coal and iron mines, to destroy the energy, character, and resourcefulness of its population; to destroy, in short, the determination of forty million people to make their living by the work of their hands. Were we not hypnotized by this extraordinary illusion, we should accept as a matter of course that the prosperity of a people depends upon such facts as the natural wealth of the country in which they live, their social discipline and industrial character, the result of years, of generations, of centuries, it may be, of tradition and slow, elaborate, selective processes; and, in addition to all these deep-seated elementary factors, upon countless commercial and financial ramifications--a special technical capacity for such-and-such a manufacture, a special aptitude for meeting the peculiarities of such and-such a market, the efficient equipment of elaborately constructed workshops, the existence of a population trained to given trades--a training not infrequently involving years, and even generations, of effort. All this, according to Mr. Harrison, is to go for nothing, and Germany is to be able to replace it in the twinkling of an eye, and forty million people are to sit down helplessly because Germany has been victorious at sea. On the morrow of her marvelous victory Germany is by some sort of miracle to find shipyards, foundries, cotton-mills, looms, factories, coal and iron mines, and all their equipment, suddenly created in order to take the trade that the most successful manufacturers and traders in the world have been generations in building up. Germany is to be able suddenly to produce three or four times what her population has hitherto been able to produce; for she must either do that or leave the markets which England has supplied heretofore still available to English effort. What has really fed these forty millions, who are to starve on the morrow of Germany's naval victory, is the fact that the coal and iron exported by them have been sent in one form or another to populations which need those products. Is that need suddenly to cease, or are the forty millions suddenly to be struck with some sort of paralysis, that all this vast industry is coming to an end? What has the defeat of English ships at sea to do with the fact that the Canadian farmer wants to buy English manufactures and pay for them with his wheat? It may be true that Germany could stop the importation of that wheat. But why should she want to do so? How would it benefit her people to do so? By what sort of miracle is she suddenly to be able to supply products which have kept forty million people busy? By what sort of miracle is she suddenly to be able to double her industrial population? And by what sort of miracle is she to be able to consume the wheat, because if she cannot take the wheat the Canadian cannot buy her products? I am aware that all this is elementary, that it is economics in words of one syllable; but what are the economics of Mr. Harrison and those who think like him when he talks in the strain of the passage that I have just quoted?

There is just one other possible meaning that the English patriot may have in his mind. He may plead that great military and naval establishments do not exist for the purpose of the conquest of territory or of destroying a rival's trade, but for "protecting" or indirectly aiding trade and industry. We are allowed to infer that in some not clearly defined way a great Power can aid the trade of its citizens by the use of the prestige which a great navy and a great army bring, and by exercising bargaining power, in the matter of tariffs, with other nations. But again the condition of the small nations in Europe gives the lie to this assumption.

It is evident that the neutral does not buy English products and refuse Germany's because England has a larger navy. If one can imagine the representatives of an English and a German firm meeting in the office of a merchant in Argentina, or Brazil, or Bulgaria, or Finland, both of them selling cutlery, the German is not going to secure the order because he is able to show the Argentinian, or the Brazilian, or the Bulgarian, or the Finn that Germany has twelve *Dreadnoughts* and England only eight. The German will take the order if, on the whole, he can make a more advantageous offer to the prospective buyer, and for no other reason whatsoever, and the buyer will go to the merchant of any nation whatever, whether he be German, or Swiss, or Belgian, or British, irrespective of the armies and navies which may lie behind the nationality of the seller. Nor does it appear that armies and navies weigh in the least when it comes to a question of a tariff bargain. Switzerland wages a tariff war with Germany, and wins. The whole history of the trade of the small nations shows that the political prestige of the great ones gives them practically no commercial advantage.

We continually talk as though carrying trade were in some special sense the result of the growth of a great navy, but Norway has a carrying trade which, relatively to her population, is nearly three times as great as Britain's, and the same reasons which would make it impossible for another nation to confiscate the gold reserve of the Bank of England would make it impossible for another nation to confiscate British shipping on the morrow of a British naval defeat. In what way can her carrying trade or any other trade be said to depend upon military power?

As I write these lines there comes to my notice a series of articles in the London *Daily Mail*, written by Mr. F. A. McKenzie, explaining how it is that England is losing the trade of Canada. In one article he quotes a number of Canadian merchants:

"We buy very little direct from England," said Mr. Harry McGee, one of the vice-presidents of the company, in answer to my questions. "We keep a staff in London of twenty, supervising our European purchases, but the orders go mostly to France, Germany, and Switzerland, and not to England."

And in a further article he notes that many orders are going to Belgium. Now the question arises: What more can a navy do that it has not done for England in Canada? And yet the trade goes to Switzerland and Belgium. Is England going to protect herself against the commercial "aggression" of Switzerland by building a dozen more *Dreadnoughts*? Suppose she could conquer Switzerland and Belgium with her *Dreadnoughts*, would not the trade of Switzerland and Belgium go on all the same? Her arms have brought her Canada--but no monopoly of the Canadian orders, which go, in part, to Switzerland.

If the traders of little nations can snap their fingers at the great war lords, why do British traders need *Dreadnoughts*? If Swiss commercial prosperity is secure from the aggression of a neighbor who outweighs Switzerland in military power a hundred to one, how comes it that the trade and industry, the very life-bread of her children, as Mr. Harrison would have us believe, of the greatest nation in history is in danger of imminent annihilation the moment she loses her military predominance?

If the statesmen of Europe would tell us *how* the military power of a great nation is used to advance the commercial interest of its citizens, would explain to us the *modus operandi,* and not refer us to large and vague phrases about "exercising due weight in the councils of the nations," we might accept their philosophy. But, until they do so, we are surely justified in assuming that their political terminology is simply a survival--an inheritance from a state of things which has, in fact, passed away.

It is facts of the nature of those I have instanced which constitute the real protection of the small State, and which are bound as they gain in general recognition to constitute the real protection from outside aggression of all States, great or small.

One financial authority from whom I have quoted noted that this elaborate financial interdependence of the modern world has grown up in spite of ourselves, "without our noticing it until we put it to some rude test." Men are fundamentally just as disposed as they were at any time to take wealth that does not belong to them, which they have not earned. But their relative interest in the matter has changed. In very primitive conditions robbery is a moderately profitable enterprise. Where the rewards of labor, owing to the inefficiency of the means of production, are small and uncertain, and where all wealth is portable, raiding and theft offer the best reward for the enterprise of the courageous; in such conditions the size of man's wealth depends a good deal on the size of his club and the agility with which he wields it. But to the man whose wealth so largely depends upon his credit and on his paper being "good paper" at the bank, dishonesty has become as precarious and profitless as honest toil was in more primitive times.

The instincts of the business man may, at bottom, be just as predatory as those of the cattle-lifter or the robber baron, but taking property by force has become one of the least profitable and the most speculative forms of enterprise upon which he could engage. The force of commercial events has rendered the thing impossible. I know that the defender of arms will reply that it is the police who have rendered it impossible. This is not true. There were as many armed men in Europe in the days when the robber baron carried on his occupation as there are in our day. To say that the policeman makes him impossible is to put the cart before the horse. What created the police and made them possible, if it was not the general recognition of the fact that disorder and aggression make trade impossible?

Just note what is taking place in South America. States in which repudiation was a commonplace of everyday politics have of recent years become as stable and as respectable as the City of London, and have come to discharge their obligations as regularly. These countries were during hundreds of years a slough of disorder and a never-ending sanguinary scramble for the spoils, and yet in a matter of fifteen or twenty years the conditions have radically changed. Does this mean that the nature of these populations has fundamentally altered in less than a generation? In that case many a militarist claim must be rejected. There is a simpler explanation.

These countries, like Brazil and the Argentine, have been drawn into the circle of international trade, exchange, and finance. Their economic relationships have become sufficiently extensive and complex to make repudiation the least profitable form of theft. The financier will tell you "they cannot afford to repudiate." If any attempt at repudiation were made, all sorts of property, either directly or indirectly connected with the orderly execution of Governmental functions, would suffer, banks would become involved, great businesses would stagger, and the whole financial community would protest. To attempt to escape the payment of a single loan would involve the business world in losses amounting to many times the value of the loan.

It is only where a community has nothing to lose, no banks, no personal fortunes dependent upon public good faith, no great businesses, no industries, that the Government can afford to repudiate its obligations or to disregard the general code of economic morality. This was the case with Argentina and Brazil a generation ago; it is still the case, to some extent, with some Central American States to-day. *It is not because the armies in these States have grown* that the public credit has improved. Their armies were greater a generation ago than they are now. It is because they know that trade and finance are built upon credit--that is, confidence in the fulfillment of obligations, upon security of tenure in titles, upon the enforcement of contract according to law--and that if credit is seriously shaken, there is not a section of the elaborate fabric which is not affected.

The more our commercial system gains in complication, the more does the common prosperity of all of us come to depend upon the reliance which can be placed on the due performance of all contracts. This is the real basis of "prestige," national and individual; circumstances stronger than ourselves are pushing us, despite what the cynical critics of our commercial civilization may say, towards the unvarying observance of this simple ideal. When we drop back from it--and such relapses occur as we should expect them to occur, especially in those societies which have just emerged from a more or less primitive state--punishment is generally swift and sure.

What was the real origin of the bank crisis of 1907 in the United States, which had for American business men such disastrous consequences? It was the loss by American financiers and American bankers of the confidence of the American public. At bottom there was no other reason. One talks of cash reserves and currency errors; but London, which does the banking of the universe, works on the smallest cash reserve in the world, because, as an American authority has put it, English bankers work with a "psychological reserve."

I quote from Mr. Withers:

It is because they (English bankers) are so safe, so straight, so sensible, from an American point of view so unenterprising, that they are able to build up a bigger credit fabric on a smaller gold basis, and even carry this building to a height which they themselves have decided to be questionable. This "psychological reserve" is the priceless possession that has been handed down through generations of good bankers, and every individual of every generation who receives it can do something to maintain and improve it.

But it was not always thus, and it is merely the many ramifications of the English commercial and financial world that have brought this about. In the end the Americans will imitate it, or they will suffer from a hopeless disadvantage in their financial competition with England. Commercial development is broadly illustrating one profound truth: that the real basis of social morality is self-interest. If English banks and insurance companies have become absolutely honest in their administration, it is because the dishonesty of any one of them threatened the prosperity of all.

Must we assume that the Governments of the world, which, presumably, are directed by men as far-sighted as bankers, are permanently to fall below the banker in their conception of enlightened self-interest? Must we assume that what is self-evident to the banker--namely, that the repudiation of engagements, or any attempt at financial plunder, is sheer stupidity and commercial suicide--is forever to remain unperceived by the ruler? Then, when he realizes this truth, shall we not at least have made some progress towards laying the foundations for a sane international polity?

The following correspondence, provoked by the first edition of this book, may throw light on some of the points dealt with in this chapter. A correspondent of London *Public Opinion* criticized a part of the thesis here dealt with as a "series of half-truths," questioning as follows:

What is "natural wealth," and how can trade be carried on with it unless there are markets for it when worked? Would the writer maintain that markets cannot be permanently or seriously affected by military conquests, especially if conquest be followed by the imposition upon the vanquished of commercial conditions framed in the interests of the victor?... Germany has derived, and continues to derive, great advantages from the most-favored-nation clause which she compelled France to insert in the Treaty of Frankfurt.... Bismarck, it is true, underestimated the financial resilience of France, and was sorely disappointed when the French paid off the indemnity with such astonishing rapidity, and thus liberated themselves from the equally crushing burden of having to maintain the German army of occupation. He regretted not having demanded an indemnity twice as large. Germany would not repeat the mistake, and any country having the misfortune to be vanquished by her in future will be likely to find its commercial prosperity compromised for decades.

To which I replied:

Will your correspondent forgive my saying that while he talks of half-truths, the whole of this passage indicates the domination of that particular half-truth which lies at the bottom of the illusion with which my book deals?

What is a market? Your correspondent evidently conceives it as a place where things are sold. That is only half the truth. It is a place where things are bought and sold, and one operation is impossible without the other, and the notion that one nation can sell for ever and never buy is simply the theory of perpetual motion applied to economics; and international trade can no more be based upon perpetual motion than can engineering. As between economically highly-organized nations a customer must also be a competitor, a fact which bayonets cannot alter. To the extent to which they destroy him as a competitor, they destroy him, speaking generally, and largely, as a customer.

The late Mr. Seddon conceived England as making her purchases with "a stream of golden sovereigns" flowing from a stock all the time getting smaller. That "practical" man, however, who so despised "mere theories," was himself the victim of a pure theory, and the picture which he conjured up from his inner consciousness has no existence in fact. England has hardly enough gold to pay one year's taxes, and if she paid for her imports in gold she would exhaust her stock in three months; and the process by which she really pays has been going on for sixty years. She is a buyer just as long as she is a seller, and if she is to afford a market to Germany she must procure the money wherewith to pay for Germany's goods by selling goods to Germany or elsewhere, and if that process of sale stops, Germany loses a market, not only the English market, but also those markets which depend in their turn upon England's capacity to buy--that is to say, to sell, for, again, the one operation is impossible without the other.

If your correspondent had had the whole process in his mind instead of half of it, I do not think that he would have written the passages I have quoted. In his endorsement of the Bismarckian conception of political economy he evidently deems that one nation's gain is the measure of another nation's loss, and that nations live by robbing their neighbors in a lesser or greater degree. This is economics in the style of Tamerlane and the Red Indian, and, happily, has no relation to the real facts of modern commercial intercourse.

The conception of one-half of the case only, dominates your correspondent's letter throughout. He says, "Germany has derived, and continues to derive, great advantage from the most-favored-nation clause which she compelled France to insert in the Treaty of Frankfurt," which is quite true, but leaves out the other half of the truth, somewhat important to our discussion--viz., that France has also greatly benefited, in that the scope of fruitless tariff war has been by so much restricted.

A further illustration: Why should Germany have been sorely disappointed at France's rapid recovery? The German people are not going to be the richer for having a poor neighbor--on the contrary, they are going to be the poorer, and there is not an economist with a reputation to lose, whatever his views of fiscal policy, who would challenge this for a moment.

How would Germany impose upon a vanquished England commercial arrangements which would impoverish the vanquished and enrich the victor? By enforcing another Frankfurt treaty, by which English ports should be kept open to German goods? But that is precisely what English ports have been for sixty years, and Germany has not been obliged to wage a costly war to effect it. Would Germany close her own markets to our goods? But, again, that is precisely what she has done--again without war, and by a right which we never dream of challenging. How is war going to affect the question one way or another? I have been asking for a detailed answer to that question from European publicists and statesmen for the last ten years, and I have never yet been answered, save by much vagueness, much fine phrasing concerning commercial supremacy, a spirited foreign policy, national prestige, and much else, which no one seems able to define, but a real policy, a *modus operandi*, a balance-sheet which one can analyze, never. And until such is forthcoming I shall continue to believe that the whole thing is based upon an illusion.

The true test of fallacies of this kind is progression. Imagine Germany (as our Jingoes seem to dream of her) absolute master of Europe, and able to dictate any policy that she pleased. How would she treat such a European empire? By impoverishing its component parts? But that would be suicidal. Where would her big industrial population find their markets?[15] If she set out to develop and enrich the component parts, these would become merely efficient competitors, and she need not have undertaken the costliest war of history to arrive at that result. This is the paradox, the futility of conquest--the great illusion which the history of our own Empire so well illustrates. We British "own" our Empire by allowing its component parts to develop themselves in their own way, and in view of their own ends, and all the empires which have pursued any other policy have only ended by impoverishing their own populations and falling to pieces.

Your correspondent asks: "Is Mr. Norman Angell prepared to maintain that Japan has derived no political or commercial advantages from her victories, and that Russia has suffered no loss from defeat?"

What I am prepared to maintain, and what the experts know to be the truth, is that the Japanese people are the poorer, not the richer for their war, and that the Russian people will gain more from defeat than they could possibly have gained by victory, since defeat will constitute a check on the economically sterile policy of military and territorial aggrandizement and turn Russian energies to social and economic development; and it is because of this fact that Russia is at the present moment, despite her desperate internal troubles, showing a capacity for economic regeneration as great as, if not greater than, that of Japan. This latter country is breaking all modern records, civilized or uncivilized, in the burdensomeness of her taxation. On the average, the Japanese people pay 30 per cent.--nearly one-third--of their net income in taxation in one form or another, and so far have they been compelled to push the progressive principle that a Japanese lucky enough to possess an income of ten thousand a year has to surrender over six thousand of it in taxation, a condition of things which would, of course, create a revolution in any European country in twenty-four hours. And this is quoted as a result so brilliant that those who question it cannot be doing so seriously![16] On the other side, for the first time in twenty years the Russian Budget shows a surplus.

This recovery of the defeated nation after wars is not even peculiar to our generation. Ten years after the Franco-Prussian War France was in a better financial position than Germany, as she is in a better financial position to-day, and though her foreign trade does not show as great expansion as that of Germany--because her population remains absolutely stationary, while that of Germany increases by leaps and bounds--the French people as a whole are more prosperous, more comfortable, more economically secure, with a greater reserve of savings, and all the moral and social advantages that go therewith, than are the Germans. In the same way the social and industrial renaissance of modern Spain dates from the day that she was defeated and lost her colonies, and it is since her defeat that Spanish securities have just doubled in value.[17] It is since England added the "gold-fields of the world" to her "possessions" that British Consols have dropped twenty points. Such is the outcome in terms of social well-being of military success and political prestige!

CHAPTER VI

THE INDEMNITY FUTILITY

The real balance-sheet of the Franco-German War--Disregard of Sir Robert Giffen's warning in interpreting the figures--What really happened in France and Germany during the decade following the war--Bismarck's disillusionment--The necessary discount to be given an indemnity--The bearing of the war and its result on German prosperity and progress.

In politics it is unfortunately true that ten dollars which can be seen bulk more largely in the public mind than a million which happen to be out of sight but are none the less real. Thus, however clearly the wastefulness of war and the impossibility of effecting by its means any permanent economic or social advantage for the conqueror may be shown, the fact that Germany was able to exact an indemnity of a billion dollars from France at the close of the war of 1870-71 is taken as conclusive evidence that a nation can "make money by war."

In 1872, Sir Robert (then Mr.) Giffen wrote a notable article summarizing the results of the Franco-German War thus: it meant to France a loss of 3500 million dollars, and to Germany a total net gain of 870 millions, a money difference in favor of Germany exceeding in value the whole amount of the British National Debt!

An arithmetical statement of this kind seems at first sight so conclusive that those who have since discussed the financial outcome of the war of 1870 have quite overlooked the fact that, if such a balance-sheet as that indicated be sound, the whole financial history of Germany and France during the forty years which have followed the war is meaningless.

The truth is, of course, that such a balance-sheet is meaningless--a verdict which does not reflect upon Sir Robert Giffen, because he drew it up in ignorance of the sequel of the war. It does, however, reflect on those who have adopted the result shown on such a balance-sheet. Indeed, Sir Robert Giffen himself made the most important reservations. He had at least an inkling of the practical difficulties of profiting by an indemnity, and indicated plainly that the nominal figures had to be very heavily discounted.

A critic[18] of an early edition of this book seems to have adopted most of Sir Robert Giffen's figures, disregarding, however, certain of his reservations, and to this critic I replied as follows:

In arriving at this balance my critic, like the company-promoting genius who promises you 150 per cent. for your money, leaves so much out of the account. There are a few items not considered, *e.g.* the increase in the French army which took place immediately after the war, and as the direct result thereof, compelled Germany to increase her army by at least one hundred thousand men, an increase which has been maintained for forty years. The expenditure throughout this time amounts to at least a billion dollars. We have already wiped out the "profit," and I have only dealt with one item yet--to this we must add,--loss of markets for Germany involved in the destruction of so many French lives and so much French wealth; loss from the general disturbance throughout Europe, and still greater loss from the fact that the unproductive expenditure on armaments throughout the greater part of Europe which has followed the war, the diversion of energies which is the result of it, has directly deprived Germany of large markets and by a general check of development indirectly deprived her of immense ones.

But it is absurd to bring figures to bear on such a system of bookkeeping as that adopted by my critic. Germany had several years' preparation for the war, and has had, as the direct result thereof and as an integral part of the general war system which her own policy supports, certain obligations during forty years. All this is ignored. Just note how the same principle would work if applied in ordinary commercial matters; because, for instance, on an estate the actual harvest only takes a fortnight, you disregard altogether the working expenses for the remaining fifty weeks of the year, charge only the actual cost of the harvest (and not all of that), deduct this from the gross proceeds of the crops, and call the result "profit"! Such "finance" is really luminous. Applied by the ordinary business man, it would in an incredibly short time put his business in the bankruptcy court and himself in gaol!

But were my critic's figures as complete as they are absurdly incomplete and misleading, I should still be unimpressed, because the facts which stare us in the face would not corroborate his statistical performance. We are examining what is from the money point of view the most successful war ever recorded in history, and if the general proposition that such a war is financially profitable were sound, and if the results of the war were anything like as brilliant as they are represented, money should be cheaper and more plentiful in Germany than in France, and credit, public and private, should be sounder. Well, it is the exact reverse which is the case. As a net result of the whole thing Germany was, ten years after the war, a good deal worse off, financially, than her vanquished rival, and was at that date trying, as she is trying to-day, to borrow money from her victim. Within twenty months of the payment of the last of the indemnity, the bank rate was higher in Berlin than in Paris, and we know that Bismarck's later life was clouded by the spectacle of what he regarded as an absurd miracle: the vanquished recovering more quickly than the victor. We have the testimony of his own speeches to this fact, and to the fact that France weathered the financial storms of 1878-9 a great deal better than did Germany. And to-day, when Germany is compelled to pay nearly 4 per cent. for money, France can secure it for 3.... We are not for the moment considering anything but the money view--the advantages and disadvantages of a certain financial operation--and by any test that you care to apply, France, the vanquished, is better off than Germany, the victor. The French people are as a whole more prosperous, more comfortable, more economically secure, with greater reserve of savings and all the moral and social advantages that go therewith, than are the Germans, a fact expressed briefly by French Rentes standing at 98 and German Consols at 83. There is something wrong with a financial operation that gives these results.

The something wrong, of course, is that in order to arrive at any financial profit at all essential facts have to be disregarded, those facts being what necessarily precedes and what necessarily follows a war of this kind. In the case of highly organized industrial nations like England and Germany, dependent for the very livelihood of great masses of their population upon the fact that neighboring nations furnish a market for their goods, a general policy of "piracy," imposing upon those neighbors an expenditure which limits their purchasing power, creates a burden of which the nation responsible for that policy of piracy pays its part. It is not France alone which has paid the greater part of the real cost of the Franco-German War, it is Europe--and particularly Germany--in the burdensome military system and the general political situation which that war has created or intensified.

But there is a more special consideration connected with the exaction of an indemnity, which demands notice, and that is the practical difficulty with regard to the transfer of an immense sum of money outside the ordinary operations of commerce.

The history of the German experience with the French indemnity suggests the question whether in every case an enormous discount on the nominal value of a large money indemnity must not be allowed owing to the practical financial difficulties of its payment and receipt, difficulties unavoidable in any circumstances which we need consider.

These difficulties were clearly foreseen by Sir Robert Giffen, though his warnings, and the important reservations that he made on this point, are generally overlooked by those who wish to make use of his conclusions.

These warnings he summarized as follows:

As regards Germany, a doubt is expressed whether the Germans will gain so much as France loses, the capital of the indemnity being transferred from individuals to the German Government, who cannot use it so profitably as individuals. It is doubted whether the practice of lending out large sums, though a preferable course to locking them up, will not in the end be injurious.

The financial operations incidental to these great losses and expenses seriously affect the money market. They have been a fruitful cause, in the first place, of spasmodic disturbance. The outbreak of war caused a monetary panic in July, 1870, by the anxiety of people who had money engagements to meet to provide against the chances of war, and there was another monetary crash in September, 1871, owing to the sudden withdrawal by the German Government of the money it had to receive. The war thus illustrates the tendency of wars in general to cause spasmodic disturbance in a market so delicately organized as that of London now is.

And it is to be noted in this connection that the difficulties of 1872 were trifling compared to what they would necessarily be in our day. In 1872, Germany was self-sufficing, little dependent upon credit; to-day undisturbed credit in Europe is the very life-blood of her industry; it is, in fact, the very food of her people, as the events of 1911 have sufficiently proved.

It is not generally realized how abundantly the whole history of the German indemnity bears out Sir Robert Giffen's warning; how this flood of gold turned indeed to dust and ashes as far as the German nation is concerned.

First, anyone familiar with financial problems might have expected that the receipt of so large a sum of money by Germany would cause prices to rise and so handicap export trade in competition with France, where the reverse process would cause prices to fall. This result was, in fact, produced. M. Paul Beaulieu and M. Léon Say[19] have both shown that this factor operated through the value of commercial bills of exchange, giving to the French exporter a bonus and to the German a handicap which affected trade most perceptibly. Captain Bernard Serrigny, who has collected in his work a wealth of evidence bearing on this subject, writes:

The rise in prices influenced seriously the cost of production, and the German manufacturers fought, in consequence, at a disadvantage with England and France. Finally the goods produced at this high cost were thrown upon the home market at the moment when the increase in the cost of living was diminishing seriously the purchasing power of the bulk of consumers. These goods had to compete, not only with home over-production due to the failure to sell abroad, but with foreign goods, which, despite the tariff, were by their lower price able to push their way into the German market, where relatively higher prices attracted them. In this competition France was particularly prominent. In France the lack of metallic money had engendered great financial caution, and had considerably lowered prices all around, so that there was a general financial and commercial condition very different from that in Germany, where the payment of the indemnity had been followed by reckless speculation. Moreover, owing to the heavy foreign payments made by France, bills drawn on foreign centres were at a premium, a premium which constituted a sensible additional profit to French exporters, so considerable in certain cases that it was worthwhile for French manufacturers to sell their goods at an actual loss in order to realize the profit on the bill of exchange. The German market was thus being captured by the French at the very moment when the Germans supposed they would, thanks to the indemnity, be starting out to capture the world.

The German economist Max Wirth ("Geschichte der Handelskrisen") expressed in 1874 his astonishment at France's financial and industrial recovery: "The most striking example of the economic force of the country is shown by the exports, which rose immediately after the signature of peace, despite a war which swallowed a hundred thousand lives and more than ten milliards (two billion dollars)." A similar conclusion is drawn by Professor Biermer ("Fürst Bismarck als Volkswirt"), who indicates that the Protectionist movement in 1879 was to a large extent due to the result of the payment of the indemnity.

This disturbance of the balance of trade, however, was only one factor among several: the financial disorganization, a fictitious expansion of expenditure creating a morbid speculation, precipitated the worst financial crisis in Germany which she has known in modern times. Monsieur Lavisse summarizes the experience thus:

Enormous sums of money were lost. If one takes the aggregate of the securities quoted on the Berlin Bourse, railroad, mining and industrial securities generally, it is by thousands of millions of marks that one must estimate the value of such securities in 1870 and 1871. But a large number of enterprises were started in Germany of which the Berlin Bourse knew nothing. Cologne, Hamburg, Frankfurt, Leipzig, Breslau, Stuttgart, had all their local groups of speculative securities; hundreds of millions must be added to the thousands of millions. These differences did not represent merely a transfer of wealth, for a great proportion of the capital sunk was lost altogether, having been eaten up in ill-considered and unattractive expenditure.... There can be no sort of doubt that the money lost in these worthless enterprises constitutes an absolute loss for Germany.

The decade from 1870-1880 was for France a great recuperative period, although for several other nations in Europe it was one of great depression, notably, after the "boom" of 1872, for Germany. No less an authority than Bismarck himself testifies to the double fact. We know that Bismarck was astonished and dismayed by seeing the regeneration of France after the war taking place more rapidly and more completely than the regeneration of Germany. This weighed so heavily upon his mind that in introducing his Protectionist Bill in 1879 he declared that Germany was "slowly bleeding to death," and that if the present process were continued she would find herself ruined. Speaking in the Reichstag on May 2, 1879, he said:

We see that France manages to support the present difficult business situation of the civilized world better than we do; that her Budget has increased since 1871 by a milliard and a half, and that thanks not only to loans; we see that she has more resources than Germany, and that, in short, over there they complain less of bad times.

And in a speech two years later (November 29, 1881) he returned to the same idea:

It was towards 1877 that I was first struck with the general and growing distress in Germany as compared with France. I saw furnaces banked, the standard of well-being reduced, and the general position of workmen becoming worse and business as a whole terribly bad.

In the book from which these extracts are taken[20] the author writes as an introduction to Bismarck's speeches:

Trade and industry were in a miserable condition. Thousands of workmen were without employment, and in the winter of 1876-77 unemployment took great proportions, and soup-kitchens and State workshops had to be established.

Every author who deals with this period seems to tell broadly the same tale, however much they may differ in detail. "If only we could get back to the general position of things before the war," said M. Block in 1879. "But salaries diminish and prices go up."[21]

At the very time that the French millions were raining in upon Germany (1873) she was suffering from a grave financial crisis, and so little effect did the transfer of the money have upon trade and finance in general, that twelve months after the payment of the last of the indemnity we find the bank rate higher in Berlin than in Paris; and, as was shown by the German economist Soetbeer, by the year 1878 far more money was in circulation in France than in Germany.[22] Hans Blum, indeed, directly ascribed the series of crises between the years 1873 and 1880 to the indemnity: "A burst of prosperity and then ruin for thousands."[23] Throughout the year 1875 the bank rate in Paris was uniformly 3 per cent. In Berlin (Preussische Bank, which preceded the Reichs Bank) it varied from 4 to 6 per cent. A similar difference is reflected by the fact that, between the years 1872 and 1877, the deposits in the State savings banks in Germany actually fell by roughly 20 per cent., while in the same period the French deposits *increased* about 20 per cent.

Two tendencies plainly show the condition of Germany during the decade which followed the war: the enormous growth of Socialism--relatively much greater than any which we have ever since seen--and the immense stimulus given to emigration.

Perhaps no thesis is commoner with the defender of war than this: that, though one may not be able in a narrow economic sense to justify an enterprise like that of 1870, the moral stimulus which victory gave to the German people is accepted as being of incalculable benefit to the race and the nation. Its alleged effect in bringing about a national solidarity, in stimulating patriotic sentiment and national pride, in the wiping out of internal differences and Heaven knows what, are claims I have dealt with at greater length elsewhere, and I wish only to note here that all this high-falutin does not stand the test of facts. The two phenomena just mentioned--the extraordinary progress of Socialism and the enormous stimulus given to emigration during the years which immediately followed the war--give the lie to all the claims in question. In 1872-73, the very years in which the moral stimulus of victory and the economic stimulus of the indemnity should have kept at home every able-bodied German, emigration was, relatively to the population, greater than it has ever been before or since, the figures for 1872 being 154,000 and for 1873 134,000.[24] And at no period since the fifties was the internal political struggle so bitter--it was a period of repression, of prescription on the one side and class-hatred on the other--"the golden age of the drill-sergeant," some German has called it.

It will be replied that, after the first decade, Germany's trade has shown an expansion which has not been shown by that of France. Those who are hypnotized by this, quietly ignore altogether one great fact or which has affected both France and Germany, not only since the war, but during the whole of the nineteenth century, and that factor is that the population of France, from causes in no way connected with the Franco-Prussian War, since the tendency was a pronounced one for fifty years before, is practically quite stationary; while the population of Germany, also for reasons in no way connected with the war, since the tendency was also pronounced half a century previously, has shown an abounding expansion. Since 1875 the population of Germany has increased by twenty million souls. That of France has not increased at all. Is it astonishing that the labor of twenty million souls makes some stir in the industrial world? Is it not evident that the necessity of earning a livelihood for this increasing population gives to German industry an expansion outside the limits of her territory which cannot be looked for in the case of a nation whose social energies are not faced with any such problem? There is this, moreover, to be borne in mind: Germany has secured her foreign trade on what are, in the terms of the relative comfort of her people, hard conditions. In other words, she has secured that trade by cutting profits, in the way that a business fighting desperately for life will cut profits, in order to secure orders, and by making sacrifices that the comfortable business man will not make. Notwithstanding the fact that France has made no sensational splash in foreign trade since the war, the standard of comfort among her people has been rising steadily, and is without doubt generally higher to-day than is that of the German people. This higher standard of comfort is reflected in her financial situation. It is Germany, the victor, which is to-day in the position of a suppliant in regard to France, and it is revealing no diplomatic secrets to say that, for many years now, Germany has been employing all the wiles of her diplomacy to obtain the official recognition of German securities on the French Bourses. France financially has, in a very real sense, the whip hand.

That is not all. Those who point triumphantly to German industrial expansion, as a proof of the benefits of war and conquest, ignore certain facts which cannot be ignored if that argument is to have any value, and they are these:

1. Such progress is not peculiar to Germany; it is shown in an equal or greater degree (I am speaking now of the general wealth and social progress of the average individual citizen) by States that have had no victorious war--the Scandinavian States, the Netherlands, Switzerland.

2. Even if it were special to Germany, which it is not, we should be entitled to ask whether certain developments of German political evolution, which *preceded the war,* and which one may fairly claim have a more direct and understandable bearing upon industrial progress, are not a much more appreciable factor in that progress than the war itself--I refer particularly, of course, to the immense change involved in the fiscal union of the German States, which was completed before the Franco-German War of 1870 had been declared; to say nothing of such other factors as the invention of the Thomas-Gilchrist process which enabled the phosphoric iron ores of Germany, previously useless, to be utilized.

3. The very serious social difficulties (which have, of course, their economic aspect) that *do* confront the German people--the intense class friction, the backwardness of parliamentary government, the survival of reactionary political ideas, wrapped up with the domination of the "Prussian ideal"--all difficulties which States whose political development has been less marked by successful war (the lesser European States just mentioned, for instance)--are not faced with in the same degree. These difficulties, special, among the great European nations, to Germany, are certainly in a large measure a legacy of the Franco-German War, a part of the general system to which that war gave rise, the general character of the political union which it provoked.

The general ascription of such real progress as Germany has made to the effects of the war and nothing else--a conclusion which calmly ignores factors which have evidently a more direct bearing--is one of those *a priori* judgments repeated, parrot fashion, without investigation or care even by publicists of repute; it is characteristic of the carelessness which dominates this whole subject. This more general consideration, which does not properly belong to the special problem of an indemnity, I have dealt with at greater length in the next section. The evidence bearing on the particular question, as to whether in practice the exaction of a large monetary indemnity from a conquered foe can ever be economically profitable or of real advantage to the conqueror, is of a simpler character. If we put the question in this form, "Was the receipt of the indemnity, in the most characteristic and successful case in history, of advantage to the conqueror?" the reply is simple enough: all the evidence plainly and conclusively shows that it was of no advantage; that the conqueror would probably have been better without it.

Even if we draw from that evidence a contrary conclusion, even if we conclude that the actual payment of the indemnity was as beneficial as all the evidence would seem to show it was mischievous; even if we could set aside completely the financial and commercial difficulties which its payment seems to have involved; if we ascribe to other causes the great financial crises which followed that payment; if we deduct no discount from the nominal value of the indemnity, but assume that every mark and thaler of it represented its full face value to Germany--even admitting all this, it is still inevitable that *the direct cost of preparing for a war and of guarding against a subsequent war of retribution must, from the nature of the case, exceed the value of the indemnity which can be exacted.* This is not merely a hypothetical statement, it is a commercial fact, supported by evidence which is familiar to us all. In order to avoid repaying, with interest, the indemnity drawn from France, Germany has had to expend upon armaments a sum of money at least equal to that indemnity. In order to exact a still larger indemnity from Great Britain, Germany would have to spend a still larger sum in preparations, and to guard against repayment would be led into indefinite expenditure, which has only to go on long enough inevitably to exceed the very definite indemnity. For, it must be remembered that the amount of an indemnity extractable from a modern community, of the credit era, has very definite limits: an insolvent community can pay more. If the Statesmen of Europe could lay on one side, for a moment, the irrelevant considerations which cloud their minds, they would see that the direct cost of acquisition by force must in these circumstances necessarily exceed in value the property acquired. When the *indirect* costs are also considered, the balance of loss becomes incalculably greater.

Those who urge that through an indemnity, war can be made to "pay" (and it is for them that this chapter is written), have before them problems and difficulties--difficulties of not merely a military, but of a financial and social character--of the very deepest kind. It was precisely in this section of the subject that German science failed in 1870. There is no evidence that much progress has been made in the study of this phase of the problem by either side since the war--indeed, there is plenty of evidence that it has been neglected. It is time that it was scientifically and systematically attacked.

Those who wish well for Europe will encourage the study, for it can have but one result: to show that less and less can war be made to pay; that all those forces of our world which daily gain in strength make it, as a commercial venture, more and more preposterous. The study of this department of international polity will tend to the same result as the study of any of its facets: the undermining of those beliefs which have in the past so often led to, and are to-day so often claimed as the motives likely to lead to, war between civilized peoples.

CHAPTER VII

HOW COLONIES ARE OWNED

Why twentieth-century methods must differ from eighteenth--The vagueness of our conceptions of statecraft--How Colonies are "owned"--Some little recognized facts--Why foreigners could not fight England for her self-governing Colonies--She does not "own" them, since they are masters of their own destiny--The paradox of conquest: England in a worse position in regard to her own Colonies than in regard to foreign nations--Her experience as the oldest and most practiced colonizer in history--Recent French experience--Could Germany hope to do what England cannot do?

The foregoing chapters dispose of the first six of the seven propositions outlined in Chapter III. There remains the seventh, dealing with the notion that in some way England's security and prosperity would be threatened by a foreign nation "taking our Colonies from us"--a thing which we are assured her rivals are burning to do, as it would involve the "breaking up of the British Empire" to their advantage.

Let us try to read some meaning into a phrase which, however childish it may appear on analysis, is very commonly in the mouths of those who are responsible for British political ideas.

In this connection it is necessary to point out--as, indeed, it is in every phase of this problem of the relationship of States--that the world has moved, that methods have changed. It is hardly possible to discuss this matter of the necessary futility of military force in the modern world for ten minutes without it being urged that as England has acquired her Colonies by the sword, it is evident that the sword may do a like service for modern States desiring Colonies. About as reasonably could one say that, as certain tribes and nations in the past enriched themselves by capturing slaves and women among neighboring tribes, the desire to capture slaves and women will always be an operative motive in warfare between nations, as though slavery had not been put economically out of court by modern industrial methods, and as though the change in social methods had not put the forcible capture of women out of court.

What was the problem confronting the merchant adventurer of the sixteenth century? There were newly-discovered foreign lands containing, as he believed, precious metals and stones and spices, and inhabited by savages or semi-savages. If other traders got those stones, it was quite evident that he could not. His colonial policy, therefore, had to be directed to two ends: first, such effective political occupation of the country that he could keep the savage or semi-savage population in check, and could exploit the territory for its wealth; and, secondly, such arrangements as would prevent other nations from searching for this wealth in precious metals, spices, etc., since, if they obtained it, he could not.

That is the story of the French and Dutch in India, and of the Spanish in South America. But as soon as there grew up in those countries an organized community living in the country itself, the whole problem changed. The Colonies, in this later stage of development, have a value to the Mother Country mainly as a market and a source of food and raw material, and if their value in those respects is to be developed to the full, they inevitably become self-governing communities in greater or less degree, and the Mother Country exploits them exactly as she exploits any other community with which she may be trading. Germany might acquire Canada, but it could no longer be a question of her taking Canada's wealth in precious metals, or in any other form, to the exclusion of other nations. Could Germany "own" Canada, she would have to "own" it in the same way that Britain does; the Germans would have to pay for every sack of wheat and every pound of beef that they might buy, just as though Canada "belonged" to England or to anybody else. Germany could not have even the meager satisfaction of Germanizing these great communities, for one knows that they are far too firmly "set." Their language, law, morals, would have to be, after German conquest, what they are now. Germany would find that the German Canada was pretty much the Canada that it is now--a country where Germans are free to go and do go; a field for Germany's expanding population.

As a matter of fact, Germany feeds her expanding population from territories like Canada and the United States and South America without sending its citizens there. The era of emigration from Germany has stopped, because the compound steam-engine has rendered emigration largely unnecessary. And it is the developments which are the necessary outcome of such forces, that have made the whole colonial problem of the twentieth century radically different from that of the eighteenth or seventeenth.

I have stated the case thus: No nation could gain any advantage by the conquest of the British Colonies, and Great Britain could not suffer material damage by their "loss," however much this would be regretted on sentimental grounds, and as rendering less easy a certain useful social co-operation between kindred peoples. For the British Colonies are, in fact, independent nations in alliance with the Mother Country, to whom they are no source of tribute or economic profit (except in the way that foreign nations are), their economic relations being settled not by the Mother Country, but by the Colonies. Economically, England would gain by their formal separation, since she would be relieved of the cost of their defense. Their loss, involving, therefore, no change in economic fact (beyond saving the Mother Country the cost of their defense), could not involve the ruin of the Empire and the starvation of the Mother Country, as those who commonly treat of such a contingency are apt to aver. As

England is not able to exact tribute or economic advantage, it is inconceivable that any other country, necessarily less experienced in colonial management, would be able to succeed where England had failed, especially in view of the past history of the Spanish, Portuguese, French, and British Colonial Empires. This history also demonstrates that the position of British Crown Colonies, in the respect which we are considering, is not sensibly different from that of the self-governing ones. It is not to be presumed, therefore, that any European nation would attempt the desperately expensive business of the conquest of England, for the purpose of making an experiment with her Colonies which all colonial history shows to be doomed to failure.

What are the facts? Great Britain is the most successful colonizing nation in the world, and the policy into which her experience has driven her is that outlined by Sir C. P. Lucas, one of the greatest authorities on colonial questions. He writes, speaking of the history of the British Colonies on the American continent, thus:

It was seen--but it might not have been seen had the United States not won their independence--that English colonists, like Greek Colonies of old, go out on terms of being equal, not subordinate, to those who are left behind; that when they have effectively planted another and a distant land, they must, within the widest limits, be left to rule themselves; that, whether they are right, or whether they are wrong--more, perhaps, when they are wrong than when they are right--they cannot be made amenable by force; that mutual good feeling, community of interest, and abstention from pressing rightful claims to their logical conclusion, can alone hold together a true Colonial Empire.

But what in the name of common sense is the advantage of conquering them if the only policy is to let them do as they like, "whether they are right, or whether they are wrong--more, perhaps, when they are wrong than when they are right"? And what avails it to conquer them if they cannot be made amenable to force? Surely this makes the whole thing a *reductio ad absurdum*. Were a Power like Germany to use force to conquer Colonies, she would find out that they were not amenable to force, and that the only working policy was to let them do exactly as they did before she conquered them, and to allow them, if they chose--and many of the British Colonies do so choose--to treat the Mother Country absolutely as a foreign country. There has recently been going on in Canada a discussion as to the position which that Dominion should hold with reference to the British in the event of war, and that discussion has made Canada's position quite plain. It has been summarized thus: "We must always be free to give or refuse support."[25]

Could a foreign nation say more? In what sense does England "own" Canada when Canadians must always be free to give or refuse their military support to England; and in what way does Canada differ from a foreign nation while England may be at war when Canada can be at peace? Mr. Asquith formally endorses this conception.[26]

This shows clearly that no Dominion is held to be bound by virtue of its allegiance to the Sovereign of the British Empire to place its forces at his disposition, no matter how real may be the emergency. If it should not desire so to do, it is free to refuse so to do. This is to convert the British Empire into a loose alliance of independent Sovereign States, which are not even bound to help each other in case of war. The military alliance between Austria and Germany is far more stringent than the tie which unites, for purposes of war, the component parts of the British Empire.

One critic, commenting on this, says:

Whatever language is used to describe this new movement of Imperial defense, it is virtually one more step towards complete national independence on the part of the Colonies. For not only will the consciousness of the assumption of this task of self-defense feed with new vigor the spirit of nationality, it will entail the further power of full control over foreign relations. This has already been virtually admitted in the case of Canada, now entitled to a determinant voice in all treaties or other engagements in which her interests are especially involved. The extension of this right to the other colonial nations may be taken as a matter of course. Home rule in national defense thus established reduces the Imperial connection to its thinnest terms.[27]

Still more significant, perhaps, is the following emphatic declaration from Mr. Balfour himself. Speaking in London, on November 6, 1911, he said:

We depend as an Empire upon the co-operation of absolutely independent Parliaments. I am not talking as a lawyer; I am talking as a politician. I believe from a legal point of view that the British Parliament is supreme over the Parliament of Canada or Australia or the Cape of South Africa, but in fact they are independent Parliaments, absolutely independent, and it is our business to recognize that and to frame the British Empire upon the co-operation of absolutely independent Parliaments.[28]

Which means, of course, that England's position with regard to Canada or Australia is just England's position with regard to any other independent State; that she has no more "ownership" in Australia than she has in Argentina. Indeed, facts of very recent English history have established quite incontrovertibly this ridiculous paradox: England has more influence--that is to say, a freer opportunity of enforcing her point of view--with foreign nations than with her own Colonies. Indeed, does not Sir C. P. Lucas's statement that "whether they are right or wrong--still more, perhaps, when they are wrong," they must be left alone, necessarily mean that her position with the Colonies is weaker than her position with foreign nations? In the present state of international feeling an English Statesman would never dream of advocating that she should submit to foreign nations when they are wrong. Recent history is illuminating on this point.

What were the larger motives that pushed England into war with the Dutch Republics? To vindicate the supremacy of the British race in South

Africa, to enforce British ideals as against Boer ideals, to secure the
rights of British Indians and other British subjects, to protect the native
against Boer oppression, to take the government of the country generally
from a people whom, at that date, she was apt to describe as "inherently
incapable of civilization." What, however, is the outcome of spending a
billion and a quarter of dollars upon the accomplishment of these objects? The present Government of the Transvaal is in the hands of the
Boer party.[29] England has achieved the union of South Africa in which
the Boer element is predominant. Britain has enforced against the British Indian in the Transvaal and Natal the same Boer regulations which
were one of her grievances before the war, and the Houses of Parliament
have ratified an Act of Union in which the Boer attitude with reference
to the native is codified and made permanent. Sir Charles Dilke, in the
debate in the House of Commons on the South African Bill, made this
quite clear. He said: "The old British principle in South Africa, as distinct
from the Boer principle, in regard to the treatment of natives, was equal
rights for all civilized men. At the beginning of the South African War the
country was told that one of its main objects, and certainly that the one
predominant factor in any treaty of peace, would be the assertion of the
British principle as against the Boer principle. Now the Boer principle
dominates throughout the whole of South Africa." Mr. Asquith, as representing the British Government, admitted that this was the case, and
that "the opinion of this country is almost unanimous in objecting to the
color bar in the Union Parliament." He went on to say that "the opinion
of the British Government and the opinion of the British people must not
be allowed to lead to any interference with a self-governing Colony." So
that, having expended in the conquest of the Transvaal a greater sum
than Germany exacted from France at the close of the Franco-Prussian
War, England has not even the right to enforce her views on those whose
contrary views were the *casus belli!*

A year or two since there was in London a deputation from the British
Indians in the Transvaal pointing out that the regulations there deprive
them of the ordinary rights of British citizens. The British Government
informed them that the Transvaal being a self-governing Colony, the Imperial Government could do nothing for them.[30] Now, it will not be forgotten that, at a time when Britain was quarrelling with Paul Krüger, one
of the liveliest of her grievances was the treatment of British Indians.
Having conquered Krüger, and now "owning" his country, do the British
themselves act as they were trying to compel Paul Krüger as a foreign
ruler to act? They do not. They (or rather the responsible Government of
the Colony, with whom they dare not interfere, although they were ready
enough to make representations to Krüger) simply and purely enforce
his own regulations. Moreover, the Australian Commonwealth and British Columbia have since taken the view with reference to British Indians
which President Krüger took, and which view England made almost a
casus belli. Yet in the case of her Colonies she does absolutely nothing.

So the process is this: The Government of a foreign territory does something which we ask it to cease doing. The refusal of the foreign Government constitutes a *casus belli*. We fight, we conquer, and the territory in question becomes one of our Colonies, and we allow the Government of that Colony to continue doing the very thing which constituted, in the case of a foreign nation, a *casus belli*.

Do we not, taking the English case as typical, arrive, therefore, at the absurdity I have already indicated--*that we are in a worse position to enforce our views in our own territory--that is to say, in our Colonies--than in foreign territory?*

Would England submit tamely if a foreign Government should exercise permanently gross oppression on an important section of her citizens? Certainly she would not. But when the Government exercising that oppression happens to be the Government of her own Colonies she does nothing, and a great British authority lays it down that, even more when the Colonial Government is wrong than when it is right, must she do nothing, and that, though wrong, the Colonial Government cannot be amenable to force. Nor can it be said that Crown Colonies differ essentially in this matter from self-governing dominions. Not only is there an irresistible tendency for Crown Colonies to acquire the practical rights of self-governing dominions, but it has become a practical impossibility to disregard their special interests. Experience is conclusive on this point.

I am not here playing with words or attempting to make paradoxes. This *reductio ad absurdum*--the fact that when she owns a territory she renounces the privilege of using force to ensure observance of her views--is becoming more and more a commonplace of British colonial government.

As to the fiscal position of the Colonies, that is precisely what their political relation is in all but name; they are foreign nations. They erect tariffs against Great Britain; they exclude large sections of British subjects absolutely (practically speaking, no British Indian is allowed to set foot in Australia, and yet British India constitutes the greater part of the British Empire), and even against British subjects from Great Britain vexatious exclusion laws are enacted. Again the question arises: Could a foreign country do more? If fiscal preference is extended to Great Britain, that preference is not the result of British "ownership" of the Colonies, but is the free act of the colonial legislators, and could as well be made by any foreign nation desiring to court closer fiscal relations with Great Britain.[31]

Is it conceivable that Germany, if the real relations between Great Britain and her Colonies were understood, would undertake the costliest war of conquest in history in order to acquire an absurd and profitless position from which she could not exact even the shadow of a material advantage?

It may be pleaded that Germany might on the morrow of conquest attempt to enforce a policy which gave her a material advantage in the

Colonies, such as Spain and Portugal attempted to create for themselves. But in that case, is it conceivable that Germany, without colonial experience, would be able to enforce a policy which Great Britain was obliged to abandon a hundred years ago? Is it imaginable that, if Great Britain has been utterly unable to carry out a policy by which the Colonies shall pay anything resembling tribute to the Mother Country, Germany, without experience, and at an enormous disadvantage in the matter of language, tradition, racial tie, and the rest, would be able to make such a policy a success? Surely, if the elements of this question were in the least understood in Germany, such a preposterous notion could not be entertained for a moment.

Does anyone seriously pretend that the present system of British Colony-holding is due to British philanthropy or high-mindedness? We all know, of course, that it is simply due to the fact that the older system of exploitation by monopoly broke down. It was a complete social, commercial, and political failure long before it was abolished by law. If England had persisted in the use of force to impose a disadvantageous situation on the Colonies, she would have followed in the trail of Spain, Portugal, and France, and she would have lost her Colonies, and her Empire would have broken up.

It took England anything from two to three centuries to learn the real colonial policy, but it would not take so long in our day for a conqueror to realize the only situation possible between one great community and another. European history, indeed, has recently furnished a striking illustration of how the forces which compel the relationship, which England has adopted towards her Colonies, are operative, even in the case of quite small Colonies, which could not be termed "great communities." Under the Méline régime in France, less than twenty years ago, a highly Protectionist policy, somewhat corresponding to the old English colonial monopoly system, was enforced in the case of certain French Colonies. None of these Colonies was very considerable--indeed, they were all quite small--and yet the forces which they represented in the matter of the life of France have sufficed to change radically the attitude of the French Government in the matter of the policy which less than twenty years ago was imposed on them. In *Le Temps* of April 5, 1911, appeared the following:

Our Colonies can consider yesterday a red-letter day. The debate in the Chamber gives hope that the stifling fiscal policy imposed on them heretofore is about to be very greatly modified. The Tariff Commission of the Chamber has hitherto been a very citadel of the blindest type of Protectionism in this matter. M. Thierry is the present President of this Commission, and yet it is from him that we learn that a new era in the Colonies is about to be inaugurated. It is a very great change, and one that may have incalculable consequences in the future development of our Colonial Empire.

The Customs Law of 1892 committed two injustices with regard to our possessions. The first was that it obliged the Colonies to receive, free of duty, goods coming from France, while it taxed colonial goods coming into France. Now, it is impossible to imagine a treaty of that kind being passed between two free countries, and if it was passed with the Colonies, it was because these Colonies were weak, and not in the position to defend themselves *vis-à-vis* the Mother Country.... The Minister of the Colonies himself, animated by a newer and better spirit, which we are so happy to see appear in our treatment of colonial questions, has promised to give all his efforts towards terminating the present bad system.

A further defect of the law of 1892 is that all the Colonies have been subjected to the same fiscal arrangement, as though there could be anything in common between countries separated by the width of the whole globe. Happily the policy was too outrageous ever to be put into full execution. Certain of our African Colonies[32] were tied by international treaties at the time that the law was voted, so that the Government was compelled to make exceptions. But Monsieur Méline's idea at this period was to bring all the Colonies under one fiscal arrangement imposed by the Mother Country, just as soon as the international treaty should have expired. The exceptions have thus furnished a most useful demonstration as to the results which flow from the two systems; the fiscal policy imposed by the Mother Country in view merely of its own immediate interest, and the fiscal policy framed to some extent by the Colony in view of its own special interests. Well, what is the result? It is this. That those Colonies which have been free to frame their own fiscal policy have enjoyed undeniable prosperity, while those which have been obliged to submit to the policy imposed by another country have been sinking into a condition of veritable ruin; they are faced by positive disaster! Only one conclusion is possible. Each Colony must be free to make those arrangements which in its view are suited to its local conditions. That is not at all what M. Méline desired, but it is what experience imposes.... It is not merely a matter of injustice. Our policy has been absurd. What is it that France desires in her Colonies? An addition of wealth and power to the Mother Country. But if we compel the Colonies to submit to disadvantageous fiscal arrangements, which result in their poverty, how can they possibly be a source of wealth and power to the Mother Country? A Colony which can sell nothing is a Colony which can buy nothing: it is a customer lost to French industry.

Every feature of the foregoing is significant and pregnant: this change of policy is not taking place because France is unable to impose force-- she is perfectly able to do so; speaking in practical terms, the Colonies have no physical force whatever to oppose to her--but this change is taking place because the imposition of force, even when completely successful and unchallenged, is economically futile. The object at which France is striving can be obtained in one way only: by an arrangement which is mutually advantageous, arrived at by the free consent of both parties, the establishment of a relationship which places a Colony fiscally, economically, on the footing of a foreign country. France is now in process of doing exactly what England has done in the case of her Colonies: she is undoing the work of conquest, surrendering bit by bit the right to impose force, because force fails in its object.

Perhaps the most significant feature of all in the French experience is this: that it has taken less than twenty years for the old colonial system, even in the case of small and relatively powerless Colonies, to break down entirely. How long would a Power like Germany be able to impose the old policy of exploitation on great and powerful communities, a hundred times greater than the French Colonies, even supposing that she could ever "conquer" them?[33]

Yet so little is the real relationship of modern Colonies understood, that I have heard it mentioned in private conversation by an English public man, whose position was such, moreover, as to enable him to give very great effect to his opinion, that one of the motives pushing Germany to war was the projected capture of South Africa, in order to seize the gold-mines, and by means of a tax of 50 per cent. on their output, secure for herself one of the chief sources of gold in the world.

One heard a good deal at the outbreak of the South African War of the part that the gold-mines played in precipitating that conflict. Alike in England and on the Continent, it was generally assumed that Great Britain was "after the gold-mines." A long correspondence took place in the London *Times* as to the real value of the mines, and speculation as to the amount of money which it was worth Great Britain's while to spend in their "capture." Well, now that England has won the war, how many gold-mines has she captured? In other words, how many shares in the gold-mines does the British Government hold? How many mines have been transferred from their then owners to the British Government, as the result of British victory? How much tribute does the Government of Westminster exact as the result of investing two hundred and fifty millions in the enterprise?

The fact is, of course, that the British Government does not hold a cent's worth of the property. The mines belong to the shareholders and to no one else, and in the conditions of the modern world it is not possible for a Government to "capture" so much as a single dollar's worth of such property as the result of a war of conquest.

Supposing that Germany or any other conqueror were to put on the output of the mines a duty of 50 per cent. What would she get, and what would be the result? The output of the South African mines to-day is, roughly, $150,000,000 a year, so that she would get about $75,000,000 a year.[34] The annual total income of Germany is calculated at something like $15,000,000,000, so that a tribute of $75,000,000 would hold about the same proportion to Germany's total income that, say, fifteen cents a day would to a man in receipt of $10,000 a year. It would represent, say, the expenditure of a man with an income of $2000 or $2500 a year upon, say, his evening cigars. Could one imagine such a householder in his right mind committing burglary and murder in order to economize a dollar a week? Yet that would be the position of the German Empire entering upon a great and costly war for the purpose of exacting $75,000,000 a year from the South African mines; or, rather, the situation for the German Empire would be a great deal worse than that. For this householder having committed burglary and murder for the sake of his dollar a week (the German Empire, that is, having entered into one of the most frightful wars of history to exact its tribute of seventy-five millions) would then find that in order to get this dollar he had to jeopardize many of the investments upon which the bulk of his income depended. On the morrow of imposing a tax of fifty per cent. on the mines there would be such a slump in a class of security now dealt in by every considerable stock exchange in the world that there would hardly be a considerable business firm in Europe unaffected thereby. In England, they know of the difficulty that a relatively mild fiscal attack, delivered rather for social and moral than economic reasons, upon a class of property like the brewing trade provokes. What sort of outcry, therefore, would be raised throughout the world when every South African mining share in the world lost at one stroke half its value, and a great many of them lost all their value? Who would invest money in the Transvaal at all if property were to be subject to that sort of shock? Investors would argue that though it be mines to-day, it might be other forms of property to-morrow, and South Africa would find herself in the position of being able hardly to borrow a quarter for any purpose whatsoever, save at usurious and extortionate rates of interest. The whole of South African trade and industry would, of course, feel the effect, and South Africa as a market would immediately begin to dwindle in importance. Those businesses bound up with South African affairs would border on the brink of ruin, and many of them topple over. Is that the way efficient Germany would set about the development of her newly-acquired Empire? She would soon find that she had a ruined Colony on her hands. If in South Africa the sturdy Dutch and English stock did not produce a George Washington with a better material and moral case for independence than George Washington ever had, then history has no meaning. If it costs England a billion and a quarter to conquer Dutch South Africa, what would it cost Germany to conquer Anglo-Dutch South Africa? Such a policy could not, of course, last six months, and Germany would end by doing what Great Britain has ended by doing--she would renounce all attempt to exact a tribute or commercial advantage other than that which is the result of free co-operation with the South African people. In other words, she would learn that the policy which Great Britain has adopted was not adopted by philanthropy, but in the hard school of bitter experience. Germany would see that the last word in colonial statesmanship is to exact nothing from your Colonies, and where the greatest colonial power of history has been unable to follow any other policy, a poor intruder in the art of colonial administration would not be likely to prove more successful, and she, too, would find that the only way to treat Colonies is to treat them as independent or foreign territories, and the only way to own them is to make no attempt at exercising any of the functions of ownership. All the reasons which gave force to this principle in the seventeenth and eighteenth centuries have been reinforced a hundredfold by the modern contrivances of credit and capital, quick communication, popular government, popular press, the conditions and cost of warfare--the whole weight, indeed, of modern progress. It is not a question here of theorizing, of the erection of an elaborate thesis, nor is it a question of arguing what the relations of Colonies ought to be. The differences between the Imperialist and the Anti-imperialist do not enter into the discussion at all. It is simply a question of what the unmistakable outstanding facts of experience have taught, and we all know, Imperialists and their opponents alike, that whatever the relations with the Colonies are to be, that relationship must be fixed by the free consent of the Colonies, by their choice, not ours. Sir J. R. Seeley notes in his book, "The Expansion of England," that because the early Spanish Colonies were in a true sense of the word "possessions," Britons acquired the habit of talking of "possessions" and "ownership," and their ideas of colonial policy were vitiated during three centuries, simply by the fatal hypnotism of an incorrect word. Is it not time that we shook off the influence of those disastrous words? Canada, Australia, New Zealand, and South Africa, are not "possessions." They are no more possessions than is Argentina or Brazil, and the nation which conquered England, which even captured London, would be hardly nearer to the conquest of Canada or Australia than if it happened to occupy Constantinople or St. Petersburg. Why, therefore, do we tolerate the loose talk which assumes that the master of London is also master of Montreal, Vancouver, Cape Town, Johannesburg, Melbourne, and Sydney? Have we not had about enough of this ignorant chatter, which is persistently blind to the simplest and most elementary facts of the case? And have not the English, of all people of the world, a most direct interest in aiding the general realization of these truths in Europe? Would not that general realization add immensely to the security of their so-called Empire?

CHAPTER VIII

THE FIGHT FOR "THE PLACE IN THE SUN"

How Germany really expands--Where her real Colonies are--How she exploits without conquest--What is the difference between an army and a police force?--The policing of the world--Germany's share of it in the Near East.

What is the practical outcome of the situation which the facts detailed in the last chapter make plain? Must nations like Germany conclude that, because there can be no duplication of the fight for empty territory which took place between European nations in the seventeenth and eighteenth centuries, and because talk of the German conquest of British Colonies is childish nonsense, Germany must therefore definitely surrender any hope of expansion, and accept a secondary position because she happens to have "come too late into the world"? Are Germans with all their activities and scientific thoroughness, and with such a lively sense of the difficulty of finding room in the world for the additional million of Germans every year quietly to accept the *status quo*?

If our thoughts were not so distorted by misleading political imagery, it is doubtful whether it would ever occur to us that such a "problem" existed.

When one nation, say England, occupies a territory, does it mean that that territory is "lost" to Germans? We know this to be an absurdity. Germany does an enormous and increasing trade with the territory that has been pre-empted by the Anglo-Saxon race. Millions of Germans in Germany gain their livelihood by virtue of German enterprise and German industry in Anglo-Saxon countries--indeed, it is the bitter and growing complaint of Englishmen that they are being driven out of these territories by the Germans; that where originally British shipping was universal in the East,[35] German shipping is now coming to occupy the prominent place; that the trade of whole territories which Englishmen originally had to themselves is now being captured by Germans, and this not merely where the fiscal arrangements are more or less under the control of the British Government, as in the Crown Colonies, but in those territories originally British but now independent, like the United States, as well as in those territories which are in reality independent, though nominally still under British control, like Australia and Canada.

Moreover, why need Germany occupy the extraordinary position of phantom "ownership," which England occupies, in order to enjoy all the real benefits which in our day result from a Colonial Empire? More Germans have found homes in the United States in the last half-century than have Englishmen in all their Colonies. It is calculated that between ten and twelve millions of the population of the United States are of direct German descent. It is true, of course, that Germans do not live under their flag, but it is equally true that they do not regret that fact, but rejoice in it! The majority of German emigrants do not desire that the land to which they go shall have the political character of the land which they leave behind. The fact that in adopting the United States they have shed something of the German tradition and created a new national type, partaking in part of the English and in part of the German, is, on the whole, very much to their advantage--and incidentally to ours.

Of course it is urged that, despite all this, the national sentiment will always desire, for the overflow of its population, territories in which that nation's language, law, and literature reign. But how far is that aspiration one of those purely political aspirations still persisting, it is true, but really the result of the momentum of old ideas, the outcome of facts long since passed away, and destined to disappear as soon as the real facts have been absorbed by the general public?

Thus a German will shout patriotically, and, if needs be, embroil his country in a war for an equatorial or Asiatic colony; the truth being that he does not think about the matter seriously. But if he and his family have to emigrate, he *does* think about it seriously, and then it is another matter; he does not choose Equatorial Africa or China; he goes to the United States, which he knows to be a far better country in which to make his home than the Cameroons or Kiau Chau could ever be. Indeed, in England's own case, are not certain foreign countries much more her real colonies for her children of the future than certain territory under her own flag? Will not her children find better and more congenial conditions, more readily build real homes, in Pennsylvania, which is "foreign," than in Bombay, which is "British"?

Of course, if by sheer military conquest it were possible to turn a United States or even a Canada into a real Germany--of German language, law, literature--the matter would assume another aspect. But the facts dealt with in the last chapter show that the day is past for conquest in that form. Quite other means must be employed. The German conqueror of the future would have to say with Napoleon: "I come too late. The nations are too firmly set." Even when the English, the greatest colonizers of the world, conquer a territory like the Transvaal or the Orange Free State, they have no resort, having conquered it, but to allow its own law, its own literature, its own language to have free play, just as though the conquest had never taken place. This was even the case with Quebec more than one hundred years ago, and Germany will have to be guided by a like rule. On the morrow of conquest she would have to proceed to establish her real ascendancy by other than military means--a thing she is free to do to-day, if she can. It cannot throughout this discussion be too often repeated that the world has been modified, and that what was possible to the Canaanites and the Romans, and even to the Normans, is no longer possible to us. The edict can no longer go forth to "slay every male child" that is born into the conquered territory, in order that the race may be exterminated. Conquest in this sense is impossible. The most marvelous colonial history in the world--British colonial history--demonstrates that in this field physical force is no longer of avail.

And Germans are beginning to realize it. "We must resign ourselves in all clearness and calm to the fact that there is no possibility of acquiring Colonies suitable for emigration," writes Dr. P. Rohrbach. He continues:

But if we cannot have such Colonies, it by no means follows that we cannot obtain the advantages, if only to a limited extent, which make these Colonies desirable. It is a mistake to regard the mere possession of extensive trans-oceanic territories, even when they are able to absorb a part of the national surplus of population, as necessarily a direct increase of power. Australia, Canada, and South Africa do not increase the power of the British Empire because they are British possessions, nor yet because they are peopled by a few million British emigrants and their descendants, but because by trade with them the wealth and with it the defensive strength of the Mother Country are increased. Colonies which do not produce that result have but little value; and countries which possess this importance for a nation, even though they are not its Colonies, are in this decisive point a substitute for colonial possessions in the ordinary sense.[36]

In fact the misleading political imagery to which I referred a few pages back has gone far to destroy our sense of reality and sense of proportion in the matter of political control of foreign territory, a fact which the diplomatic turmoil of 1911 most certainly illustrated. I had occasion at the time to emphasize it in the following terms:

The Press of Europe and America is very busy discussing the lessons of the diplomatic conflict which has just ended, and the military conflict which has just begun. And the outstanding impression which one gets from most of these essays in high politics--whether French, Italian, or British--is that we have been and still are witnessing part of a great world movement, the setting in motion of Titanic forces "deep-set in primordial needs and impulses."

For months those in the secrets of the Chancelleries have spoken with bated breath--as though in the presence of some vision of Armageddon. On the strength of this mere talk of war by the three nations, vast commercial interests have been embarrassed, fortunes have been lost and won on the Bourses, banks have suspended payment, some thousands have been ruined; while the fact that the fourth and fifth nations have actually gone to war has raised all sorts of further possibilities of conflict, not alone in Europe, but in Asia, with remoter danger of religious fanaticism and all its sequelæ. International bitterness and suspicion in general have been intensified, and the one certain result of the whole thing is that immense burdens will be added in the shape of further taxation for armaments to the already heavy ones carried by the five or six nations concerned. For two or three hundred millions of people in Europe, life, which with all the problems of high prices, labor wars, unsolved social difficulties, is none too easy as it is, will be made harder still.

The needs, therefore, that can have provoked a conflict of these dimensions must be "primordial" indeed. In fact one authority assures us that what we have seen going on is "the struggle for life among men"--that struggle which has its parallel in the whole of sentient existence.

Well, I put it to you, as a matter worth just a moment or two of consideration, that this conflict is about nothing of the sort; that it is about a perfectly futile matter, one which the immense majority of the German, English, French, Italian, and Turkish people could afford to treat with the completest indifference. For, to the vast majority of these 250,000,000 people more or less, it does not matter two straws whether Morocco or some vague African swamp near the Equator is administered by German, French, Italian, or Turkish officials, so long as it is well administered. Or rather one should go further: if French, German, or Italian colonization of the past is any guide, the nation which wins in the contest for territory of this sort has added a wealth-draining incubus.

This, of course, is preposterous; I am losing sight of the need for making provision for the future expansion of the race, for each party to "find its place in the sun"; and Heaven knows what!

The European Press was full of these phrases at the time, and I attempted to weigh their real meaning by a comparison of French and German history in the matter of national "expansion" during the last thirty or forty years.

France has got a new empire, we are told; she has won a great victory; she is growing and expanding and is richer by something which her rivals are the poorer for not having.

Let us assume that she makes the same success of Morocco that she has made of her other possessions, of, say, Tunis, which represents one of the most successful of those operations of colonial expansion which have marked her history during the last forty years. What has been the precise effect on French prosperity?

In thirty years, at a cost of many millions (it is part of successful colonial administration in France never to let it be known what the Colonies really cost), France has founded in Tunis a Colony, in which to-day there are, excluding soldiers and officials, about 25,000 genuine French colonists; just the number by which the French population in France-- the real France--is diminishing every year! And the value of Tunis as a market does not even amount to the sum which France spends directly on its occupation and administration, to say nothing of the indirect extension of military burdens which its conquest involved; and, of course, the market which it represents would still exist in some form, though England--or even Germany--administered the country.

In other words, France loses every year in her home population a Colony equivalent to Tunis--if we measure Colonies in terms of communities made up of the race which has sprung from the Mother Country. And yet, if once in a generation her rulers and diplomats can point to 25,000 Frenchmen living artificially and exotically under conditions which must in the long-run be inimical to their race, it is pointed to as "expansion" and as evidence that France is maintaining her position as a Great Power. In a few years, as history goes, unless there is some complete change in tendencies, which at present seem as strong as ever, the French race, as we know it, will have ceased to exist, swamped without the firing, may be, of a single shot, by the Germans, Belgians, English, Italians, and Jews. There are to-day more Germans in France than there are Frenchmen in all the Colonies that France has acquired in the last half-century, and German trade with France outweighs enormously the trade of France with all French Colonies. France is to-day a better Colony for the Germans than they could make of any exotic Colony which France owns.

"They *tell* me," said a French Deputy recently (in a not quite original *mot*), "that the Germans are at Agadir. I *know* they are in the Champs-Elysées." Which, of course, is in reality a much more serious matter.

On the other side we are to assume that Germany has during the period of France's expansion,--since the war--not expanded at all. That she has been throttled and cramped--that she has not had her place in the sun; and that is why she must fight for it and endanger the security of her neighbors.

Well, I put it to you again that all this in reality is false: that Germany has not been cramped or throttled; that, on the contrary, as we recognize when we get away from the mirage of the map, her expansion has been the wonder of the world. She has added twenty millions to her population--one-half the present population of France--during a period in which the French population has actually diminished. Of all the nations in Europe, she has cut the biggest slice in the development of world trade, industry, and influence. Despite the fact that she has not "expanded" in the sense of mere political dominion, a proportion of her population, equivalent to the white population of the whole Colonial British Empire, make their living, or the best part of it, from the development and exploitation of territory outside her borders. These facts are not new, they have been made the text of thousands of political sermons preached in England itself during the last few years; but one side of their significance seems to have been missed.

We get, then, this: On the one side a nation extending enormously its political dominion, and yet diminishing in national force--if by national force we mean the growth of a sturdy, enterprising, vigorous people. (I am not denying that France is both wealthy and comfortable, to a greater degree it may be than her rival; but that is another story.) On the other side, we get immense expansion expressed in terms of those things--a growing and vigorous population, and the possibility of feeding them--and yet the political dominion, speaking practically, has hardly been extended at all.

Such a condition of things, if the common jargon of high politics means anything, is preposterous. It takes nearly all meaning out of most that we hear about "primordial needs" and the rest of it.

As a matter of fact, we touch here one of the vital confusions, which is at the bottom of most of the present political trouble between nations, and shows the power of the old ideas and the old phraseology.

In the days of the sailing ship and the lumbering wagon dragging slowly over all but impassable roads, for one country to derive any considerable profit from another it had practically to administer it politically. But the compound steam-engine, the railway, the telegraph, have profoundly modified the elements of the whole problem. In the modern world political dominion is playing a more and more effaced rôle as a factor in commerce; the non-political factors have in practice made it all but inoperative. It is the case with every modern nation, actually, that the outside territories which it exploits most successfully are precisely those of which it does not "own" a foot. Even with the most characteristically colonial of all--Great Britain--the greater part of her overseas trade is done with countries which she makes no attempt to "own," control, coerce, or dominate--and incidentally she has ceased to do any of those things with her Colonies.

Millions of Germans in Prussia and Westphalia derive profit or make their living out of countries to which their political dominion in no way extends. The modern German exploits South America by remaining at home. Where, forsaking this principle, he attempts to work through political power, he approaches futility. German Colonies are Colonies *pour rire*. The Government has to bribe Germans to go to them; her trade with them is microscopic; and if the twenty millions who have been added to Germany's population since the war had had to depend on their country's political conquest, they would have had to starve. What feeds them are countries which Germany has never "owned," and never hopes to "own": Brazil, Argentina, the United States, India, Australia, Canada, Russia, France, and England. (Germany, which never spent a mark on its political conquest, to-day draws more tribute from South America than does Spain, which has poured out mountains of treasure and oceans of blood in its conquest.) These are Germany's real Colonies. Yet the immense interests which they represent, of really primordial concern to Germany, without which so many of her people would be actually without food, are for the diplomats and the soldiers quite secondary ones; the immense trade which they represent owes nothing to the diplomat, to Agadir incidents, to *Dreadnoughts*: it is the unaided work of the merchant and the manufacturer. All this diplomatic and military conflict and rivalry, this waste of wealth, the unspeakable foulness which Tripoli is revealing, are reserved for things which both sides to the quarrel could sacrifice, not merely without loss, but with profit. And Italy, whose statesmen have been faithful to all the old "axioms" (Heaven save the mark!) will discover it rapidly enough. Even her defenders are ceasing now to urge that she can possibly derive any real benefit from this colossal ineptitude.

Is it not time that the man in the street--verily, I believe, less deluded by diplomatic jargon than his betters, less the slave of an obsolete phraseology--insisted that the experts in the high places acquired some sense of the reality of things, of proportions, some sense of figures, a little knowledge of industrial history, of the real processes of human co-operation?

But are we to assume that the extension of a European nation's authority overseas can never be worthwhile; or that it could, or should, never be the occasion for conflict between nations; or that the rôle of, say, England in India or Egypt, is neither useful nor profitable?

In the second part of this book I have attempted to uncover the general principle--which sadly needs establishing in politics--serving to indicate clearly the advantageous and disadvantageous employment of force. Because force plays an undoubted rôle in human development and co-operation, it is sweepingly concluded that military force and the struggle between groups must always be a normal feature of human society.

To a critic, who maintained that the armies of the world were necessary and justifiable on the same grounds as the police forces of the world ("Even in communities such as London, where, in our civic capacity, we have nearly realized all your ideals, we still maintain and are constantly improving our police force"), I replied:

When we learn that London, instead of using its police for the running in of burglars and "drunks," is using them to lead an attack on Birmingham for the purpose of capturing that city as part of a policy of "municipal expansion," or "Civic Imperialism," or "Pan-Londonism," or what not; or is using its force to repel an attack by the Birmingham police acting as the result of a similar policy on the part of the Birmingham patriots--when that happens you can safely approximate a police force to a European army. But until it does, it is quite evident that the two--the army and the police force--have in reality diametrically opposed rôles. The police exist as an instrument of social co-operation; the armies as the natural outcome of the quaint illusion that though one city could never enrich itself by "capturing" or "subjugating" another, in some unexplained way one country can enrich itself by capturing or subjugating another.

In the existing condition of things in England this illustration covers the whole case; the citizens of London would have no imaginable interest in "conquering" Birmingham, or *vice versa*. But suppose there arose in the cities of the North such a condition of disorder that London could not carry on its ordinary work and trade; then London, if it had the power, *would* have an interest in sending its police into Birmingham, presuming that this could be done. The citizens of London would have a tangible interest in the maintenance of order in the North--they would be the richer for it.

Order was just as well maintained in Alsace-Lorraine before the German conquest as it was after, and for that reason Germany has not benefited by the conquest. But order was not maintained in California, and would not have been as well maintained under Mexican as under American rule, and for that reason America has benefited by the conquest of California. France has benefited by the conquest of Algeria, England by that of India, because in each case the arms were employed not, properly speaking, for conquest at all, but for police purposes, for the establishment and maintenance of order; and, so far as they achieved that object, their rôle was a useful one.

How does this distinction affect the practical problem under discussion? Most fundamentally. Germany has no need to maintain order in England, nor England in Germany, and the latent struggle therefore between these two countries is futile. It is not the result of any inherent necessity of either people; it is the result merely of that woeful confusion which dominates statecraft to-day, and it is bound, so soon as that confusion is cleared up, to come to an end.

Where the condition of a territory is such that the social and economic co-operation of other countries with it is impossible, we may expect the intervention of military force, not as the result of the "annexationist illusion," but as the outcome of real social forces pushing to the maintenance of order. That is the story of England in Egypt, or, for that matter, in India. But foreign nations have no need to maintain order in the British Colonies, nor in the United States; and though there might be some such necessity in the case of countries like Venezuela, the last few years have taught us that by bringing these countries into the great economic currents of the world, and so setting up in them a whole body of interests in favor of order, more can be done than by forcible conquest. We occasionally hear rumors of German designs in Brazil and elsewhere, but even the modicum of education possessed by the average European statesman makes it plain to him that these nations are, like the others, "too firmly set" for military occupation and conquest by an alien people.

It is one of the humors of the whole Anglo-German conflict that so much has the British public been concerned with the myths and bogies of the matter that it seems calmly to have ignored the realities. While even the wildest Pan-German has never cast his eyes in the direction of Canada, he has cast them, and does cast them, in the direction of Asia Minor; and the political activities of Germany may center on that area, for precisely the reasons which result from the distinction between policing and conquest, which I have drawn. German industry is coming to have dominating interests in the Near East, and as those interests--her markets and investments--increase, the necessity for better order in, and the better organization of, those territories increases in corresponding degree. Germany may need to police Asia Minor.

What interest have we in attempting to prevent her? It may be urged that she would close the markets of those territories against us. But even if she attempted it, which she is never likely to do, a Protectionist Asia Minor organized with German efficiency would be better from the point of view of trade than a Free Trade Asia Minor organized à la Turque. Protectionist Germany is one of the best markets in Europe. If a second Germany were created in the Near East, if Turkey had a population with the German purchasing power and the German tariff, the markets would be worth some two hundred to two hundred and fifty millions instead of some fifty to seventy-five. Why should we try to prevent Germany increasing our trade?

It is true that we touch here the whole problem of the fight for the open door in the undeveloped territories. But the real difficulty in this problem is not the open door at all, but the fact that Germany is beating England--or England fears she is beating her in those territories where she has the same tariff to meet that Germany has, or even a smaller one; and that she is even beating England in the territories that the English already "own"--in their Colonies, in the East, in India. How, therefore, would England's final crushing of Germany in the military sense change anything? Suppose England crushed her so completely that she "owned" Asia Minor and Persia as completely as she owns India or Hong Kong, would not the German merchant continue to beat her even then, as he is beating her now, in that part of the East over which she already holds political sway? Again, how would the disappearance of the German navy affect the problem one way or the other?

Moreover, in this talk of the open door in the undeveloped territories, we again seem to lose all our sense of proportion. English trade is in relative importance first with the great nations--the United States, France, Germany, Argentina, South America generally--after that with the white Colonies; after that with the organized East; and last of all, and to a very small extent, with the countries concerned in this squabble for the open door--territories in which the trade really is so small as hardly to pay for the making and upkeep of a dozen battleships.

When the man in the street, or, for that matter, the journalistic pundit, talks commercial diplomacy, his arithmetic seems to fall from him. Some years since the question of the relative position of the three Powers in Samoa exercised the minds of these wiseacres, who got fearfully warlike both in England and in the United States. Yet the trade of the whole island is not worth that of an obscure Massachusetts village, and the notion that naval budgets should be increased to "maintain our position," the notion that either of the countries concerned should really think it worthwhile to build so much as a single battleship the more for such a purpose, is not throwing away a sprat to catch a whale, but throwing away a whale to catch a sprat--and then not catching it. For even when you *have* the predominant political position, even when you *have* got your extra *Dreadnought* or extra dozen *Dreadnoughts*, it is the more efficiently organized nation on the commercial side that will take the trade. And while England is getting excited over the trade of territories that matter very little, rivals, including Germany, will be quietly walking off with the trade that *does* matter, will be increasing their hold upon such

markets as the United States, Argentina, South America, and the lesser
Continental States.

If we really examined these questions without the old meaningless pre-
possessions, we should see that it is more to the general interest to have
an orderly and organized Asia Minor under German tutelage than to have
an unorganized and disorderly one which should be independent. Perhaps it would be best of all that Great Britain should do the organizing,
or share it with Germany, though England has her hands full in that
respect--Egypt and India are problems enough. Why should England forbid Germany to do in a small degree what she has done in a large degree?
Sir Harry H. Johnston, in the *Nineteenth Century* for December, 1910,
comes a great deal nearer to touching the real kernel of the problem that
is preoccupying Germany than any of the writers on the Anglo-German
conflict of whom I know. As the result of careful investigation, he admits
that Germany's real objective is not, properly speaking, England or England's Colonies at all, but the undeveloped lands of the Balkan Peninsula, Asia Minor, Mesopotamia, down even to the mouth of the Euphrates.
He adds that the best informed Germans use this language to him:

In regard to England, we would recall a phrase dropped by ex-President
Roosevelt at an important public speech in London, a phrase which for
some reason was not reported by the London Press. Roosevelt said that
the best guarantee for Great Britain on the Nile is the presence of Germany on the Euphrates. Putting aside the usual hypocrisies of the Teu-
tonic peoples, you know that this is so. You know that we ought to make
common cause in our dealing with the backward races of the world. Let
Britain and Germany once come to an agreement in regard to the question of the Near East, and the world can scarcely again be disturbed by
any great war in any part of the globe, if such a war is contrary to the
interests of the two Empires.

Such, declares Sir Harry, is German opinion. And in all human probability, so far as sixty-five million people can be said to have the same
opinion, he is absolutely right.

It is because the work of policing backward or disorderly populations
is so often confused with the annexationist illusion that the danger of
squabbles in the matter is a real one. Not the fact that England is doing a real and useful work for the world at large in policing India creates jealousy of her work there, but the notion that in some way she
"possesses" this territory, and draws tribute and exclusive advantage
therefrom. When Europe is a little more educated in these matters, the
European populations will realize that they have no primordial interest
in furnishing the policemen. German public opinion will see that, even if
such a thing were possible, the German people would gain no advantage
by replacing England in India, especially as the final result of the administrative work of Europe in the Near and Far East will be to make populations like those of Asia Minor in the last resort their own policemen.
Should some Power, acting as policeman, ignoring the lessons of history,

try again the experiment tried by Spain in South America and later by England in North America, should she try to create for herself exclusive privileges and monopolies, the other nations have means of retaliation apart from the military ones--in the numberless instruments which the economic and financial relationships of nations furnish.

PART II

THE HUMAN NATURE AND MORALS OF THE CASE

CHAPTER I

THE PSYCHOLOGICAL CASE FOR WAR

The non-economic motives of war--Moral and psychological--The importance of these pleas--English, German, and American exponents--The biological plea.

Perhaps the commonest plea urged in objection to the case presented in the first part of this book is that the real motives of nations in going to war are not economic at all; that their conflicts arise from moral causes, using that word in its largest sense; that they are the outcome of conflicting views of rights; or that they arise from, not merely non-economic, but also non-rational causes--from vanity, rivalry, pride of place, the desire to be first, to occupy a great situation in the world, to have power or prestige; from quick resentment of insult or injury; from temper; the unreasoned desire, which comes of quarrel or disagreement, to dominate a rival at all costs; from the "inherent hostility" that exists between rival nations; from the contagion of sheer passion, the blind strife of mutually hating men; and generally because men and nations always have fought and always will, and because, like the animals in Watt's doggerel, "it is their nature to."

An expression of the first point of view is embodied in the criticism of an earlier edition of this book, in which the critic says:

The cause of war is spiritual, not material.... The great wars arose from conflicts as to rights, and the dangerous causes of war are the existence of antagonistic ideas of rights or righteousness.... It is for moral ideas that men are most ready to make sacrifices.[37]

A similar criticism is made by Admiral Mahan.[38]

In the same way the London *Spectator* while admitting the truth of the principles outlined in the first part of this book, deems that such facts do not seriously affect the basic cause of war:

Just as individuals quarrel among themselves, and fight as bitterly as the police and the law courts will allow them, not because they think it will make them rich, but because their blood is up, and they want to stand up for what they believe to be their rights, or to revenge themselves for wrongs done to them, as they think, by their fellows, so nations will fight, even though it is demonstrable that they will get no material gain thereby.... They want sometimes freedom, sometimes power. Sometimes a passion for expansion or dominion comes over them. Sometimes they seem impelled to fight for fighting's sake, or, as their leaders and rhetoricians vaguely say, to fulfill their destinies.... Men fight sometimes for the love of fighting, sometimes for great and noble causes, and sometimes for bad causes, but practically never with an account-book and a balance-sheet in their hands.

I desire to give every possible weight to this plea, and not to shirk a detail of it, and I think that the pages that follow cover every one of the points here raised. But there is a whole school of philosophy which goes much farther than the *Spectator*. The view just cited rather implies that though it is a fact that men settle their differences by force and passion, instead of by reason, it is a regrettable fact. But the school to which I refer urges that men should be encouraged to fight, and that war is the preferable solution. War, declare these philosophers, is a valuable discipline for the nations, and it is not desirable to see human conflict shifted from the plane of physical force. They urge that humanity will be permanently the poorer when, as one of them has put it, the great struggles of mankind become merely the struggles of "talk and money-bags."

Parenthetically, it should be pointed out that the matter has a good deal more than academic interest. This philosophy constitutes a constant element of resistance to that reform of political thought and tradition in Europe which must be the necessary precedent of a sounder condition. Not merely, of course, do international situations become infinitely more dangerous when you get, on both sides of the frontier, a general "belief in war for war's sake," but a tendency is directly created to discredit the use of patience, a quality as much needed in the relationship of nations as in that of individuals; and further there is a tendency to justify political action making for war as against action that might avoid it. All these pleas, biological and otherwise, are powerful factors in creating an atmosphere and temperament in Europe favorable to war and unfavorable to international agreement. For, be it noted, this philosophy is not special to any one country: one finds it plentifully expressed in England and America, as well as in France and Germany. It is a European doctrine, part of that "mind of Europe," of which someone has spoken, that, among other factors, determines the character of European civilization generally.

This particular point of view has received a notable re-statement quite recently[39] from General Bernhardi, a distinguished cavalry General, and probably the most influential German writer on current strategic and tactical problems, in his book, "Deutschland und der nächste Krieg."[40] He therein gives very candid expression to the opinion that Germany must, regardless of the rights and interests of other peoples, fight her way to predominance. One of the chapters is headed, "The Duty to Make War." He describes the peace movement in Germany as "poisonous," and proclaims the doctrine that the duties and tasks of the German people cannot be fulfilled save by the sword. "The duty of self-assertion is by no means exhausted in the mere repelling of hostile attacks. It includes the need of securing to the whole people, which the State embraces, the possibility of existence and development." It is desirable, declares the author, that conquest shall be effected by war, and not by peaceful means; Silesia would not have had the same value for Prussia if Frederick the Great had obtained it from an Arbitration Court. The attempt to abolish war is not only "immoral and unworthy of humanity," it is an attempt to deprive man of his highest possession--the right to stake physical life for ideal ends. The German people "must learn to see that the maintenance of peace cannot be, and must never be, the goal of policy."

Similar efforts are being made in England by English writers to secure the acceptance of this doctrine of force. Many passages almost duplicating those of Bernhardi, or at least extolling the general doctrine of force, may be found in the writings of such Anglo-Saxon authors as Admiral Mahan and Professor Spenser Wilkinson.[41]

A scientific color is often given to the philosophy of force, as expressed by the authors just referred to, by an appeal to evolutionary and biological laws.

It is urged that the condition of man's advance in the past has been the survival of the fit by struggle and warfare, and that in that struggle it is precisely those endowed with combativeness and readiness to fight who have survived. Thus the tendency to combat is not a mere human perversity, but is part of the self-protective instinct rooted in a profound biological law--the struggle of nations for survival.

This point of view is expressed by S.R. Steinmetz in his "Philosophie des Krieges." War, according to this author, is an ordeal instituted by God, who weighs the nations in its balance. It is the essential function of the State, and the only function in which peoples can employ all their powers at once and convergently. No victory is possible save as the resultant of a totality of virtues; no defeat for which some vice or weakness is not responsible. Fidelity, cohesiveness, tenacity, heroism, conscience, education, inventiveness, economy, wealth, physical health and vigor--there is no moral or intellectual point of superiority that does not tell when "God holds His assizes, and hurls the peoples one upon another" (Die Weltgeschichte ist das Weltgericht); and Dr. Steinmetz does not believe that in the long-run chance and luck play any part in apportioning the issues.

It is urged that international hostility is merely the psychological stimulus to that combativeness which is a necessary element of existence, and that though, like other elemental instincts--our animal appetites, for instance--it may in some of its manifestations be ugly enough, it makes for survival, and is to that extent a part of the great plan. Too great a readiness to accept the "friendly assurances" of another nation and an undue absence of distrust would, in accordance with a sort of Gresham's Law in international relationships, make steadily for the disappearance of the humane and friendly communities in favor of the truculent and brutal. If friendliness and good-feeling towards other nations led us to relax our self-defensive efforts, the quarrelsome communities would see, in this slackening, an opportunity to commit aggression, and there would be a tendency, therefore, for the least civilized to wipe out the most. Animosity and hostility between nations is a corrective of this sentimental slackness, and to that extent it plays a useful rôle, however ugly it may appear--"not pretty, but useful, like the dustman." Though the material and economic motives which prompt conflict may no longer obtain, other than economic motives will be found for collision, so profound is the psychological stimulus thereto.

Some such view as this has found lurid expression in the recent work of an American soldier, Homer Lea.[42] The author urges not only that war is inevitable, but that any systematic attempt to prevent it is merely an unwise meddling with the universal law.

National entities, in their birth, activities, and death, are controlled by the same laws that govern all life--plant, animal, or national--the law of struggle, the law of survival. These laws, so universal as regards life and time, so unalterable in causation and consummation, are only variable in the duration of national existence as the knowledge of and obedience to them is proportionately true or false. Plans to thwart them, to shortcut them, to circumvent, to cozen, to deny, to scorn and violate them, is folly such as man's conceit alone makes possible. Never has this been tried-- and man is ever at it--but what the end has been gangrenous and fatal.

In theory international arbitration denies the inexorability of natural laws, and would substitute for them the veriest Cagliostroic formulas, or would, with the vanity of Canute, sit down on the ocean-side of life and command the ebb and flow of its tides to cease.

The idea of international arbitration as a substitute for natural laws that govern the existence of political entities arises not only from a denial of their fiats and an ignorance of their application, but from a total misconception of war, its causes, and its meaning.

Homer Lea's thesis is emphasized in the introduction to his work, written by another American soldier, General John P. Storey:

A few idealists may have visions that with advancing civilization war and its dread horrors will cease. Civilization has not changed human nature. The nature of man makes war inevitable. Armed strife will not disappear from the earth until human nature changes.

"Weltstadt und Friedensproblem," the book of Professor Baron Karl von Stengel, a jurist who was one of Germany's delegates at the First Hague Peace Conference, contains a chapter entitled "The Significance of War for Development of Humanity," in which the author says:

War has more often facilitated than hindered progress. Athens and Rome, not only in spite of, but just because of their many wars, rose to the zenith of civilization. Great States like Germany and Italy are welded into nationalities only through blood and iron.

Storm purifies the air and destroys the frail trees, leaving the sturdy oaks standing. War is the test of a nation's political, physical, and intellectual worth. The State in which there is much that is rotten may vegetate for a while in peace, but in war its weakness is revealed.

Germany's preparations for war have not resulted in economic disaster, but in unexampled economic expansion, unquestionably because of our demonstrated superiority over France. It is better to spend money on armaments and battleships than luxury, motormania, and other sensual living.

We know that Moltke expressed a similar view in his famous letter to Bluntschli. "A perpetual peace," declared the Field-Marshal, "is a dream, and not even a beautiful dream. War is one of the elements of order in the world, established by God. The noblest virtues of men are developed therein. Without war the world would degenerate and disappear in a morass of materialism."[43]

At the very time that Moltke was voicing this sentiment, a precisely similar one was being voiced by no less a person than Ernest Renan. In his "La Réforme Intellectuelle et Morale" (Paris: Lévy, 1871, p. 111) he writes:

If the foolishness, negligence, idleness, and short-sightedness of States did not involve their occasional collision, it is difficult to imagine the degree of degeneracy to which the human race would descend. War is one of the conditions of progress, the sting which prevents a country from going to sleep, and compels satisfied mediocrity itself to awaken from its apathy. Man is only sustained by effort and struggle. The day that humanity achieves a great pacific Roman Empire, having no external enemies, that day its morality and its intelligence will be placed in the very greatest peril.

In our own times a philosophy not very dissimilar has been voiced in the public declarations of ex-President Roosevelt. I choose a few phrases from his speeches and writings, at random:

We despise a nation, just as we despise a man, who submits to insult. What is true of a man ought to be true of a nation.[44]

We must play a great part in the world, and especially ... perform those deeds of blood, of valor, which above everything else bring national renown.

We do not admire a man of timid peace.

By war alone can we acquire those virile qualities necessary to win in the stern strife of actual life.

In this world the nation that is trained to a career of unwarlike and isolated ease is bound to go down in the end before other nations which have not lost the manly and adventurous qualities.[45]

Professor William James covers the whole ground of these claims in the following passage:

The war party is assuredly right in affirming that the martial virtues, although originally gained by the race through war, are absolute and permanent human goods. Patriotic pride and ambition in their military form are, after all, only specifications of a more universal and enduring competitive passion.... Pacifism makes no converts from the military party. The military party denies neither the bestiality, nor the horror, nor the expense; it only says that these things tell but half the story. It only says that war is worth these things; that, taking human nature as a whole, war is its best protection against its weaker and more cowardly self, and that mankind cannot afford to adopt a peace economy.... Militarism is the great preserver of our ideals of hardihood, and human life without hardihood would be contemptible.... This natural feeling forms, I think, the innermost soul of army writings. Without any exception known to me, militarist authors take a highly mystical view of their subject, and regard war as a biological or sociological necessity.... Our ancestors have bred pugnacity into our bone and marrow and thousands of years of peace won't breed it out of us.[46]

Even famous English clergymen have voiced the same view. Charles Kingsley, in his defense of the Crimean War as a "just war against tyrants and oppressors," wrote: "For the Lord Jesus Christ is not only the Prince of Peace, He is the Prince of War, too. He is the Lord of Hosts, the God of armies, and whoever fights in a just war against tyrants and oppressors is fighting on Christ's side, and Christ is fighting on his side. Christ is his captain and his leader, and he can be in no better service. Be sure of it, for the Bible tells you so."[47]

Canon Newbolt, Dean Farrar, and the Archbishop of Armagh, have all written not dissimilarly.

The whole case may be summarized thus:

1. Nations fight for opposing conceptions of right: it is the moral conflict of men.

2. They fight from non-rational causes of a lower kind: from vanity, rivalry, pride of place, the desire to occupy a great situation in the world, or from sheer hostility to dissimilar people--the blind strife of mutually hating men.

3. These causes justify war, or render it inevitable. The first is admirable in itself, the second is inevitable, in that the peoples readiest to fight, and showing most energy in fighting, replace the more peacefully inclined, and the warlike type tends thus permanently to survive; "the warlike nations inherit the earth."

Or it may be put deductively, thus: Since struggle is the law of life, and a condition of survival as much with nations as with other organisms, pugnacity, which is merely intense energy in struggle, a readiness to accept struggle in its acutest form, must necessarily be a quality marking those individuals successful in the vital contests. It is this deep-seated, biological law which renders impossible the acceptance by mankind of the literal injunction to turn the other cheek to the smiter, or for human nature ever to conform to the ideal implied in that injunction; since, were it accepted, the best men and nations--in the sense of the kindliest and most humane--would be placed at the mercy of the most brutal, who, eliminating the least brutal, would stamp the survivors with their own brutality and re-establish the militarist virtues. For this reason a readiness to fight, which means the qualities of rivalry and pride and combativeness, hardihood, tenacity, and heroism--what we know as the manly qualities--must in any case survive as the race survives, and, since this stands in the way of the predominance of the purely brutal, it is a necessary part of the highest morality.

Despite the apparent force of these propositions, they are founded upon a gross misreading of certain facts, and especially upon a gross misapplication of a certain biological analogy.

CHAPTER II

THE PSYCHOLOGICAL CASE FOR PEACE

The shifting ground of pro-war arguments--The narrowing gulf between the material and moral ideals--The non-rational causes of war--False biological analogies--The real law of man's struggle: struggle with Nature, not with other men--Outline sketch of man's advance and main operating factor therein--The progress towards elimination of physical force--Co-operation across frontiers and its psychological result--Impossible to fix limits of community--Such limits irresistibly expanding--Break up of State homogeneity--State limits no longer coinciding with real conflicts between men.

Those who have followed at all closely the peace advocacy of the last few years will have observed a curious shifting of ground on the part of its opponents. Until quite recently, most peace advocacy being based on moral, not material grounds, pacifists were generally criticized as unduly idealistic, sentimental, oblivious to the hard necessities of men in a hard world of struggle, and disposed to ask too much of human nature in the way of altruistic self-sacrifice on behalf of an idealistic dogma. We were given to understand that while peace might represent a great moral ideal, man's evil passions and cupidity would always stand in the way of its achievement. The citations I have given in Chapter II. of the first part of this book prove sufficiently, I think, that this was, until quite recently, overwhelmingly the point of view of those who defended war as an unavoidable part of human struggle.

During the last few years, however, the defense of war has been made for the most part on very different grounds. Peace, we are told by those who oppose the pacifist movement, may embody the material interests of men, but the spiritual nature of mankind will stand in the way of its ever being achieved! Pacifism, far from being branded as too idealistic and sentimental, is now scorned as "sordidly material."

I do not desire, in calling attention to this fact, merely to score a cheap jibe. I want, on the contrary, to do every justice to the point of view of those who urge that moral motives push men into war. I have never, indeed, taken the ground that the defender of war is morally inferior to the defender of peace, or that much is to be gained by emphasizing the moral superiority of the peace ideal. Too often has it been assumed in pacifist advocacy that what is needed in order to clear up the difficulties in the international field, is a better moral tone, a greater kindliness, and so forth--for that assumption ignores the fact that the emotion of humanity repelling it from war may be more than counteracted by the equally strong moral emotion that we connect with patriotism. The patriot admits that war may occasion suffering, but urges that men should be prepared to endure suffering for their country. As I pointed out in the first chapter of this book, the pacifist appeal to humanity so often fails because the militarist pleads that he too is working and suffering for humanity.

My object in calling attention to this unconscious shifting of ground, on the part of the advocate of war, is merely to suggest that the growth of events during the last generation has rendered the economic case for war practically untenable, and has consequently compelled those who defend war to shift their defense. Nor, of course, am I urging that the sentimental defense of war is a modern doctrine--the quotations made in the last chapter show that not to be the case--but merely that greater emphasis is now placed upon the moral case.

Thus, writing in 1912, Admiral Mahan criticizes this book as follows:

The purpose of armaments, in the minds of those maintaining them, is not primarily an economical advantage, in the sense of depriving a neighboring State of its own, or fear of such consequences to itself through the deliberate aggression of a rival having that particular end in view.... The fundamental proposition of the book is a mistake. Nations are under no illusion as to the unprofitableness of war in itself.... The entire conception of the work is itself an illusion, based upon a profound misreading of human action. To regard the world as governed by self-interest only is to live in a non-existent world, an ideal world, a world possessed by an idea much less worthy than those which mankind, to do it bare justice, persistently entertains.[48]

Yet hardly four years previously Admiral Mahan had himself outlined the elements of international politics as follows:

It is as true now as when Washington penned the words, and will always be true, that it is vain to expect nations to act consistently from any motive other than that of interest. This under the name of Realism is the frankly avowed motive of German statecraft. It follows from this directly that the study of interests--international interest--is the one basis of sound, of provident, policy for statesmen....

The old predatory instinct, that he should take who has the power, survives ... and moral force is not sufficient to determine issues unless supported by physical. Governments are corporations, and corporations have no souls ... they must put first the rival interests of their own wards ... their own people. Commercial and industrial predominance forces a nation to seek markets, and, where possible, to control them to its own advantage by preponderating force, the ultimate expression of which is possession ... an inevitable link in a chain of logical sequences: industry, markets, control, navy bases.[49]

Admiral Mahan, it is true, anticipates this criticism by pleading the complex character of human nature (which no one denies). He says: "Bronze is copper, and bronze is tin." But he entirely overlooks the fact that if one withholds copper or one withholds tin it is no longer bronze.

The present author has never taken the ground that all international action can be explained in the terms of one narrow motive, but he does take the ground that if you can profoundly modify the bearing of a constituent, as important as the one to which Admiral Mahan has himself, in his own work, attributed such weight, you will profoundly modify the whole texture and character of international relations. Thus, even though it were true that the thesis here elaborated were as narrowly economic as the criticism I have quoted would imply, it would, nevertheless, have, on Admiral Mahan's own showing, a very profound bearing on the problems of international statecraft.

Not only do the principles elaborated here postulate no such narrow conception of human motive, but it is essential to realize that you cannot separate a problem of interest from a problem of right or morality in the absolute fashion that Admiral Mahan would imply, because right and morality connote the protection and promotion of the general interest.

A nation, a people, we are given to understand, have higher motives than money or "self-interest." What do we mean when we speak of the money of a nation, or the self-interest of a community? We mean--and in such a discussion as this can mean nothing else--better conditions for the great mass of the people, the fullest possible lives, the abolition or attenuation of poverty and of narrow circumstances; that the millions shall be better housed and clothed and fed, more capable of making provision for sickness and old age, with lives prolonged and cheered--and not merely this, but also that they shall be better educated, with character disciplined by steady labor and a better use of leisure; a general social atmosphere which shall make possible family affection, individual dignity and courtesy and the graces of life, not only among the few, but among the many.

Now, do these things constitute, as a national policy, an inspiring aim, or not? They are, speaking in terms of communities, pure self-interest--bound up with economic problems, with money. Does Admiral Mahan mean us to take him at his word when he would attach to such efforts the same discredit that one implies in talking of a mercenary individual? Would he have us believe that the typical great movements of our time--Socialism, Trades Unionism, Syndicalism, Insurance Acts, Land Reforms, Old Age Pensions, Charity Organization, improved Education--bound up as they all are with economic problems--are not the objects which, more and more, are absorbing the best activities of Christendom?

In the pages which follow, I have attempted to show that the activities which lie outside the range of these things--the religious wars, movements like those which promoted the Crusades, or the sort of tradition which we associate with the duel (which has, in fact, disappeared from Anglo-Saxon society)--do not, and cannot, any longer form part of the impulse creating the long-sustained conflicts between large groups which a European war implies. I have attempted roughly to indicate certain processes at work; to show, among other things, that in the changing character of men's ideals there is a distinct narrowing of the gulf which is supposed to separate ideal and material aims. Early ideals, whether in the field of politics or religion, are generally dissociated from any aim of general well-being. In early politics, ideals are concerned simply with personal allegiance to some dynastic chief, a feudal lord, or a monarch; the well-being of a community does not enter into the matter at all. Later the chief must embody in his person that well-being, or he does not obtain the allegiance of a community of any enlightenment; later, the well-being of the community becomes the end in itself, without being embodied in the person of an hereditary chief, so that the people realize that their efforts, instead of being directed to the protection of the personal interests of some chief, are as a matter of fact directed to the protection of their own interests, and their altruism has become communal self-interest, since the self-sacrifice of the community for the sake of the community is a contradiction in terms. In the religious sphere a similar development has occurred. Early religious ideals have no relation to the material betterment of mankind. The early Christian thought it meritorious to live a sterile life at the top of a pillar, eaten by vermin, just as the Hindoo saint to-day thinks it meritorious to live an equally sterile life upon a bed of spikes. But as the early Christian ideal progressed, sacrifices having no end connected with the betterment of mankind lost their appeal. Our admiration now goes, not to the recluse who does nothing for mankind, but rather to the priest who gives his life to bring a ray of comfort to a leper settlement. The Christian saint who would allow the nails of his fingers to grow through the palms of his clasped hands would excite, not our admiration, but our revolt. More and more is religious effort being subjected to this test: Does it make for the improvement of society? If not, it stands condemned. Political ideals are inevitably undergoing a similar development, and will be more and more subjected to a similar test.[50]

I am aware that very often at present they are not thus tested. Dominated as our political thought is by Roman and feudal imagery--hypnotized by symbols and analogies which the necessary development of organized society has rendered obsolete--the ideals even of democracies are still often pure abstractions, divorced from any aim calculated to advance the moral or material betterment of mankind. The craze for sheer size of territory, the mere extent of administrative area, is still deemed a thing deserving immense, incalculable sacrifices.

Even these ideals, however, firmly set as they are in our language and tradition, are rapidly yielding to the necessary force of events. A generation ago it would have been inconceivable that a people or a monarch should calmly see part of its country secede and establish itself as a separate political entity without attempting to prevent it by force of arms. Yet this is what happened, a year or two ago, in the Scandinavian peninsula. For forty years Germany has added to her own difficulties and to those of the European situation for the purpose of including Alsace and Lorraine in its Federation, but even there, obeying the tendency which is world-wide, an attempt has been made to create a constitutional and autonomous government. The history of the British Empire for fifty years has been a process of undoing the work of conquest. Colonies are now neither colonies nor possessions; they are independent States. England, which for centuries has made such sacrifices to retain Ireland, is now making great sacrifices in order to make her secession workable. To each political arrangement, to each political ideal, the final test will be applied: does it, or does it not, make for the widest interests of the mass of the people involved?

It is true that those who emphasize the psychological causes of war might rejoin with another distinction. They might urge that, though the questions dividing nations had more or less their origin in an economic problem, the economic question becomes itself a moral question, a question of right. It was not the few pence of the tax on tea that the Colonies fought about, but the question of right which its payment involved. So with nations. War, ineffective to achieve an economic end, unprofitable in the sense that the cost involved in the defense of a given economic point exceeds the monetary value of that point, will still be fought because a point, trifling in the economic sense, is all important from the point of view of right; and though there is no real division of interests between nations, though those interests are in reality interdependent, minor differences provoking a sudden and uncontrolled flash of temper suffice to provoke war. War is the outcome of the "hot fits" of men, "of the devil that is in them."

Although militarist literature on this, as on most similar points, shows flagrant contradictions, even that literature is against the view that war is the outcome of the sheer sudden temper of nations. Most of the popular, and all of the scientific, militarist writers take the contrary view. Mr. Blatchford and his school normally represent a typical militarist policy, like that of Germany, as actuated by a cold, deep, Machiavellian, unsentimental, calculated opportunism, as diverse from a wild, irrational explosion of feeling as possible. Mr. Blatchford writes:

German policy, based upon the teachings of Clausewitz, may be expressed in two questions, the questions laid down by Clausewitz: "Is it expedient to do this? Have we the power to do it?" If it will benefit the Fatherland to break up the British Empire, then it is expedient to break up the British Empire. Clausewitz taught Germany that "war is a part of policy." He taught that policy is a system of bargaining or negotiating, backed by arms. Clausewitz does not discuss the moral aspect of war; he deals with power and expediency. His pupils take his lead. They do not read poems on the blessings of peace; they do not spend ink on philanthropic theories.

All the more scientific writers, without an exception, so far as I am aware, repudiate its "accidental" character. They one and all, from Grotius to Von der Goltz, take the view that it results from definite and determinable laws, like all the great processes of human development.

Von der Goltz ("On the Conduct of War") says:

One must never lose sight of the fact that war is the consequence and continuation of policy. One will act on the defensive strategically or rest on the defensive according as the policy has been offensive or defensive. An offensive and defensive policy is in its turn indicated by the line of conduct dictated historically. We see this very clearly in antiquity by the example furnished us in the Persians and Romans. In their wars we see the strategical rôle following the bend of the historical rôle. The people which in its historical development has arrived at the stage of inertia, or even retrogression, will not carry on a policy of offence, but merely one of defense; a nation in that situation will wait to be attacked, and its strategy will consequently be defensive, and from a defensive strategy will follow necessarily a defensive tactic.

Lord Esher has expressed a like thought.[51]

But whether wars result from sheer temper, national "hot fits," or not, it is quite certain that the lengthy preparation for war, the condition of armed peace, the burden of armaments which is almost worse than an occasional war, does not result therefrom.

The paraphernalia of war in the modern world cannot be improvised on the spur of the moment to meet each gust of ill-feeling, and be dropped when it is over. The building of battleships, the discussion of budgets and the voting of them, the training of armies, the preparation of a campaign, are a long business, and more and more in our day does each distinctive campaign involve a special and distinctive preparation. The pundits declare that the German battleships have been especially built with a view to work in the North Sea. In any case, we know that the conflict with Germany has been going on for ten years. This is surely a rather prolonged "hot fit." The truth is that war in the modern world is the outcome of armed peace, and involves, with all its elaborate machinery of yearly budgets, and slowly built warships and forts, and slowly trained armies, fixity of policy and purpose extending over years, and sometimes generations. Men do not make these sacrifices month after month, year after year, pay taxes, and upset Governments and fight in Parliament for a mere passing whim; and as conflicts necessarily become more scientific, we shall in the nature of things be forced to prepare everything more thoroughly, and have clearer and sounder ideas as to their essence, their cause, and their effects, and to watch more closely their relation to national motive and policy. The final justification for all these immense, humdrum, workaday sacrifices must be more and more national well-being.

This does not imply, as some critics allege, the conclusion that an Englishman is to say: "Since I might be just as well off under the Germans, let them come"; but that the German will say: "Since I shall be no better off for the going, I will not go."

Indeed, the case of the authorities cited in the preceding chapter is marked by a false form of statement. Those who plead for war on moral grounds say: "War will go on because men will defend their ideals, moral, political, social, and religious." It should be stated thus: "War will go on because men will always attack the spiritual possessions of other men," because, of course, the necessity for defense arises from the fact that these possessions are in danger of attack.

Put in the second form, however, the case breaks down almost of itself. The least informed of us realizes that the whole trend of history is against the tendency for men to attack the ideals and the beliefs of other men. In the religious domain that tendency is plain, so much so that the imposition of religious ideals or beliefs by force has practically been abandoned in Europe, and the causes which have wrought this change of attitude in the European mind are just as operative in the field of politics.

Those causes have been, in the religious field, of a twofold nature, both having direct bearing on the problem with which we are dealing. The first cause is that at which I have already hinted, the general shifting of the ideals from sterile aims to those concerned with the improvement of society; the second one being that development of communication which has destroyed the spiritual homogeneity of States.

A given movement of religious opinion is not confined to one State, transforming it completely, while another current of opinion transforms completely in another sense another State; but it goes on piecemeal, *pari passu*, in the various States. Very early in the religious development of Europe there ceased to be such a thing as a purely Catholic or a purely Protestant State: the religious struggle went on inside the political frontiers--between the people of the same State. The struggle of political and social ideas must take a like course. Those struggles of ideas will be carried out, not between States, but between different groups in the same State, those groups acting in intellectual co-operation with corresponding groups in other States. This intellectual co-operation across frontiers is a necessary outcome of the similar economic co-operation athwart frontiers which the physical division of labor, owing to the development of communication, has set up. It has become impossible for the army of a State to embody the fight for an ideal, for the simple reason that the great moral questions of our time can no longer be postulated in national terms. What follows will make this plain.

There remains a final moral claim for war: that it is a needed moral discipline for nations, the supreme test for the survival of the fittest.

In the first chapter of this section, I have pointed out the importance of this plea in determining the general character of European public opinion, on which alone depends the survival or the disappearance of the militarist regimen. Yet in strict logic there is no need to rebut this claim in detail at all, for only a small fraction of those who believe in it have the courage of their convictions.

The defender of large armaments always justifies his position on the ground that such armaments ensure peace. *Si vis pacem*, etc. As between war and peace he has made his choice, and he has chosen, as the definite object of his endeavors, peace. Having directed his efforts to secure peace, he must accept whatever disadvantages there may lie in that state. He is prepared to admit that, of the two states, peace is preferable, and it is peace towards which our efforts should be directed. Having decided on that aim, what utility is there in showing that it is an undesirable one?

We must, as a matter of fact, be honest for our opponent. We must assume that in an alternative, where his action would determine the issue of war or peace, he will allow that action to be influenced by the general consideration that war might make for the moral advantage of his country. More important even than this consideration is that of the general national temper, to which his philosophy, however little in keeping with his professed policy and desire, necessarily gives rise. For these reasons it is worthwhile to consider in detail the biological case which he presents.

The illusion underlying that case arises from the indiscriminate application of scientific formulæ.

Struggle is the law of survival with man, as elsewhere, but it is the struggle of man with the universe, not man with man. Dog does not eat dog--even tigers do not live on one another. Both dogs and tigers live upon their prey.

It is true that as against this it is argued that dogs struggle with one another for the same prey--if the supply of food runs short the weakest dog, or the weakest tiger, starves. But an analogy between this state and one in which co-operation is a direct means of increasing the supply of food, obviously breaks down. If dogs and tigers were groups, organized on the basis of the division of labor, even the weak dogs and tigers could, conceivably, perform functions which would increase the food supply of the group as a whole, and, conceivably, their existence would render the security of that supply greater than would their elimination. If to-day a territory like England supports in comfort, a population of 45,000,000, where in other times rival groups, numbering at most two or three millions, found themselves struggling with one another for a bare subsistence, the greater quantity of food and the greater security of the supply is not due to any process of elimination of Wessex men by Northumbrian men, but is due precisely to the fact that this rivalry has been replaced by common action against their prey, the forces of nature. The obvious facts of the development of communities show that there is a progressive replacement of rivalry by co-operation, and that the vitality of the social organism increases in direct ratio to the efficiency of the co-operation, and to the abandonment of the rivalry, between its parts.[52]

All crude analogies between the processes of plant and animal survival and social survival are vitiated, therefore, by disregarding the dynamic element of conscious co-operation.

That mankind as a whole represents the organism and the planet the environment, to which he is more and more adapting himself, is the only conclusion that consorts with the facts. If struggle between men is the true reading of the law of life, those facts are absolutely inexplicable, for he is drifting away from conflict, from the use of physical force, and towards co-operation. This much is unchallengeable, as the facts which follow will show.

But in that case, if struggle for extermination of rivals between men is the law of life, mankind is setting at naught the natural law, and must be on the way to extinction.

Happily the natural law in this matter has been misread. The individual in his sociological aspect is not the complete organism. He who attempts to live without association with his fellows dies. Nor is the nation the complete organism. If Britain attempted to live without co-operation with other nations, half the population would starve. The completer the co-operation the greater the vitality; the more imperfect the co-operation the less the vitality. Now, a body, the various parts of which are so interdependent that without co-ordination vitality is reduced or death ensures, must be regarded, in so far as the functions in question are concerned, not as a collection of rival organisms, but as one. This is in accord with what we know of the character of living organisms in their conflict with environment. The higher the organism, the greater the elaboration and interdependence of its part, the greater the need for co-ordination.[53]

If we take this as the reading of the biological law, the whole thing becomes plain; man's irresistible drift away from conflict and towards co-operation is but the completer adaptation of the organism (man) to its environment (the planet, wild nature), resulting in a more intense vitality.

The psychological development involved in man's struggle along these lines may best be stated by an outline sketch of the character of his advance.

When I kill my prisoner (cannibalism was a very common characteristic of early man), it is in "human nature" to keep him for my own larder without sharing him. It is the extreme form of the use of force, the extreme form of human individualism. But putrefaction sets in before I can consume him (it is as well to recall these real difficulties of the early man, because, of course, "human nature does not change"), and I am left without food.

But my two neighbors, each with his butchered prisoner, are in a similar difficulty, and though I could quite easily defend my larder, we deem it better on the next occasion to join forces and kill one prisoner at a time. I share mine with the other two; they share theirs with me. There is no waste through putrefaction. It is the earliest form of the surrender of the use of force in favor of co-operation--the first attenuation of the tendency to act on impulse. But when the three prisoners are consumed, and no more happen to be available, it strikes us that on the whole we should have done better to make them catch game and dig roots for us. The next prisoners that are caught are not killed--a further diminution of impulse and the factor of physical force--they are only enslaved, and the pugnacity which in the first case went to kill them is now diverted to keeping them at work. But the pugnacity is so little controlled by rationalism that the slaves starve, and prove incapable of useful work. They are better treated; there is a diminution of pugnacity. They become sufficiently manageable for the masters themselves, while the slaves are digging roots, to do a little hunting. The pugnacity recently expended on the slaves is redirected to keeping hostile tribes from capturing them--a difficult matter, because the slaves themselves show a disposition to try a change of mastership. They are bribed into good behavior by better treatment: a further diminution of force, a further drift towards co-operation; they give labor, we give food and protection. As the tribes enlarge, it is found that those have most cohesion where the position of slaves is recognized by definite rights and privileges. Slavery becomes serfdom or villainy. The lord gives land and protection, the serf labor and military service: a further drift from force, a further drift towards co-operation, exchange. With the introduction of money even the form of force disappears: the laborer pays rent and the lord pays his soldiers. It is free exchange on both sides, and economic force has replaced physical force. The further the drift from force towards simple economic interest the better the result for the effort expended. The Tartar khan, who seizes by force the wealth in his State, giving no adequate return, soon has none to seize. Men will not work to create what they cannot enjoy, so that, finally, the khan has to kill a man by torture in order to obtain a sum which is the thousandth part of what a London tradesman will spend to secure a title carrying no right to the exercise of force from a Sovereign who has lost all right to the use or exercise of physical force, the head of the wealthiest country in the world, the sources of whose wealth are the most removed from any process involving the exercise of physical force.

But while this process is going on inside the tribe, or group, or nation, force and hostility as between differing tribes or nations remain; but not undiminished. At first it suffices for the fuzzy head of a rival tradesman to appear above the bushes for primitive man to want to hit it. He is a foreigner: kill him. Later, he only wants to kill him if he is at war with his tribe. There are periods of peace: diminution of hostility. In the first conflicts all of the other tribe are killed--men, women, and children. Force and pugnacity are absolute. But the use of slaves, both as laborers and as concubines, attentuates this; there is a diminution of force. The women of the hostile tribe bear children by the conqueror: there is a diminution of pugnacity. At the next raid into the hostile territory it is found that there is nothing to take, because everything has been killed or carried off. So on later raids the conqueror kills the chiefs only (a further diminution of pugnacity, a further drift from mere impulse), or merely dispossesses them of their lands, which he divides among his followers (Norman Conquest type). We have already passed the stage of extermination.[54] The conqueror simply absorbs the conquered--or the conquered absorbs the conqueror, whichever you like. It is no longer the case of one gobbling up the other. Neither is gobbled. In the next stage we do not even dispossess the chiefs--a further sacrifice of physical force--we merely impose tribute. But the conquering nation soon finds itself in the position of the khan in his own State--the more he squeezes the less he gets, until, finally, the cost of getting the money by military means exceeds what is obtained. It was the case of Spain in Spanish America--the more territory she "owned" the poorer she became. The wise conqueror, then, finds that better than the exaction of tribute is an exclusive market--old English colonial type. But in the process of ensuring exclusiveness more is lost than is gained: the colonies are allowed to choose their own system--further drift from the use of force, further drift from hostility and pugnacity. Final result: complete abandonment of physical force, co-operation on basis of mutual profit the only relationship, with reference not merely to colonies which have become in fact foreign States, but also to States foreign in name as well as in fact. We have arrived not at the intensification of the struggle between men, but at a condition of vital dependence upon the prosperity of foreigners. Could England by some magic kill all foreigners, half the British population would starve. This is not a condition making indefinitely for hostility to foreigners; still less is it a condition in which such hostility finds its justification in any real instinct of self-preservation or in any deep-seated biological law. With each new intensification of dependence between the parts of the organism must go that psychological development which has marked every stage of the progress in the past, from the day that we killed our prisoner in order to eat him, and refused to share him with our fellow, to the day that the telegraph and the bank have rendered military force economically futile.

But the foregoing does not include all the facts, or all the factors. If Russia does England an injury--sinks a fishing fleet in time of peace, for instance--it is no satisfaction to Englishmen to go out and kill a lot of Frenchmen or Irishmen. They want to kill Russians. If, however, they knew a little less geography--if, for instance, they were Chinese Boxers, it would not matter in the least which they killed, because to the Chinaman all alike are "foreign devils"; his knowledge of the case does not enable him to differentiate between the various nationalities of Europeans. In the case of a wronged negro in the Congo the collective responsibility is still wider; for a wrong inflicted by one white man he will avenge himself on any other--American, German, English, French, Dutch, Belgian, or Chinese. As our knowledge increases, our sense of the collective responsibility of outside groups narrows. But immediately we start on this differentiation there is no stopping. The English yokel is satisfied if he can "get a whack at them foreigners"--Germans will do if Russians are not available. The more educated man wants Russians; but if he stops a moment longer, he will see that in killing Russian peasants he might as well be killing so many Hindoos, for all they had to do with the matter. He then wants to get at the Russian Government. But so do a great many

Russians--Liberals, Reformers, etc. He then sees that the real conflict is not English against Russians at all, but the interest of all law-abiding folk--Russian and English alike--against oppression, corruption, and incompetence. To give the Russian Government an opportunity of going to war would only strengthen its hands against those with whom he was in sympathy--the Reformers. As war would increase the influence of the reactionary party in Russia, it would do nothing to prevent the recurrence of such incidents, and so quite the wrong party would suffer. Were the real facts and the real responsibilities understood, a Liberal people would reply to such an aggression by taking every means which the social and economic relationship of the two States afforded to enable Russian Liberals to hang a few Russian Admirals and establish a Russian Liberal Government. In any case, the realization of the fact attenuates hostility. In the same way, as they become more familiar with the facts, the English will attenuate their hostility to "Germans." An English patriot recently said, "We must smash Prussianism." The majority of Germans are in cordial agreement with him, and are working to that end. But if England went to war for that purpose, Germans would be compelled to fight for Prussianism. War between States for a political ideal of this kind is not only futile, it is the sure means of perpetuating the very condition which it would bring to an end. International hostilities repose for the most part upon our conception of the foreign State, with which we are quarrelling, as a homogeneous personality, having the same character of responsibility as an individual, whereas the variety of interests, both material and moral, regardless of State boundaries, renders the analogy between nations and individuals an utterly false one.

Indeed, when the co-operation between the parts of the social organism is as complete as our mechanical development has recently made it, it is impossible to fix the limits not merely of the economic interests, but of the moral interest of the community, and to say what is one community and what is another. Certainly the State limits no longer define the limits of the community; and yet it is only the State limits which international antagonism predicates. If the Louisiana cotton crop fails, a part of Lancashire starves. There is closer community of interest in a vital matter between Lancashire and Louisiana than between Louisiana and, say, Iowa, parts of the same State. There is much closer intercommunication between Britain and the United States in all that touches social and moral development than between Britain and, say, Bengal, part of the same State. An English nobleman has more community of thought and feeling with a European continental aristocrat (will marry his daughter, for instance) than he would think of claiming with such "fellow" British countrymen as a Bengal Babu, a Jamaica negro, or even a Dorset yokel. A professor at Oxford will have closer community of feeling with a member of the French Academy than with, say, a Whitechapel publican. One may go further, and say that a British subject of Quebec has closer contact with Paris than with London; the British subject of Dutch-speaking

Africa with Holland than with England; the British subject of Hong Kong with Pekin than with London; of Egypt, with Constantinople than with London, and so on. In a thousand respects, association cuts across State boundaries, which are purely conventional, and renders the biological division of mankind into independent and warring States a scientific ineptitude.

Allied factors, introduced by the character of modern intercourse, have already gone far to render territorial conquest futile for the satisfaction of natural human pride and vanity. Just as in the economic sphere, factors peculiar to our generation have rendered the old analogy between States and persons a false one, so do these factors render the analogy in the sentimental sphere a false one. While the individual of great possessions does in fact obtain, by reason of his wealth, a deference which satisfies his pride and vanity, the individual of the great nation has no such sentimental advantage as against the citizen of the small nation. No one thinks of respecting the Russian mujik because he belongs to a great nation, or despising a Scandinavian or Belgian gentleman because he belongs to a small one; and any society will accord prestige to the nobleman of Norway, Holland, Belgium, Spain, or even Portugal, which it refuses to an American "Climber." The nobleman of any country will marry the noblewoman of another more readily than a woman from a lower class of his own country. The prestige of the foreign country rarely counts for anything in the matter, when it comes to the real facts of everyday life, so shallow is the real sentiment which now divides States. Just as in material things community of interest and relationship cut clear across State boundaries, so inevitably will the psychic community of interest come so to do.

Just as, in the material domain, the real biological law, which is association and co-operation between individuals of the same species in the struggle with their environment, has pushed men in their material struggle to conform with that law, so will it do so in the sentimental sphere. We shall come to realize that the real psychic and moral divisions are not as between nations, but as between opposing conceptions of life. Even admitting that man's nature will never lose the combativeness, hostility, and animosity which are so large a part of it (although the manifestations of such feelings have so greatly changed within the historical period as almost to have changed in character), what we shall see is the diversion of those psychological qualities to the real, instead of the artificial, conflict of mankind. We shall see that at the bottom of any conflict between the armies or Governments of Germany and England lies not the opposition of "German" interests to "English" interests, but the conflict in both States between democracy and autocracy, or between Socialism and Individualism, or reaction and progress, however one's sociological sympathies may classify it. That is the real division in both countries, and for Germans to conquer English, or English Germans, would not advance the solution of such a conflict one iota; and as such conflict becomes more acute, the German individualist will see that it is more important to protect his freedom and property against the Socialist and trade unionist, who can and do attack them, than against the British Army, which cannot. In the same way the British Tory will be more concerned with what Mr. Lloyd George's Budgets can do than with what the Germans can do.[55] From the realization of these things to the realization on the part of the British democrat that what stands in the way of his securing for social expenditure enormous sums, that now go to armaments, is mainly a lack of co-operation between himself and the democrats of a hostile nation who are in a like case, is but a step, and a step that, if history has any meaning, is bound shortly to be taken. When it is taken, property, capital, Individualism will have to give to its international organization, already far-reaching, a still more definite form, in which international differences will play no part. And when that condition is reached, both peoples will find inconceivable the idea that artificial State divisions (which are coming more and more to approximate to mere administrative divisions, leaving free scope within them or across them for the development of genuine nationality) could ever in any way define the real conflicts of mankind.

There remains, of course, the question of time; that these developments will take "thousands" or "hundreds" of years. Yet the interdependence of modern nations is the growth of little more than fifty years. A century ago England could have been self-supporting, and little the worse for it. One must not overlook the Law of Acceleration. The age of man on the earth is placed variously at from thirty thousand to three hundred thousand years. He has in some respects developed more in the last two hundred years than in all the preceding ages. We see more change now in ten years than originally in ten thousand. Who shall foretell the developments of a generation?

CHAPTER III

UNCHANGING HUMAN NATURE

The progress from cannibalism to Herbert Spencer--The disappearance of religious oppression by government--Disappearance of the duel--The Crusaders and the Holy Sepulcher--The wail of militarist writers at man's drift away from militancy.

All of us who have had occasion to discuss this subject are familiar with the catch-phrases with which the whole matter is so often dismissed. "You cannot change human nature," "What man always has been during thousands of years, he always will be," are the sort of dicta generally delivered as self-evident propositions that do not need discussion. Or if, in deference to the fact that very profound changes, in which human nature is involved, *have* taken place in the habits of mankind, the statement of the proposition is somewhat less dogmatic, we are given to understand that any serious modification of the tendency to go to war can only be looked for in "thousands of years."

What are the facts? They are these:

That the alleged unchangeability of human nature in this matter is not borne out; that man's pugnacity though not disappearing, is very visibly, under the forces of mechanical and social development, being transformed and diverted from ends that are wasteful and destructive to ends that are less wasteful, which render easier that co-operation between men in the struggle with their environment which is the condition of their survival and advance; that changes which, in the historical period, have been extraordinarily rapid are necessarily quickening--quickening in geometrical rather than in arithmetical ratio.

With very great courtesy, one is impelled to ask those who argue that human nature in all its manifestations must remain unchanged how they interpret history. We have seen man progress from the mere animal fighting with other animals, seizing his food by force, seizing also by force his females, eating his own kind, the sons of the family struggling with the father for the possession of the father's wives; we have seen this incoherent welter of animal struggle at least partly abandoned for settled industry, and partly surviving as a more organized tribal warfare or a more ordered pillaging, like that of the Vikings and the Huns; we have seen even these pillagers abandon in part their pillaging for ordered industry, and in part for the more ceremonial conflict of feudal struggle; we have seen even the feudal conflict abandoned in favor of dynastic and religious and territorial conflict, and then dynastic and religious conflict abandoned. There remains now only the conflict of States, and that, too,

at a time when the character and conception of the State are being profoundly modified.

Human nature may not change, whatever that vague phrase may
mean; but human nature is a complex factor. It includes numberless
motives, many of which are modified in relation to the rest as circumstances change; so that the manifestations of human nature change out
of all recognition. Do we mean by the phrase that "human nature does
not change" that the feelings of the paleolithic man who ate the bodies of
his enemies and of his own children are the same as those of a Herbert
Spencer, or even of the modern New Yorker who catches his subway train
to business in the morning? If human nature does not change, may we
therefore expect the city clerk to brain his mother and serve her up for
dinner, or suppose that Lord Roberts or Lord Kitchener is in the habit,
while on campaign, of catching the babies of his enemies on spear-heads,
or driving his motor-car over the bodies of young girls, like the leaders of
the old Northmen in their ox-wagons.

What *do* these phrases mean? These, and many like them, are repeated
in a knowing way with an air of great wisdom and profundity by journal-
ists and writers of repute, and one may find them blatant any day in our
newspapers and reviews; yet the most cursory examination proves them
to be neither wise nor profound, but simply parrot-like catch-phrases
which lack common sense, and fly in the face of facts of everyday experience.

The truth is that the facts of the world as they stare us in the face
show that, in our common attitude, we not only overlook the modifications in human nature, which have occurred historically since yesterday-
-occurred even in our generation--but we also ignore the modification of
human nature which mere differences of social habit and custom and
outlook effect. Take the case of the duel. Even educated people in Germany, France, and Italy, will tell you that it is "not in human nature" to
expect a man of gentle birth to abandon the habit of the duel; the notion
that honorable people should ever so place their honor at the mercy of
whoever may care to insult them is, they assure you, both childish and
sordid. With them the matter will not bear discussion.

Yet the great societies which exist in England, North America, Austra-
lia--the whole Anglo-Saxon world, in fact--have abandoned the duel, and
we cannot lump the whole Anglo-Saxon race as either sordid or childish.

That such a change as this, which must have conflicted with human
pugnacity in its most insidious form,--pride and personal vanity, the traditions of an aristocratic status, every one of the psychological factors
now involved in international conflict--has been effected in our own generation should surely give pause to those who dismiss as chimerical any
hope that rationalism will ever dominate the conduct of nations.

Discussing the impossibility of allowing arbitration to cover all causes
of difference, Mr. Roosevelt remarked, in justification of large armaments:
"We despise a nation, just as we despise a man, who fails to resent an in-

sult."[56] Mr. Roosevelt seems to forget that the duel with us is extinct. Do *we*, the English-speaking people of the world, to whom presumably Mr. Roosevelt must have been referring, despise a man who fails to resent an insult by arms? Would we not, on the contrary, despise the man who should do so? Yet so recent is this charge that it has not yet reached the majority of Europeans.

The vague talk of national honor, as a quality under the especial protection of the soldier, shows, perhaps more clearly than aught else, how much our notions concerning international politics have fallen behind the notions that dominate us in everyday life. When an individual begins to rave about his honor, we may be pretty sure he is about to do some irrational, most likely some disreputable deed. The word is like an oath, serving with its vague yet large meaning to intoxicate the fancy. Its vagueness and elasticity make it possible to regard a given incident, at will, as either harmless or a *casus belli.* Our sense of proportion in these matters approximates to that of the schoolboy. The passing jeer of a foreign journalist, a foolish cartoon, is sufficient to start the dogs of war baying up and down the land.[57] We call it "maintaining the national prestige," "enforcing respect," and I know not what other high-sounding name. It amounts to the same thing in the end.

The one distinctive advance in civil society achieved by the Anglo-Saxon world is fairly betokened by the passing away of this old notion of a peculiar possession in the way of honor, which has to be guarded by arms. It stands out as the one clear moral gain of the nineteenth century; and, when we observe the notion resurging in the minds of men, we may reasonably expect to find that it marks one of those reversions in development which so often occur in the realm of mind as well as in that of organic forms.

Two or three generations since, this progress, even among Anglo-Saxons, towards a rational standard of conduct in this matter, as between individuals, would have seemed as unreasonable as do the hopes of international peace in our day. Even to-day the continental officer is as firmly convinced as ever that the maintenance of personal dignity is impossible save by the help of the duel. He will ask in triumph, "What will you do if one of your own order openly insults you? Can you preserve your self-respect by summoning him to the police-court?" And the question is taken as settling the matter offhand.

The survival, where national prestige is concerned, of the standards of the *code duello* is daily brought before us by the rhetoric of the patriots. Our army and our navy, not the good faith of our statesmen, are the "guardians of our national honor." Like the duellist, the patriot would have us believe that a dishonorable act is made honorable if the party suffering by the dishonor be killed. The patriot is careful to withdraw from the operation of possible arbitration all questions which could affect the "national honor." An "insult to the flag" must be "wiped out in blood." Small nations, which in the nature of the case cannot so resent the insults of great empires, have apparently no right to such a possession as "honor." It is the peculiar prerogative of world-wide empires. The patriots who would thus resent "insults to the flag" may well be asked whether they would condemn the conduct of the German lieutenant who kills the unarmed civilian in cold blood "for the honor of the uniform."

It does not seem to have struck the patriot that, as personal dignity and conduct have not suffered but been improved by the abandonment of the principle of the duel, there is little reason to suppose that international conduct, or national dignity, would suffer by a similar change of standards.

The whole philosophy underlying the duel, where personal relations are concerned, excites in our day the infinite derision of all Anglo-Saxons. Yet these same Anglo-Saxons maintain it as rigorously as ever in the relations of States.

Profound as is the change involved in the Anglo-Saxon abandonment of the duel, a still more universal change, affecting still more nearly our psychological impulses, has been effected within a relatively recent historical period. I refer to the abandonment, by the Governments of Europe, of their right to prescribe the religious belief of their citizens. For hundreds of years, generation after generation, it was regarded as an evident part of a ruler's right and duty to dictate what his subjects should believe.

As Lecky has pointed out, the preoccupation which, for numberless generations, was the center round which all other interests revolved has simply and purely disappeared; coalitions which were once the most serious occupation of statesmen now exist only in the speculations of the expounders of prophecy. Among all the elements of affinity and repulsion that regulate the combinations of nations, dogmatic influences which were once supreme can scarcely be said to exist. There is a change here reaching down into the most fundamental impulses of the human mind. "Until the seventeenth century every mental discussion, which philosophy pronounces to be essential to legitimate research, was almost uniformly branded as a sin, and a large proportion of the most deadly intellectual vices were deliberately inculcated as virtues."

Anyone who argued that the differences between Catholics and Protestants were not such as force could settle, and that the time would come when man would realize this truth, and regard a religious war between European States as a wild and unimaginable anachronism, would have been put down as a futile doctrinaire, completely ignoring the most elementary facts of "unchanging human nature."

There is one striking incident of the religious struggle of States which illustrates vividly the change which has come over the spirit of man. For nearly two hundred years Christians fought the Infidel for the conquest of the Holy Sepulcher. All the nations of Europe joined in this great endeavor. It seemed to be the one thing which could unite them, and for generations, so profound was the impulse which produced the movement, the struggle went on. There is nothing in history, perhaps, quite comparable to it. Suppose that during this struggle one had told a European statesman of that age that the time would come when, assembled in a room, the representatives of a Europe, which had made itself the absolute master of the Infidel, could by a single stroke of the pen secure the Holy Sepulcher for all time to Christendom, but that, having discussed the matter cursorily twenty minutes or so, they would decide that on the whole it was not worthwhile! Had such a thing been told to a mediæval statesman, he would certainly have regarded the prophecy as that of a madman. Yet this, of course, is precisely what has taken place.[58]

A glance over the common incidents of Europe's history will show the profound change which has visibly taken place, not only in the minds, but in the hearts of men. Things which even in our stage of civilization would no longer be possible, owing to that change in human nature which the military dogmatist denies, were commonplace incidents with our grandfathers. Indeed, the modifications in the religious attitude just touched on assuredly arise from an emotional as much as from an intellectual change. A theology which could declare that the unborn child would suffer eternal torment in the fires of hell for no crime, other than that of its conception, would be in our day impossible on merely emotional grounds.[59] What was once deemed a mere truism would now be viewed with horror and indignation. Again, as Lecky says, "For a great change has silently swept over Christendom. Without disturbance, an old doctrine has passed away from among the realizations of mankind."

Not only in the religious sphere do we see this progress. In a civilization, which was in many respects an admirable one, it was possible for 400 slaves to be slaughtered because one of them had committed some offence; for a lady of fashion to gratify a momentary caprice by ordering a slave to be crucified; and, a generation or two since, for whole populations to turn torture into a public amusement[60] and a public festival; for kings, historically yesterday, to assist personally at the tortures of persons accused of witchcraft. It is related by Pitcairn, in his "Criminal Trials of Scotland," that James I. of Scotland personally presided over the tortures of one, Dr. Fian, accused of having caused a storm at sea. The bones of the prisoner's legs were broken into small pieces in the boot, and it was the King himself who suggested the following variation and witnessed the execution of it: the nails of both hands were seized by a pair of pincers and torn from the fingers, and into the bleeding stump of each finger two needles were thrust up to their heads!

Does anyone seriously contend that the conditions of modern life have not modified psychology in these matters? Does anyone seriously deny that our wider outlook, which is the result of somewhat larger conceptions and wider reading, has wrought such a change that the repetition of things like these in London, or in Edinburgh, or in Berlin, has become impossible?

Or, is it seriously argued that we may witness a repetition of these events, that we are quite capable at any moment of taking pleasure in burning alive a beautiful child? Does the Catholic or the Protestant really stand in danger of such things from his religious rival? If human nature is unchanged by the progress of ideas, then he does, and Europe's general adoption of religious freedom is a mistake, and each sect should arm against the other in the old way, and the only real hope of religious peace and safety is in the domination of an absolutely universal Church. This was, indeed, the plea of the old inquisitor, just as it is the plea of the *Spectator* to-day, that the only hope of political peace is in the domination of an absolutely universal power:

There is only one way to end war and preparation for war, and that is, as we have said, by a universal monarchy. If we can imagine one country--let us say Russia for the sake of argument--so powerful that she could disarm the rest of the world, and then maintain a force big enough to forbid any Power to invade the rights of any other Power ... no doubt we should have universal peace.[61]

This dictum recalls one, equally emphatic, once voiced by a colleague of the late Procurator of the Holy Synod in Russia, who said:

There is only one way to ensure religious peace in the State, to compel all in that State to conform to the State religion. Those that will not conform must, in the interests of peace, be driven out.

Mr. Lecky, who of all authors has written most suggestively, perhaps, on the disappearance of religious persecution, has pointed out that the strife between opposing religious bodies arose out of a religious spirit which, though often high-minded and disinterested (he protests with energy against the notion that persecution as a whole was dictated by interested motives), was unpurified by rationalism; and he adds that the irrationality which once characterized the religious sentiment has now been replaced by the irrationality of patriotism. Mr. Lecky says:

If we take a broad view of the course of history, and examine the relations of great bodies of men, we find that religion and patriotism are the chief moral influences to which they have been subjected, and that the separate modifications and mutual interaction of these two agents may almost be said to constitute the moral history of mankind.

Is it to be expected that the rationalization and humanization which have taken place in the more complex domain of religious doctrine and belief will not also take place in the domain of patriotism? More especially, as the same author points out, since it was the necessities of material interest which brought about the reform in the first domain, and since "not only does interest, as distinct from passion, gain a greater empire with advancing civilization, but passion itself is mainly guided by its power."

Have we not abundant evidence, indeed, that the passion of patriotism, as divorced from material interest, is being modified by the pressure of material interest? Are not the numberless facts of national interdependence, which I have indicated here, pushing inevitably to that result? And are we not justified in concluding that, just as the progress of rationalism has made it possible for the various religious groups to live together, to exist side by side without physical conflict; just as there has been in that domain no necessary choice between universal domination or unending strife, so in like manner will the progress of political rationalism mark the evolution of the relationship of political groups; that the struggle for domination will cease because it will be realized that physical domination is futile, and that instead of either universal strife or universal domination there will come, without formal treaties or Holy Alliances, the general determination for each to go his way undisturbed in his political allegiance, as he is now undisturbed in his religious allegiance?

Perhaps the very strongest evidence that the whole drift of human tendencies is away from such conflict as is represented by war between States is to be found in the writings of those who declare war to be inevitable. Among the writers quoted in the first chapter of this section, there is not one who, if his arguments are examined carefully, does not show that he realizes, consciously, or subconsciously, that man's disposition to fight, far from being unchanged, is becoming rapidly enfeebled. Take, for instance, one of the latest works voicing the philosophy that war is inevitable; that, indeed, it is both wicked and childish to try to prevent it.[62] Notwithstanding that the inevitability of war is the thesis of his book, Homer Lea entitles the first section "The Decline of Militancy," and shows clearly, in fact, that the commercial activities of the world lead directly away from war.

Trade, ducats, and mortgages are regarded as far greater assets and sources of power than armies or navies. They produce national effeminacy and effeteness.

Now, as this tendency is common to all nations of Christendom--indeed, of the world--since commercial and industrial development is world-wide, it necessarily means, if it is true of any one nation, that the world as a whole is drifting away from the tendency to warfare.

A large part of Homer Lea's book is a sort of Carlylean girding at what he terms "protoplasmic gourmandizing and retching" (otherwise the busy American industrial and social life of his countrymen). He declares that, when a country makes wealth, production, and industries its sole aim, it becomes "a glutton among nations, vulgar, swinish, arrogant"; "commercialism, having seized hold of the American people, overshadows it, and tends to destroy not only the aspirations and world-wide career open to the nation, but the Republic itself." "Patriotism in the true sense" (i.e., the desire to go and kill other people) Homer Lea declares almost dead in the United States. The national ideals, even of the native-born American, are deplorably low:

There exists not only individual prejudice against military ideals, but public antipathy; antagonism of politicians, newspapers, churches, colleges, labor unions, theorists, and organized societies. They combat the military spirit as if it were a public evil and a national crime.

In that case, what, in the name of all that is muddleheaded, becomes

of the "unchanging tendency towards warfare"? What is all this curious rhetoric of Homer Lea's (and I have dealt with him at some length,
because his principles if not his language are those which characterize
much similar literature in England, France, Germany, and the continent
of Europe generally) but an admission that the whole tendency is not,
as he would have us believe, towards war, but away from it? Here is an
author who tells us that war is to be forever inevitable, and in the same
breath that men are rapidly conceiving not only a "slothful indifference"
to fighting, but a profound antipathy to the military ideal.

Of course, Homer Lea implies that this tendency is peculiar to the
American Republic, and is for that reason dangerous to his country; but,
as a matter of fact, Homer Lea's book might be a free translation of much
nationalist literature of either France or Germany.[63] I cannot recall a
single author of either of the four great countries who, treating of the
inevitability of war, does not bewail the falling away of his own country
from the military ideal, or, at least, the tendency so to fall away. Thus the
English journalist reviewing in the *Daily Mail* Homer Lea's book cannot
refrain from saying:

Is it necessary to point out that there is a moral in all this for us as well
as for the American? Surely almost all that Mr. Lea says applies to Great
Britain as forcibly as to the United States. We too have lain dreaming.
We have let our ideals tarnish. We have grown gluttonous, also.... Shame
and folly are upon us as well as upon our brethren. Let us hasten with
all our energy to cleanse ourselves of them, that we can look the future
in the face without fear.

Exactly the same note dominates the literature of an English protagonist like Mr. Blatchford, the militarist socialist. He talks of the "fatal apathy" of the British people. "The people," he says, breaking out in anger
at the small disposition they show to kill other people, "are conceited,
self-indulgent, decadent, and greedy. They will shout for the Empire, but
they will not fight for it."[64] A glance at such publications as *Blackwood's*,
the *National Review*, the London *Spectator*, the London *World*, will reveal
precisely similar outbursts.

Of course, Mr. Blatchford declares that the Germans are very different,
and that what Mr. Lea (in talking of *his* country) calls the "gourmandizing
and retching" is not at all true of Germany. As a matter of fact, however,
the phrase I have quoted might have been "lifted" from the work of any
average Pan-German, or even from more responsible quarters. Have Mr.
Blatchford and Mr. Lea forgotten that no less a person than Prince von
Bülow, in a speech made in the Prussian Diet, used almost the words I
have quoted from Mr. Blatchford, and dwelt at length on the self-indul-
gence and degeneracy, the rage for luxury, etc., which possess modern
Germany, and told how the old qualities which had marked the founders
of the Empire were disappearing?[65]

Indeed, do not a great part of the governing classes of Germany almost
daily bewail the infiltration of anti-militarist doctrines among the Ger-

man people, and does not the extraordinary increase in the Socialist vote justify the complaint?

A precisely analogous plea is made by the Nationalist writer in France when he rails at the pacifist tendencies of *his* country, and points to the contrasting warlike activities of neighbouring nations. A glance at a copy of practically any Nationalist or Conservative paper in France will furnish ample evidence of this. Hardly a day passes but that the *Echo de Paris, Gaulois, Figaro, Journal des Débats, Patrie*, or *Presse*, sounds this note, while one may find it rampant in the works of such serious writers as Paul Bourget, Faguet, Le Bon, Barrès, Brunetière, Paul Adam, to say nothing of more popular publicists like Deroulède, Millevoye, Drumont, etc.

All these advocates of war, therefore--American, English, German, French--are at one in declaring that foreign countries are very warlike, but that their own country, "sunk in sloth," is drifting away from war. As presumably they know more of their own country than of others, their own testimony involves mutual destruction of their own theories. They are thus unwilling witnesses to the truth, which is that we are all alike--English, Americans, Germans, French--losing the psychological impulse to war, just as we have lost the psychological impulse to kill our neighbors on account of religious differences, and (at least in the case of the Anglo-Saxon) to kill our neighbors in duels for some cause of wounded vanity.

How, indeed, could it be otherwise? How can modern life, with its overpowering proportion of industrial activities and its infinitesimal proportion of military ones, keep alive the instincts associated with war as against those developed by peace?

Not only evolution, but common sense and common observation, teaches us that we develop most those qualities which we exercise most, which serve us best in the occupation in which we are most engaged. A race of seamen is not developed by agricultural pursuits, carried on hundreds of miles from the sea.

Take the case of what is reputed (quite wrongly, incidentally) to be the most military nation in Europe--Germany. The immense majority of adult Germans--practically, all who make up what we know as Germany--have never seen a battle, and in all human probability never will see one. In forty years eight thousand Germans have been in the field about twelve months--against naked blacks.[66] So that the proportion of warlike activities to peaceful activities works out at one to hundreds of thousands. I wish it were possible to illustrate this diagrammatically; but it could not be done in this book, because, if a single dot the size of a full-stop were to be used to illustrate the expenditure of time in actual war, I should have to fill most of the book with dots to illustrate the time spent by the balance of the population in peace activities.[67]

In that case, how can we possibly expect to keep alive warlike qualities, when all our interests and activities--all our environments, in short--are peace-like?

In other words, the occupations which develop the qualities of industry and peace are so much in excess of those which would develop the qualities we associate with war that that excess has almost now passed beyond any ordinary means of visual illustration, and has entirely passed beyond any ordinary human capacity fully to appreciate. Peace is with us now nearly always; war is with us rarely, yet we are told that it is the qualities of war which will survive, and the qualities of peace which will be subsidiary.

I am not forgetting, of course, the military training, the barrack life which is to keep alive the military tradition. I have dealt with that question in the next chapter. It suffices for the moment to note that that training is defended on the grounds (notably among those who would introduce it into England)--(1) that it ensures peace; (2) that it renders a population more efficient in the arts of peace--that is to say, perpetuates that condition of "slothful ease" which we are told is so dangerous to our characters, in which we are bound to lose the "warlike qualities," and which renders society still more "gourmandizing" in Mr. Lea's contemptuous phrase, still more "Cobdenite" in Mr. Leo Maxse's. One cannot have it both ways. If long-continued peace is enervating, it is mere self-stultification to plead for conscription on the ground that it will still further prolong that enervating condition. If Mr. Leo Maxse sneers at industrial society and the peace ideal-- "the Cobdenite ideal of buying cheap and selling dear"--he must not defend German conscription (though he does) on the ground that it renders German commerce more efficient--that, in other words, it advances that "Cobdenite ideal." In that case, the drift away from war will be stronger than ever. Perhaps some of all this inconsistency was in Mr. Roosevelt's mind when he declared that by "war alone" can man develop those manly qualities, etc. If conscription really does prolong peace and increase our aptitude for the arts of peace, then conscription itself is but a factor in man's temperamental drift away from war, in the change of his nature towards peace.

It is not because man is degenerate or swinish or gluttonous (such language, indeed, applied as it is by Mr. Lea to the larger and better part of the human race, suggests a not very high-minded ill-temper at the stubbornness of facts which rhetoric does not affect) that he is showing less and less disposition to fight, but because he is condemned by the real "primordial law" to earn his bread by the sweat of his brow, and his nature in consequence develops those qualities which the bulk of his interests and capacities demand and favor.

Finally, of course, we are told that even though these forces are at work, they must take "thousands of years" to operate. This dogmatism ignores the Law of Acceleration, as true in the domain of sociology as in that of physics, which I have touched on at the close of the preceding chapter. The most recent evidence would seem to show that man as a fire-using animal dates back to the Tertiary epoch--say, three hundred thousand years. Now, in all that touches this discussion, man in Northern Europe (in Great Britain, say) remained unchanged for two hundred and ninety-eight thousand of those years. In the last two thousand years he changed more than in the two hundred and ninety-eight thousand preceding, and in one hundred he has changed more, perhaps, than in the preceding two thousand. The comparison becomes more understandable if we resolve it into hours. For, say, fifty years the man was a cannibal savage or a wild animal, hunting other wild animals, and then in the space of three months he became John Smith of Des Moines, attending church, passing laws, using the telephone, and so on. That is the history of European mankind. And in the face of it, the wiseacres talk sapiently, and lay it down as a self-evident and demonstrable fact that inter-State war, which, by reason of the mechanics of our civilization, accomplishes nothing and can accomplish nothing, will forever be unassailable because, once man has got the habit of doing a thing, he will go on doing it, although the reason which in the first instance prompted it has long since disappeared--because, in short, of the "unchangeability of human nature."

CHAPTER IV

DO THE WARLIKE NATIONS INHERIT THE EARTH?

The confident dogmatism of militarist writers on this subject--The facts--The lessons of Spanish America--How conquest makes for the survival of the unfit--Spanish method and English method in the New World--The virtues of military training--The Dreyfus case--The threatened Germanization of England-- "The war which made Germany great and Germans small."

The militarist authorities I have quoted in the preceding chapter admit, therefore, and admit very largely, man's drift, in a sentimental sense, away from war. But that drift, they declare, is degeneration; without those qualities which "war alone," in Mr. Roosevelt's phrase, can develop, man will "rot and decay."

This plea is, of course, directly germane to our subject. To say that the qualities which we associate with war, and nothing else but war, are necessary to assure a nation success in its struggles with other nations is equivalent to saying that those who drift away from war will go down before those whose warlike activity can conserve those qualities essential to survival; and this is but another way of saying that men must always remain warlike if they are to survive, that the warlike nations inherit the earth; that men's pugnacity, therefore, is the outcome of the great natural law of survival, and that a decline of pugnacity marks in any nation a retrogression and not an advance in its struggle for survival. I have already indicated (Chapter II., Part II.) the outlines of the proposition, which leaves no escape from this conclusion. This is the scientific basis of the proposition voiced by the authorities I have quoted--Mr. Roosevelt, Von Moltke, Renan, Nietzsche, and various of the warlike clergy[68]--and it lies at the very bottom of the plea that man's nature, in so far as it touches the tendency of men as a whole to go to war, does not change; that the warlike qualities are a necessary part of human vitality in the struggle for existence; that, in short, all that we know of the law of evolution forbids the conclusion that man will ever lose this warlike pugnacity, or that nations will survive other than by the struggle of physical force.

The view is best voiced, perhaps, by Homer Lea, whom I have already quoted. He says, in his "Valor of Ignorance":

As physical vigor represents the strength of man in his struggle for existence, in the same sense military vigor constitutes the strength of nations; ideals, laws, constitutions are but temporary effulgences [P. 11]. The deterioration of the military force and the consequent destruction of the militant spirit have been concurrent with national decay [P. 24].

International disagreements are ... the result of the primordial conditions that sooner or later cause war ... the law of struggle, the law of survival, universal, unalterable ... to thwart them, to short-cut them, to circumvent them, to cozen, to deny, to scorn, to violate them, is folly such as man's conceit alone makes possible.... Arbitration denies the inexorability of natural laws ... that govern the existence of political entities [Pp. 76, 77]. Laws that govern the militancy of a people are not of man's framing, but follow the primitive ordinances of nature that govern all forms of life, from simple protozoa, awash in the sea, to the empires of man.[69]

I have already indicated the grave misconception which lies at the bottom of the interpretation of the evolutionary law here indicated. What we are concerned with now is to deal with the facts on which this alleged general principle is inductively based. We have seen from the foregoing chapter that man's nature certainly does change; the next step is to show, from the facts of the present-day world, that the warlike qualities do not make for survival, that the warlike nations do not inherit the earth.

Which are the military nations? We generally think of them in Europe as Germany and France, or perhaps also Russia, Austria, and Italy. Admittedly (vide all the English and American military pundits and economists) England is the least militarized nation in Europe, the United States perhaps in the world. It is, above all, Germany that appeals to us as the type of the military nation, one in which the stern school of war makes for the preservation of the "manly and adventurous qualities."

The facts want a little closer examination. What is a career of unwarlike ease, in Mr. Roosevelt's phrase? In the last chapter we saw that during the last forty years eight thousand out of sixty million Germans have been engaged in warfare during a trifle over a year, and that against Hottentots or Hereros--a proportion of war days per German to peace days per German which is as one to some hundreds of thousands. So that if we are to take Germany as the type of the military nation, and if we are to accept Mr. Roosevelt's dictum that by war alone can we acquire "those virile qualities necessary to win in the stern strife of actual life," we shall nevertheless be doomed to lose them, for under conditions like those of Germany how many of us can ever see war, or can pretend to fall under its influence? As already pointed out, the men who really give the tone to the German nation, to German life and conduct--that is to say, the majority of adult Germans--have never seen a battle and never will see one. France has done much better. Not only has she seen infinitely more actual fighting, but her population is much more militarized than that of Germany, 50 per cent. more, in fact, since, in order to maintain from a population of forty millions the same effective military force as Germany does with sixty millions, 1-1/2 per cent. of the French population is under arms as against 1 per cent. of the German.[70]

Still more military in organization and in recent practical experience is Russia, and more military than Russia is Turkey, and more military than

Turkey as a whole are the semi-independent sections of Turkey, Arabia, and Albania, and then, perhaps, comes Morocco.

On the Western Hemisphere we can draw a like table as to the "warlike, adventurous, manly, and progressive peoples" as compared with the "peaceful, craven, slothful, and decadent." The least warlike of all, the nation which has had the least training in war, the least experience of it, which has been the least purified by it, is Canada. After that comes the United States, and after that the best--(excuse me, I mean, of course, the worst--*i.e.*, the least warlike)--of the Spanish American republics like Brazil and Argentina; while the most warlike of all, and consequently the most "manly and progressive," are the "Sambo" republics, like San Domingo, Nicaragua, Colombia, and Venezuela. They are always fighting. If they cannot manage to get up a fight between one another, the various parties in each republic will fight between themselves. Here we get the real thing. The soldiers do not pass their lives in practicing the goose-step, cleaning harness, pipeclaying belts, but in giving and taking hard pounding. Several of these progressive republics have never known a year since they declared their independence from Spain in which they have not had a war. And quite a considerable proportion of the populations spend their lives in fighting. During the first twenty years of Venezuela's independent existence she fought no less than one hundred and twenty important battles, either with her neighbors or with herself, and she has maintained the average pretty well ever since. Every election is a fight--none of your "mouth-fighting," none of your craven talking-shops for them. Good, honest, hard, manly knocks, with anything from one to five thousand dead and wounded left on the field. The presidents of these strenuous republics are not poltroons of politicians, but soldiers--men of blood and iron with a vengeance, men after Mr. Roosevelt's own heart, all following "the good old rule, the simple plan." These are the people who have taken Carlyle's advice to "shut up the talking-shops." *They* fight it out like men; *they* talk with Gatling-guns and Mausers. Oh, they are a very fine, manly, military lot! If fighting makes for survival, they should completely oust from the field Canada and the United States, one of which has never had a real battle for the best part of its hundred years of craven, sordid, peaceful life, and the other of which Homer Lea assures us is surely dying, because of its tendency to avoid fighting.

Mr. Lea does not make any secret of the fact (and if he did, some of his rhetoric would display it) that he is out of sympathy with predominant American ideals. He might emigrate to Venezuela, or Colombia, or Nicaragua. He would be able to prove to each military dictator in turn that, in converting the country into a shambles, far from committing a foul crime for which such dictators should be, and are, held in execration by civilized men the world over, they are, on the contrary, but obeying one of God's commands in tune with all the immutable laws of the universe. I desire to write in all seriousness, but, to one who happens to have seen at first hand something of the conditions which arise from a real military conception of civilization, it is very difficult. How does Mr. Roosevelt, who declares that "by war alone can we acquire those virile qualities necessary to win in the stern strife of actual life"; how does Von Stengel, who declares that "war is a test of a nation's health, political, physical, and moral"; how do our militarists, who infer that the military state is so much finer than the Cobdenite one of commercial pursuits; how does M. Ernest Renan, who declares that war is the condition of progress, and that under peace we should sink to a degree of degeneracy difficult to realize; and how do the various English clergymen who voice a like philosophy reconcile their creed with military Spanish America? How can they urge that non-military industrialism, which, with all its shortcomings, has on the Western Continent given us Canada and the United States, makes for decadence and degeneration, while militarism and the qualities and instincts that go with it have given us Venezuela and San Domingo? Do we not all recognize that industrialism--Mr. Lea's "gourmandizing and retching" notwithstanding--is the one thing which will save these military republics; that the one condition of their advance is that they shall give up the stupid and sordid gold-braid militarism and turn to honest work?

If ever there was a justification for Herbert Spencer's sweeping generalization that "advance to the highest forms of man and society depends on the decline of militancy and the growth of industrialism," it is to be found in the history of the South and Central American Republics. Indeed, Spanish America at the present moment affords more lessons than we seem to be drawing, and, if militancy makes for advance and survival, it is a most extraordinary thing that all who are in any way concerned with those countries, all who live in them and whose future is wrapped up in them, can never sufficiently express their thankfulness that at last there seems to be a tendency with some of them to get away from the blood and valor nonsense which has been their curse for three centuries, and to exchange the military ideal for the Cobdenite one of buying cheap and selling dear which excites so much contempt.

Some years ago an Italian lawyer, a certain Tomasso Caivano, wrote a letter detailing his experiences and memories of twenty years' life in Venezuela and the neighboring republics, and his general conclusions have for this discussion a direct relevancy. As a sort of farewell exhortation to the Venezuelans, he wrote:

The curse of your civilization is the soldier and the soldier's temper. It is impossible for two of you, still less for two parties, to carry on a discussion without one wanting to fight the other about the matter in hand. You regard it as a derogation of dignity to consider the point of view of the other side, and to attempt to meet it, if it is possible to fight about it. You deem that personal valor atones for all defects. The soldier of evil character is more considered amongst you than the civilian of good character, and military adventure is deemed more honorable than honest labor. You overlook the worst corruption, the worst oppression, in your leaders if only they gild it with military fanfaronade and declamation about bravery and destiny and patriotism. Not until there is a change in this spirit will you cease to be the victims of evil oppression. Not until your general populace--your peasantry and your workers--refuse thus to be led to slaughter in quarrels of which they know and care nothing, but into which they are led because they also prefer fighting to work--not until all this happens will those beautiful lands which are among the most fertile on God's earth support a happy and prosperous people living in contentment and secure possession of the fruits of their labor.[71]

Spanish America seems at last in a fair way to throwing off the domination of the soldier and awakening from these nightmares of successive military despotisms tempered by assassination, though, in abandoning, in Signor Caivano's words, "military adventure for honest labor," she will necessarily have less to do with those deeds of blood and valor of which her history has been so full. But those in South America who matter are not mourning. Really they are not.[72]

The situation can be duplicated absolutely on the other side of the hemisphere. Change a few names, and you get Arabia or Morocco. Listen to this from a recent London *Times* article:[73]

The fact is that for many years past Turkey has almost invariably been at war in some part or other of Arabia.... At the present moment Turkey is actually conducting three separate small campaigns within Arabia or upon its borders, and a fourth series of minor operations in Mesopotamia. The last-named movement is against the Kurdish tribes of the Mosul district.... Another, and more important, advance is against the truculent Muntefik Arabs of the Euphrates delta.... The fourth, and by far the largest, campaign is the unending warfare in the province of Yemen, north of Aden, where the Turks have been fighting intermittently for more than a decade. The peoples of Arabia are also indulging in conflict on their own account. The interminable feud between the rival potentates of Nedjd, Ibn Saud of Riadh and Ibn Rashid of Hail, has broken out afresh, and the tribes of the coastal province of El Katar are supposed to have plunged into the fray. The Muntefik Arabs, not content with worrying the Turks, are harrying the territories of Sheikh Murbarak of Koweit. In the far south the Sultan of Shehr and Mokalla, a feudatory of the British Government, is conducting a tiny war against a hostile tribe in the mysterious Hadramaut. In the west the Beduin are spasmodically menacing certain sections of the Hedjaz Railway, which they very much dislike.... Ten years ago the Ibn Rashids were nominally masters of a great deal of Arabia, and grew so aggressive that they tried to seize Koweit. The fiery old Sheikh of Koweit marched against them, and alternately won and lost. He had his revenge. He sent an audacious scion of the Ibn Sauds to the old Wahabi capital of Riadh, and by a remarkable stratagem the youth captured the stronghold with only fifty men. The rival parties have been fighting at intervals ever since.

And so on and so on to the extent of a column. So that what Venezuela and Nicaragua are to the American Continent, Arabia, Albania, Armenia, Montenegro, and Morocco are to the Eastern Hemisphere. We find exactly the same rule--that just as one gets away from militancy one gets towards advance and civilization; as men lose the tendency to fight they gain the tendency to work, and it is by working with one another, and not by fighting against each other, that men advance.

Take the progression away from militancy, and it gives us a table something like this:

Arabia and Morocco. Turkish territory as a whole. The more unruly Balkan States. Montenegro. Russia. Spain. Italy. Austria. France. Germany. Scandinavia. Holland. Belgium. England. The United States. Canada.

Do Mr. Roosevelt, Admiral Mahan, Baron von Stengel, Marshal von Moltke, Mr. Homer Lea, and the English clergymen seriously argue that this list should be reversed, and that Arabia and Turkey should be taken as the types of progressive nations, and England and Germany and Scandinavia as the decadent?

It may be urged that my list is not absolutely accurate, in that England, having fought more little wars (though the conflict with the Boers, waged with a small, pastoral people, shows how a little war may drain a great country), is more militarized than Germany, which has not been fighting at all. But I have tried in a very rough fashion to arrive at the degree of militancy in each State, and the absence of actual fighting in the case of Germany (as in that of the smaller States) is balanced by the fact of the military training of her people. As I have indicated, France is more military than Germany, both in the extent to which her people are put through the mill of universal military training, and by virtue of the fact that she has done so much more small fighting than Germany (Madagascar, Tonkin, Africa, etc.); while, of course, Turkey and the Balkan States are still more military in both senses--more actual fighting, more military training.

Perhaps the militarist will argue that, while useless and unjust wars make for degeneration, just wars are a moral regeneration. But did a nation, group, tribe, family, or individual ever yet enter into a war which he did not think just? The British, or most of them, believed the war against the Boers just, but most of the authorities in favor of war in general, outside of Great Britain, believed it unjust. Nowhere do you find such deathless, absolute, unwavering belief in the justice of war as in those conflicts which all Christendom knows to be at once unjust and unnecessary. I refer to the religious wars of Mohammedan fanaticism.

Do you suppose that when Nicaragua goes to war with San Salvador, or Costa Rica or Colombia with Peru, or Peru with Chili, or Chili with Argentina, they do not each and every one of them believe that they are fighting for immutable and deathless principles? The civilization of most of them is, of course, as like as two peas, and there is no more reason, except their dislike of rational thought and hard work, why they should fight with one another, than that Illinois should fight with Indiana, despite

Homer Lea's fine words as to the primordial character of national differences; to one another they are as alike, and whether San Salvador beats Costa Rica or Costa Rica, San Salvador, does not, so far as essentials are concerned, matter a continental. But their rhetoric of patriotism--the sacrifice, and the deathless glory, and the rest of it--is often just as sincere as ours. That is the tragedy of it, and it is that which gives to the solution of the problem in Spanish America its real difficulty.

But even if we admit that warfare à l'espagnole may be degrading, and that just wars are ennobling and necessary to our moral welfare, we should nevertheless be condemned to degeneracy and decline. A just war implies that someone must act unjustly towards us, but as the general condition improves--as it is improving in Europe as compared with Central and South America, or Morocco, or Arabia--we shall get less and less "moral purification"; as men become less and less disposed to make unjustifiable attacks, they will become more and more degenerate. In such incoherence are we landed by the pessimistic and impossible philosophy that men will decay and die unless they go on killing each other.

What is the fundamental error at the base of the theory that war makes for the survival of the fit--that warfare is any necessary expression of the law of survival? It is the illusion induced by the hypnotism of a terminology which is obsolete. The same factor which leads us so astray in the economic domain leads us astray in this also.

Conquest does not make for the elimination of the conquered; the weakest do not go to the wall, though that is the process which those who adopt the formula of evolution in this matter have in their minds.

Great Britain has conquered India. Does that mean that the inferior race is replaced by the superior? Not the least in the world; the inferior race not only survives, but is given an extra lease of life by virtue of the conquest. If ever the Asiatic threatens the white race, it will be thanks in no small part to the work of race conservation which England's conquests in the East have involved. War, therefore, does not make for the elimination of the unfit and the survival of the fit. It would be truer to say that it makes for the survival of the unfit.

What is the real process of war? You carefully select from the general population on both sides the healthiest, sturdiest, the physically and mentally soundest, those possessing precisely the virile and manly qualities which you desire to preserve, and, having thus selected the élite of the two populations, you exterminate them by battle and disease, and leave the worst of both sides to amalgamate in the process of conquest or defeat--because, in so far as the final amalgamation is concerned, both processes have the same result--and from this amalgam of the worst of both sides you create the new nation or the new society which is to carry on the race. Even supposing the better nation wins, the fact of conquest results only in the absorption of the inferior qualities of the beaten nation--inferior presumably because beaten, and inferior because we have killed off their selected best and absorbed the rest, since we no longer exterminate the women, the children, the old men, and those too weak or too feeble to go into the army.[74]

You have only to carry on this process long enough and persistently enough to weed out completely from both sides the type of man to whom alone we can look for the conservation of virility, physical vigor, and hardihood. That such a process did play no small rôle in the degeneration of Rome and the populations on which the crux of the Empire reposed there can hardly be any reasonable doubt. And the process of degeneration on the part of the conqueror is aided by this additional factor: If the conqueror profits much by his conquest, as the Romans in one sense did, it is the conqueror who is threatened by the enervating effect of the soft and luxurious life; while it is the conquered who is forced to labor for the conqueror, and learns in consequence those qualities of steady industry which are certainly a better moral training than living upon the fruits of others, upon labor extorted at the sword's point. It is the conqueror who becomes effete, and it is the conquered who learns discipline and the qualities making for a well-ordered State.

To say of war, therefore, as does Baron von Stengel, that it destroys the frail trees, leaving the sturdy oaks standing, is merely to state with absolute confidence the exact reverse of the truth; to take advantage of loose catch-phrases, which by inattention not only distort common thought in these matters, but often turn the truth upside down. Our everyday ideas are full of illustrations of the same thing. For hundreds of years we talked of the "riper wisdom of the ancients," implying that this generation is the youth in experience, and that the early ages had the accumulated experience--the exact reverse, of course, of the truth. Yet "the learning of the ancients" and "the wisdom of our forefathers" was a common catch-phrase, even in the British Parliament, until an English country parson killed this nonsense by ridicule.[75]

I do not urge that the somewhat simple, elementary, selective process which I have described accounts in itself for the decadence of military Powers. That is only a part of the process; the whole of it is somewhat more complicated, in that the process of elimination of the good in favor of the bad is quite as much sociological as biological; that is to say, if during long periods a nation gives itself up to war, trade languishes, the population loses the habit of steady industry, government and administration become corrupt, abuses escape punishment, and the real sources of a people's strength and expansion dwindle. What has caused the relative failure and decline of Spanish, Portuguese, and French expansion in Asia and the New World, and the relative success of English expansion therein? Was it the mere hazards of war which gave to Great Britain the domination of India and half of the New World? That is surely a superficial reading of history. It was, rather, that the methods and processes of Spain, Portugal, and France were military, while those of the Anglo-Saxon world were commercial and peaceful. Is it not a commonplace that in India, quite as much as in the New World, the trader and the settler drove out the soldier and the conqueror? The difference between the two methods was that one was a process of conquest, and the other of colonizing, or non-military administration for commercial purposes. The one embodied the sordid Cobdenite idea, which so excites the scorn of the militarists, and the other the lofty military ideal. The one was parasitism; the other co-operation.[76]

Those who confound the power of a nation with the size of its army and navy are mistaking the check-book for the money. A child, seeing its father paying bills in checks, assumes that you need only plenty of check-books in order to have plenty of money; it does not see that for the check-book to have power there must be unseen resources on which to draw. Of what use is domination unless there be individual capacity, social training, industrial resources, to profit thereby? How can you have these things if energy is wasted in military adventure? Is not the failure of Spain explicable by the fact that she failed to realize this truth? For three centuries she attempted to live upon conquest, upon the force of her arms, and year after year got poorer in the process and her modern social renaissance dates from the time when she lost the last of her American colonies. It is since the loss of Cuba and the Philippines that Spanish national securities have doubled in value. (At the outbreak of the Hispano-American War Spanish Fours were at 45; they have since touched par.) If Spain has shown in the last decade a social renaissance, not shown perhaps for a hundred and fifty years, it is because a nation still less military than Germany, and still more purely industrial, has compelled Spain once and for all to surrender all dreams of empire and conquest. The circumstances of the last surrender are eloquent in this connection as showing how even in warfare itself the industrial training and the industrial tradition--the Cobdenite ideal of militarist scorn--are more than a match for the training of a society in which military activities are predominant. If it be true that it was the German schoolmaster who conquered at Sedan, it was the Chicago merchant who conquered at Manila. The writer happens to have been in touch both with Spaniards and Americans at the time of the war, and well remembers the scorn with which the Spaniards referred to the notion that the Yankee pork-butchers could possibly conquer a nation of their military tradition, and to the idea that tradesmen would ever be a match for the soldiery and pride of old Spain. And French opinion was not so very different.[77] Shortly after the war I wrote in an American journal as follows:

Spain represents the outcome of some centuries devoted mainly to military activity. No one can say that she has been unmilitary or at all deficient in those qualities which we associate with soldiers and soldiering. Yet, if such qualities in any way make for national efficiency, for the conservation of national force, the history of Spain is absolutely inexplicable. In their late contest with America, Spaniards showed no lack of the distinctive military virtues. Spain's inferiority--apart from deficiency of men and money--was precisely in those qualities which industrial-

ism has bred in the unmilitary American. Authentic stories of wretched equipment, inadequate supplies, and bad leadership show to what
depths of inefficiency the Spanish service, military and naval, had fallen.
We are justified in believing that a much smaller nation than Spain, but
one possessing a more industrial and less military training, would have
done much better, both as regards resistance to America and the defense
of her own colonies. The present position of Holland in Asia seems to
prove this. The Dutch, whose traditions are industrial and non-military
for the most part, have shown greater power and efficiency as a nation
than the Spanish, who are more numerous.

Here, as always, it is shown that, in considering national efficiency,
even as expressed in military power, the economic problem cannot be
divorced from the military, and that it is a fatal mistake to suppose that
the power of a nation depends solely upon the power of its public bodies,
or that it can be judged simply from the size of its army. A large army
may, indeed, be a sign of a national--that is, military--weakness. Warfare in these days is a business like other activities, and no courage, no
heroism, no "glorious past," no "immortal traditions," will atone for deficient rations and fraudulent administration. Good civilian qualities are
the ones that will in the end win a nation's battles. The Spaniard is the
last one in the world to see this. He talks and dreams of Castilian bravery and Spanish honor, and is above shopkeeping details.... A writer on
contemporary Spain remarks that any intelligent middle-class Spaniard
will admit every charge of incompetence which can be brought against
the conduct of public affairs. "Yes, we have a wretched Government. In
any other country somebody would be shot." This is the hopeless military
creed: killing somebody is the only remedy.

Here we see a trace of that intellectual legacy which Spain has left to
the New World, and which has stamped itself so indelibly on the history
of Spanish America. On a later occasion in this connection I wrote as
follows:

To appreciate the outcome of much soldiering, the condition in which
persistent military training may leave a race, one should study Spanish America. Here we have a collection of some score of States, all very
much alike in social and political make-up. Most of the South American
States so resemble one another in language, laws, institutions, that to
an outsider it would seem not to matter a straw under which particular six-months-old republic one should live; whether one be under the
Government of the pronunciamento-created President of Colombia, or
under that of the President of Venezuela, one's condition would appear
to be much the same. Apparently no particular country has anything
which differentiates it from another, and, consequently, anything to protect against the other. Actually, the Governments might all change places
and the people be none the wiser. Yet, so hypnotized, are these little
States by the "necessity for self-protection," by the glamour of armaments, that there is not one without a relatively elaborate and expensive

military establishment to protect it from the rest.

No conditions seem so propitious for a practical confederation as those of Spanish America; with a few exceptions, the virtual unity of language, laws, general race-ideals, would seem to render protection of frontiers supererogatory. Yet the citizens give untold wealth, service, life, and suffering to be protected against a Government exactly like their own. All this waste of life and energy has gone on without it ever occurring to one of these States that it would be preferable to be annexed a thousand times over, so trifling would be the resulting change in their condition, than continue the everlasting and futile tribute of blood and treasure. Over some absolutely unimportant matter--like that of the Patagonian roads, which nearly brought Argentina and Chili to grips the other day--as much patriotic devotion will be expended as ever the Old Guard lavished in protecting the honor of the Tricolor. Battles will be fought which will make all the struggles in South Africa appear mean in comparison. Actions in which the dead are counted in thousands will excite no more comment in the world than that produced by a skirmish in Natal, in which a score of yeomen are captured and released.[78]

In the decade since the foregoing was written things have enormously improved in South America. Why? For the simple reason, as pointed out in **Chapter V** of the first part of this book, that Spanish America is being brought more and more into the economic movement of the world; and with the establishment of factories, in which large capital has been sunk, banks, businesses, etc., the whole attitude of mind of those interested in these ventures is changed. The Jingo, the military adventurer, the fomentor of trouble, are seen for what they are--not as patriots, but as representing exceedingly mischievous and maleficent forces.

This general truth has two facets: if long warfare diverts a people from the capacity for industry, so in the long run economic pressure--the influences, that is, which turn the energies of people to preoccupation with social well-being--is fatal to the military tradition. Neither tendency is constant; warfare produces poverty; poverty pushes to thrift and work, which result in wealth; wealth creates leisure and pride and pushes to warfare.

Where Nature does not respond readily to industrial effort, where it is, at least apparently, more profitable to plunder than to work, the military tradition survives. The Beduin has been a bandit since the time of Abraham, for the simple reason that the desert does not support industrial life nor respond to industrial effort. The only career offering a fair apparent return for effort is plunder. In Morocco, in Arabia, in all very poor pastoral countries, the same phenomenon is exhibited; in mountainous countries which are arid and are removed from the economic centers, *idem*. The same may have been to some extent the case in Prussia before the era of coal and iron; but the fact that to-day 99 per cent. of the population is normally engaged in trade and industry, and 1 per cent. only in military preparation, and some fraction too small to be properly estimated engaged in actual war, shows how far she has outgrown such a state--shows, incidentally, what little chance the ideal and tradition represented by 1 per cent. or some fractional percentage has against interests and activities represented by 99 per cent. The recent history of South and Central America, because it is recent, and because the factors are less complicated, illustrates best the tendency with which we are dealing. Spanish America inherited the military tradition in all its vigor. As I have already pointed out, the Spanish occupation of the American Continent was a process of conquest rather than of colonizing; and while the mother country got poorer and poorer by the process of conquest, the new countries also impoverished themselves in adherence to the same fatal illusion. The glamour of conquest was, of course, Spain's ruin. So long as it was possible for her to live on extorted bullion, neither social nor industrial development seemed possible. Despite the common idea to the contrary, Germany has known how to keep this fatal hypnotism at bay, and, far from allowing her military activities to absorb her industrial, it is precisely the military activities which are in a fair way now to being absorbed by the industrial and commercial, and her world commerce has its foundation, not in tribute or bullion exacted at the sword's point, but in sound and honest exchange. So that to-day the legitimate commercial tribute which Germany, who never sent a soldier there, exacts from Spanish America is immensely greater than that which goes to Spain, who poured out blood and treasure during three centuries on these territories. In this way, again, do the warlike nations inherit the earth!

If Germany is never to duplicate Spain's decadence, it is precisely because (1) she has never had, historically, Spain's temptation to live by conquest, and (2) because, having to live by honest industry, her commercial hold, even upon the territories conquered by Spain, is more firmly set than that of Spain herself.

How may we sum up the whole case, keeping in mind every empire that ever existed--the Assyrian, the Babylonian, the Mede and Persian, the Macedonian, the Roman, the Frank, the Saxon, the Spanish, the Portuguese, the Bourbon, the Napoleonic? In all and every one of them we may see the same process, which is this: If it remains military it decays; if it prospers and takes its share of the work of the world it ceases to be military. There is no other reading of history.

That history furnishes no justification for the plea that pugnacity and antagonism between nations is bound up in any way with the real process of national survival, shows clearly enough that nations nurtured normally in peace are more than a match for nations nurtured normally in war; that communities of non-military tradition and instincts, like the Anglo-Saxon communities of the New World, show elements of survival stronger than those possessed by communities animated by the military tradition, like the Spanish and Portuguese nations of the New World; that the position of the industrial nations in Europe as compared with the military gives no justification for the plea that the warlike qualities make for survival. It is clearly evident that there is no biological justification in the terms of man's political evolution for the perpetuation of antagonism between nations, nor any justification for the plea that the diminution of such antagonism runs counter to the teachings of the "natural law." There is no such natural law; in accordance with natural laws, men are being thrust irresistibly towards co-operation between communities and not towards conflict.

There remains the argument that, though the conflict itself may make for degeneration, the preparation for that conflict makes for survival, for the improvement of human nature. I have already touched upon the hopeless confusion which comes of the plea that, while long-continued peace is bad, military preparations find justification in that they insure peace.

Almost every defense of militarism includes a sneer at the ideal of peace because it involves the Cobdenite state of buying cheap and selling dear. But, with equal regularity, the advocate of the military system goes on to argue for great armaments, not as a means of promoting war, that valuable school, etc., but as the best means of securing peace; in other words, that condition of "buying cheap and selling dear" which but a moment before he has condemned as so defective. As though to make the stultification complete, he pleads for the peace value of military training, on the ground that German commerce has benefited from it--that, in other words, it has promoted the "Cobdenite ideal." The analysis of the reasoning, as has been brilliantly shown by Mr. John M. Robertson,[79] gives a result something like this: (1) War is a great school of morals, therefore we must have great armaments to insure peace; (2) to secure peace engenders the Cobdenite ideal, which is bad, therefore we should adopt conscription, (a) because it is the best safeguard of peace, (b) because it is a training for commerce--the Cobdenite ideal.

Is it true that barrack training--the sort of school which the competition of armaments during the last generation has imposed on the people of Continental Europe--makes for moral health? Is it likely that a "perpetual rehearsal for something never likely to come off, and when it comes off is not like the rehearsal," should be a training for life's realities? Is it likely that such a process would have the stamp and touch of closeness to real things? Is it likely that the mechanical routine of artificial occupations, artificial crimes, artificial virtues, artificial punishments should form any training for the battle of real life?[80] What of the Dreyfus case? What of the abominable scandals that have marked German military life of late years? If peace military training is such a fine school, how could the London *Times* write thus of France after she had submitted to a generation of a very severe form of it:

A thrill of horror and shame ran through the whole civilized world outside France when the result of the Rennes Court-Martial became known.... By their (the officers') own admission, whether flung defiantly at the judges, their inferiors, or wrung from them under cross-examination, Dreyfus's chief accusers were convicted of gross and fraudulent illegalities which, anywhere, would have sufficed, not only to discredit their testimony--had they any serious testimony to offer--but to transfer them speedily from the witness-box to the prisoner's dock.... Their vaunted honor "rooted in dishonor stood." ... Five judges out of the seven have once more demonstrated the truth of the astounding axiom first propounded during the Zola trial, that "military justice is not as other justice." ... We have no hesitation in saying that the Rennes Court-Martial constitutes in itself the grossest, and, viewed in the light of the surrounding circumstances, the most appalling prostitution of justice which the world has witnessed in modern times.... Flagrantly, deliberately, mercilessly trampled justice underfoot.... The verdict, which is a slap in the face to the public opinion of the civilized world, to the conscience of humanity.... France is henceforth on her trial before history. Arraigned at the bar of a tribunal far higher than that before which Dreyfus stood, it rests with her to show whether she will undo this great wrong and rehabilitate her fair name, or whether she will stand irrevocably condemned and disgraced by allowing it to be consummated. We can less than ever afford to underrate the forces against truth and justice.... Hypnotized by the wild tales perpetually dinned into all credulous ears of an international "syndicate of treason," conspiring against the honor of the army and the safety of France, the conscience of the French nation has been numbed, and its intelligence atrophied.... Amongst those statesmen who are in touch with the outside world in the Senate and Chamber there must be some that will remind her that nations, no more than individuals, cannot bear the burden of universal scorn and live.... France cannot close her ears to the voice of the civilized world, for that voice is the voice of history.[81]

And what the *Times* said then all England was saying, and not only all England, but all America.

And has Germany escaped a like condemnation? We commonly assume that the Dreyfus case could not be duplicated in Germany. But this is not the opinion of very many Germans themselves. Indeed, just before the Dreyfus case reached its crisis, the Kotze scandal--in its way just as grave as the Dreyfus affair, and revealing a moral condition just as serious--prompted the London *Times* to declare that "certain features of German civilization are such as to make it difficult for Englishmen to understand how the whole State does not collapse from sheer rottenness." If that could be said of the Kotze affair, what shall be said of the state of things which has been revealed by Maximilien Harden among others?

Need it be said that the writer of these lines does not desire to represent Germans as a whole as more corrupt than their neighbors? But impartial observers are not of opinion, and very many Germans are not of opinion, that there has been either economic, social, or moral advantage to the German people from the victories of 1870 and the state of regimentation which the sequel has imposed. This is surely evidenced by the actual position of affairs in the German Empire, the complex difficulty with which the German people are now struggling, the growing discontent, the growing influence of those elements which are nurtured in discontent, the growth on one side of radical intransigence and on the other of almost feudal autocracy, the failure to effect normally and easily those democratic developments which have been effected in almost every other European State, the danger for the future which such a situation represents, the precariousness of German finance, the relatively small profit which her population as a whole has received from the greatly increased foreign trade--all this, and much more, confirms that view. England has of late seemed to have been affected with the German superstition. With the curious perversity that marks "patriotic" judgments, the whole tendency of the English has been to make comparisons with Germany to the disadvantage of themselves and of other European countries. Yet if Germans themselves are to be believed, much of that superiority which the English see in Germany is as purely non-existent as the phantom German war-balloon to which the British Press devoted serious columns, to the phantom army corps in Epping Forest, to the phantom stories of arms in London cellars, and to the German spy which English patriots see in every Italian waiter.[82]

Despite the hypnotism which German "progress" seems to exercise on the minds of English Jingoes, the German people themselves, as distinct from the small group of Prussian Junkers, are not in the least enamored of it, as is proved by the unparalleled growth of the social-democratic element, which is the negation of military imperialism, and which, as the figures in Prussia prove, receives support not from one class of the population merely, but from the mercantile, industrial, and professional classes as well. The agitation for electoral reform in Prussia shows how acute the conflict has become; on the one side the increasing democratic element showing more and more of a revolutionary tendency, and on the other side the Prussian autocracy showing less and less disposition to yield. Does anyone really believe that the situation will remain there, that the Democratic parties will continue to grow in numbers and be content forever to be ridden down by the "booted Prussian," and that German democracy will indefinitely accept a situation in which it will be always possible--in the words of the Junker, von Oldenburg, member of the Reichstag--for the German Emperor to say to a Lieutenant, "Take ten men and close the Reichstag"?

What must be the German's appreciation of the value of military victory and militarization when, mainly because of it, he finds himself engaged in a struggle which elsewhere less militarized nations settled a generation since? And what has the English defender of the militarist regimen, who holds the German system up for imitation, to say of it as a school of national discipline, when the Imperial Chancellor himself defends the refusal of democratic suffrage like that obtaining in England on the ground that the Prussian people have not yet acquired those qualities of public discipline which make it workable in England?[83]

Yet what Prussia, in the opinion of the Chancellor, is not yet fit for, Scandinavian nations, Switzerland, Holland, Belgium, have fitted themselves for without the aid of military victory and subsequent regimentation. Did not someone once say that the war had made Germany great and Germans small?

When we ascribe so large a measure of Germany's social progress (which no one, so far as I know, is concerned to deny) to the victories and regimentation, why do we conveniently overlook the social progress of the small States which I have just mentioned, where such progress on the material side has certainly been as great as, and on the moral side greater than, in Germany? Why do we overlook the fact that, if Germany has done well in certain social organizations, Scandinavia and Switzerland have done better? And why do we overlook the fact that, if regimentation is of such social value, it has been so completely inoperative in States which are more highly militarized even than Germany--in Spain, Italy, Austria, Turkey, and Russia?

But even assuming--a very large assumption--that regimentation has played the rôle in German progress which English Germano-maniacs would have us believe, is there any justification for supposing that a like process would be in any way adaptable to English conditions social, moral, material, and historical?

The position of Germany since the war of 1870--what it has stood for in the generation since victory, and what it stood for in the generations that followed defeat--furnishes a much-needed lesson as to the outcome of the philosophy of force. Practically all impartial observers of Germany are in agreement with Mr. Harbutt Dawson when he writes as follows:

It is questionable whether unified Germany counts as much to-day as an intellectual and moral agent in the world as when it was little better than a geographical expression.... Germany has at command an apparently inexhaustible reserve of physical and material force, but the real influence and power which it exerts is disproportionately small. The history of civilization is full of proofs that the two things are not synonymous. A nation's mere force is, on ultimate analysis, its sum of brute strength. This force may, indeed, go with intrinsic power, yet such power can never depend permanently on force, and the test is easy to apply.... No one who genuinely admires the best in the German character, and who wishes well to the German people, will seek to minimize the extent of the loss which would appear to have befallen the old national ideals; hence the discontent of the enlightened classes with the political laws under which they live--a discontent often vague and indefinite, the discontent of men who do not know clearly what is wrong or what they want, but feel that a free play is denied them which belongs to the dignity and worth and essence of human personality.

"Is there a German culture to-day?" asks Fuchs.[84] "We Germans are able to perfect all works of civilizing power as well as, and indeed better than, the best in other nations. Yet nothing that the heroes of labor execute goes beyond our own border." And the most extraordinary thing is that those who do not in the least deny this condition to which Germany has fallen--who, indeed, exaggerate it, and ask us with triumph to look upon the brutality of German method and German conception--ask us to go and follow Germany's example!

Most British pro-armament agitation is based upon the plea that Germany is dominated by a philosophy of force. They point to books like those of General Bernhardi, idealizing the employment of force, and then urge a policy of replying by force--and force only--which would, of course, justify in Germany the Bernhardi school, and by the reaction of opposing forces stereotype the philosophy in Europe and make it part of the general European tradition. England stands in danger of becoming Prussianized by virtue of the fact of fighting Prussianism, or rather by virtue of the fact that, instead of fighting it with the intellectual tools that won religious freedom in Europe, she insists upon confining her efforts to the tools of physical force.

Some of the acutest foreign students of English progress--men like Edmond Demolins--ascribe it to the very range of qualities which the German system is bound to crush; their aptitude for initiative, their reliance upon their own efforts, their sturdy resistance to State interference (already weakening), their impatience with bureaucracy and red tape (also weakening), all of which is wrapped up with general rebelliousness to regimentation.

Though the English base part of the defense of armaments on the plea that, economic interest apart, they desire to live their own life in their own way, to develop in their own fashion, do they not run some danger that with this mania for the imitation of German method they may Germanize England, though never a German soldier land on their soil?

Of course, it is always assumed that, though the English may adopt the French and German system of conscription, they could never fall a victim to the defects of those systems, and that the scandals which break out from time to time in France and Germany could never be duplicated by *their* barrack system, and that the military atmosphere of their own barracks, the training in their own army, would always be wholesome. But what do even its defenders say?

Mr. Blatchford himself says:[85]

Barrack life is bad. Barrack life will always be bad. It is never good for a lot of men to live together apart from home influences and feminine. It is not good for women to live or work in communities of women. The sexes react upon each other; each provides for the other a natural restraint, a wholesome incentive.... The barracks and the garrison town are not good for young men. The young soldier, fenced and hemmed in by a discipline unnecessarily severe, and often stupid, has at the same time an amount of license which is dangerous to all but those of strong good sense and strong will. I have seen clean, good, nice boys come into the Army and go to the devil in less than a year. I am no Puritan. I am a man of the world; but any sensible and honest man who has been in the Army will know at once that what I am saying is entirely true, and is the truth expressed with much restraint and moderation. A few hours in a barrack-room would teach a civilian more than all the soldier stories ever written. When I joined the Army I was unusually unsophisticated for a boy of twenty. I had been brought up by a mother. I had attended Sunday-school and chapel. I had lived a quiet, sheltered life, and I had an astonishing amount to learn. The language of the barrack-room shocked me, appalled me. I could not understand half I heard; I could not credit much that I saw. When I began to realize the truth, I took my courage in both hands and went about the world I had come into with open eyes. So I learnt the facts, but I must not tell them.[86]

CHAPTER V

THE DIMINISHING FACTOR OF PHYSICAL FORCE: PSYCHOLOGICAL RESULTS

Diminishing factor of physical force--Though diminishing, physical force has always had an important rôle in human affairs--What is underlying principle, determining advantageous and disadvantageous use of physical force?--Force that aids co-operation in accord with law of man's advance: force that is exercised for parasitism in conflict with such law and disadvantageous for both parties--Historical process of the abandonment of physical force--The Khan and the London tradesman--Ancient Rome and modern Britain--The sentimental defense of war as the purifier of human life--The facts--The redirection of human pugnacity.

Despite the general tendency indicated by the facts dealt with in the preceding chapter, it will be urged (with perfect justice) that, though the methods of Anglo-Saxondom as compared with those of the Spanish, Portuguese, and French Empires, may have been mainly commercial and industrial rather than military, war was a necessary part of expansion; that but for some fighting the Anglo-Saxons would have been ousted from North America or Asia, or would never have gained a footing there.

Does this, however, prevent us establishing, on the basis of the facts exposed in the preceding chapter, a general principle sufficiently definite to serve as a practical guide in policy, and to indicate reliably a general tendency in human affairs? Assuredly not. The principle which explains the uselessness of much of the force exerted by the military type of empire, and justifies in large part that employed by Britain, is neither obscure nor uncertain, although empiricism, rule of thumb (which is the curse of political thinking in our days, and more than anything else stands in the way of real progress), gets over the difficulty by declaring that no principle in human affairs can be pushed to its logical or theoretical conclusion; that what may be "right in theory" is wrong in practice.

Thus Mr. Roosevelt, who expresses with such admirable force and vigor the average thoughts of his hearers or readers, takes generally this line: We must be peaceful, but not too peaceful; warlike, but not too warlike; moral, but not too moral.[87]

By such verbal mystification we are encouraged to shirk the rough and stony places along the hard road of thinking. If we cannot carry a principle to its logical conclusion, at what point are we to stop? One will fix one and another will fix another with equal justice. What is it to be "moderately" peaceful, or "moderately" warlike? Temperament and predilection can stretch such limitations indefinitely. This sort of thing only darkens counsel.

If a theory is right, it can be pushed to its logical conclusion; indeed, the only real test of its value is that it *can* be pushed to its logical conclusion. If it is wrong in practice, it is wrong in theory, for the right theory will take cognizance of all the facts, not only of one set.

In Chapter II of this part (pp. 186-192), I have very broadly indicated the process by which the employment of physical force in the affairs of the world has been a constantly diminishing factor since the day that primitive man killed his fellow-man in order to eat him. Yet throughout the whole process the employment of force has been an integral part of progress, until even to-day in the most advanced nations force--the police-force--is an integral part of their civilization.

What, then, is the principle determining the advantageous and the disadvantageous employment of force?

Preceding the outline sketch just referred to is another sketch indicating the real biological law of man's survival and advance; the key to that law is found in co-operation between men and struggle with nature. Mankind as a whole is the organism which needs to co-ordinate its parts in order to insure greater vitality by better adaptation to its environment.

Here, then, we get the key: force employed to secure completer co-operation between the parts, to facilitate exchange, makes for advance; force which runs counter to such co-operation, which attempts to replace the mutual benefit of exchange by compulsion, which is in any way a form of parasitism, makes for retrogression.

Why is the employment of force by the police justified? Because the bandit refuses to co-operate. He does not offer an exchange; he wants to live as a parasite, to take by force, and give nothing in exchange. If he increased in numbers, co-operation between the various parts of the organism would be impossible; he makes for disintegration. He must be restrained, and so long as the police use their force in such restraint they are merely insuring co-operation. The police are not attempting to settle things by force; they are preventing things from being settled in that way.

Now, suppose that this police-force becomes the army of a political Power, and the diplomats of that Power say to a smaller one: "We outnumber you; we are going to annex your territory, and you are going to pay us tribute." And the smaller Power says: "What are you going to give us for that tribute?" And the larger replies: "Nothing. You are weak; we are strong; we gobble you up. It is the law of life; always has been--always will be to the end."

Now that police-force, become an army, is no longer making for co-operation; it has simply and purely taken the place of the bandits; and to approximate such an army to a police-force, and to say that because both operations involve the employment of force they both stand equally justified, is to ignore half the facts, and to be guilty of those lazy generalizations which we associate with savagery.[88]

But the difference is more than a moral one. If the reader will again return to the little sketch referred to above, he will probably agree that the diplomats of the larger Power are acting in an extraordinarily stupid fashion. I say nothing of their sham philosophy (which happens, however, to be that of European statecraft to-day), by which this aggression is made to appear in keeping with the law of man's struggle for life, when, as a matter of fact, it is the very negation of that law; but we know *now* that they are taking a course which gives the least result, even from *their* point of view, for the effort expended.

Here we get the key also to the difference between the respective histories of the military empires, like Spain, France, and Portugal, and the more industrial type, like England, which has been touched upon in the preceding chapter. Not the mere hazard of war, not a question of mere efficiency in the employment of force, has given to Great Britain influence in half a world, and taken it from Spain, but a radical, fundamental difference in underlying principles however imperfectly realized. England's exercise of force has approximated on the whole to the rôle of police; Spain's to that of the diplomats of the supposititious Power just referred to. England's has made for co-operation; Spain's for the embarrassment of co-operation. England's has been in keeping with the real law of man's struggle; Spain's in keeping with the sham law which the "blood and iron" empiricists are forever throwing at our heads. For what has happened to all attempts to live on extorted tribute? They have all failed--failed miserably and utterly[89]--to such an extent that to-day the exaction of tribute has become an economic impossibility.

If, however, our supposititious diplomats, instead of asking for tribute, had said: "Your country is in disorder; your police-force is insufficient; our merchants are robbed and killed; we will lend you police and help you to maintain order; you will pay the police their just wage, and that is all;" and had honestly kept to this office, their exercise of force would have aided human co-operation, not checked it. Again, it would have been a struggle, not against man, but against the use of force; the "predominant Power" would have been living, not on other men, but by more efficient organization of man's fight with nature.

That is why, in the first section of this book, I have laid emphasis on the truth that the justification of past wars has no bearing on the problem which confronts us: the precise degree of fighting which was necessary a hundred and fifty years ago is a somewhat academic problem. The degree of fighting which is necessary to-day is the problem which confronts us, and a great many factors have been introduced into it since England won India and lost part of North America. The face of the world has changed, and the factors of conflict have changed radically: to ignore that is to ignore facts and to be guided by the worst form of theorizing and sentimentalism--the theorizing that will not recognize the facts. England does not need to maintain order in Germany, nor Germany in France; and the struggle between those nations is no part of man's struggle with nature--has no justification in the real law of human struggle; it is an anachronism; it finds its justification in a sham philosophy that will not bear the test of facts, and, responding to no real need and achieving no real purpose, is bound with increasing enlightenment to come to an end.

I wish it were not everlastingly necessary to reiterate the fact that the world has moved. Yet for the purposes of this discussion it is necessary. If to-day an Italian warship were suddenly to bombard Liverpool without warning, the Bourse in Rome would present a condition, and the bank-rate in Rome would take a drop that would ruin tens of thousands of Italians--do far more injury, probably, to Italy than to England. Yet if five hundred years ago Italian pirates had landed from the Thames and sacked London itself, not an Italian in Italy would have been a penny the worse for it.

Is it seriously urged that in the matter of the exercise of physical force, therefore, there is no difference in these two conditions: and is it seriously urged that the psychological phenomena which go with the exercise of physical force are to remain unaffected?

The preceding chapter is, indeed, the historical justification of the economic truths established in the first section of this book in the terms of the facts of the present-day world, which show that the predominating factor in survival is shifting from the physical to the intellectual plane. This evolutionary process has now reached a point in international affairs which involves the complete economic futility of military force. In the last chapter but one I dealt with the psychological consequence of this profound change in the nature of man's normal activities, showing that his nature is coming more and more to adapt itself to what he normally and for the greater part of his life--in most cases all his life--is engaged in, and is losing the impulses concerned with an abnormal and unusual occupation.

Why have I presented the facts in this order, and dealt with the psychological result involved in this change before the change itself? I have adopted this order of treatment because the believer in war justifies his dogmatism for the most part by an appeal to what he alleges is the one dominating fact of the situation--i.e., that human nature is unchanging. Well, as will be seen from the chapter on that subject, that alleged fact does not bear investigation. Human nature is changing out of all recognition. Not only is man fighting less, but he is using all forms of physical compulsion less, and as a very natural result is losing those psychological attributes that go with the employment of physical force. And he is coming to employ physical force less because accumulated evidence is pushing him more and more to the conclusion that he can accomplish more easily that which he strives for by other means.

Few of us realize to what extent economic pressure--and I use that term in its just sense, as meaning, not only the struggle for money, but everything implied therein, well-being, social consideration, and the rest--has replaced physical force in human affairs. The primitive mind could not conceive a world in which everything was not regulated by force: even the great minds of antiquity could not believe the world would be an industrious one unless the great mass were made industrious by the use of physical force--*i.e.*, by slavery. Three-fourths of those who peopled what is now Italy in Rome's palmiest days were slaves, chained in the fields when at work, chained at night in their dormitories, with those who were porters chained to the doorways. It was a society of slavery--fighting slaves, working slaves, cultivating slaves, official slaves, and Gibbon adds that the Emperor himself was a slave, "the first slave to the ceremonies he imposed." Great and penetrating as were many of the minds of antiquity, none of them show much conception of any condition of society in which the economic impulse could replace physical compulsion.[90] Had they been told that the time would come when the world would work very much harder under the impulse of an abstract thing known as economic interest, they would have regarded such a statement as that of a mere sentimental theorist. Indeed, one need not go so far: if one had told an American slaveholder of sixty years ago that the time would come when the South would produce more cotton under the free pressure of economic forces than under slavery, he would have made a like reply. He would probably have declared that "a good cowhide whip beats all economic pressure"--pretty much the sort of thing that one may hear from the mouth of the average militarist to-day. Very "practical" and virile, of course, but it has the disadvantage of not being true.

The presumed necessity for physical compulsion did not stop at slavery. As we have already seen, it was accepted as an axiom in statecraft that men's religious beliefs had to be forcibly restrained, and not merely their religious belief, but their very clothing; and we have hundreds of years of complicated sumptuary laws, hundreds of years, also, of forcible control or, rather, the attempted forcible control of prices and trade, the elaborate system of monopolies, absolute prohibition of the entrance into the country of certain foreign goods, the violation of which prohibition was treated as a penal offence. We had even the use of forced money, the refusal to accept which was treated as a penal offence. In many countries for years it was a crime to send gold abroad, all indicating the domination of the mind of man by the same curious obsession that man's life must be ruled by physical force, and it is only very slowly and very painfully that we have arrived at the truth that men will work best when left to unseen and invisible forces. A world in which physical force was withdrawn from the regulation of men's labor, faith, clothes, trade, language, travel, would have been absolutely inconceivable to even the best minds during the three or four thousand years of history which mainly concern us. What is the central explanation of the profound change involved here-- the shifting of the pivot in all human affairs, in so far as they touch both the individual and the community, from physical ponderable forces to economic imponderable forces? It is surely that, strange as it may seem, the latter forces accomplish the desired result more efficiently and more readily than do the former, which even when they are not completely futile are in comparison wasteful and stultifying. It is the law of the economy of effort. Indeed, the use of physical force usually involves in those employing it the same limitation of freedom (even if in lesser degree) as that which it is desired to impose. Herbert Spencer illustrates the process in the following suggestive passage:

The exercise of mastery inevitably entails on the master himself some sort of slavery more or less pronounced. The uncultured masses and even the greater part of the cultured will regard this statement as absurd, and though many who have read history with an eye to essentials rather than to trivialities know that this is a paradox in the right sense--that is, true in fact though not seeming true--even they are not fully conscious of the mass of evidence establishing it, and will be all the better for having illustrations recalled. Let me begin with the earliest and simplest which serves to symbolize the whole.

Here is a prisoner, with his hands tied and a cord round his neck (as suggested by figures in Assyrian bas-reliefs), being led home by his savage conqueror, who intends to make him a slave. The one you say is captive and the other free. Are you quite sure the other is free? He holds one end of the cord and, unless he means his captive to escape, he must continue to be fastened by keeping hold of the cord in such way that it cannot easily be detached. He must be himself tied to the captive while the captive is tied to him. In other ways his activities are impeded and certain burdens are imposed on him. A wild animal crosses the track and he cannot pursue. If he wishes to drink of the adjacent stream he must tie up his captive, lest advantage be taken of his defenseless position. Moreover, he has to provide food for both. In various ways he is no longer, then, completely at liberty; and these worries adumbrate in a simple manner the universal truth that the instrumentalities by which the subordination of others is effected themselves subordinate the victor, the master, or the ruler.[91]

Thus it comes that all nations attempting to live by conquest end by being themselves the victims of a military tyranny precisely similar to that which they hope to inflict; or, in other terms, that the attempt to impose by force of arms a disadvantageous commercial situation to the advantage of the conqueror ends in the conqueror's falling a victim to the very disadvantages from which he hoped by a process of spoliation to profit.

But the truth that economic force always in the long run outweighs physical or military force is illustrated by the simple fact of the universal use of money--the fact that the use of money is not a thing which we choose or can shake off, but a thing imposed by the operation of forces stronger than our volition, stronger than the tyranny of the cruelest tyrant who ever reigned by blood and iron. I think it is one of the most astounding things, to the man who takes a fairly fresh mind to the study of history, that the most absolute despots--men who can command the lives of their subjects with a completeness and a nonchalance of which the modern Western world furnishes no parallel--cannot command money. One asks oneself, indeed, why such an absolute ruler, able as he is by the sheer might of his position and by the sheer force of his power to take everything that exists in his kingdom, and able as he is to exact every sort and character of service, needs money, which is the means of obtaining goods or services by a freely consented exchange. Yet, as we know, it is precisely, in ancient as in modern times, the most absolute despot who is often the most financially embarrassed.[92] Is not this a demonstration that in reality physical force is operative in only very narrow limits? It is no mere rhetoric, but the cold truth, to say that under absolutism it is a simple thing to get men's lives, but often impossible to get money. And the more, apparently, that physical force was exercised, the more difficult did the command of money become. And for a very simple reason--a reason which reveals in rudimentary form that principle of the economic futility of military power with which we are dealing. The phenomenon is best illustrated by a concrete case. If one go to-day into one of the independent despotisms of Central Asia one will find generally a picture of the most abject poverty. Why? Because the ruler has absolute power to take wealth whenever he sees it, to take it by any means whatever--torture, death--up to the completest limit of uncontrolled physical force. What is the result? The wealth is not created, and torture itself cannot produce a thing which is non-existent. Step across the frontier into a State under British or Russian protection, where the Khan has some sort of limits imposed on his powers. The difference is immediately perceptible: evidence of wealth and comfort in relative profusion, and, other things being equal, the ruler, whose physical force over his subjects is limited, is a great deal richer than the ruler whose physical force over his subjects is unlimited. In other words, the farther one gets away from physical force, in the acquisition of wealth, the greater is the result for the effort expended. At the one end of the scale you get the despot in rags, exercising sway over what is probably a potentially rich territory, reduced to having to kill a man by torture in order to obtain a sum which at the other end of the scale a London tradesman will spend on a restaurant dinner for the purpose of sitting at table with a duke--or the thousandth part of the sum which the same tradesman will spend in philanthropy or otherwise, for the sake of acquiring an empty title from a monarch who has lost all power of exercising any physical force whatsoever.

Which process, judged by all things that men desire, gives the better result, the physical force of blood and iron which we see, or the intellectual or psychic force which we cannot see? The principle which operates in the limited fashion which I have indicated, operates with no less force in the larger domain of modern international politics. The wealth of the world is not represented by a fixed amount of gold or money now in the possession of one Power, and now in the possession of another, but depends on all the unchecked multiple activities of a community for the time being. Check that activity, whether by imposing tribute, or disadvantageous commercial conditions, or an unwelcome administration which sets up sterile political agitation, and you get less wealth--less wealth for the conqueror, as well as less for the conquered. The broadest statement of the case is that all experience--especially the experience indicated in the last chapter--shows that in trade by free consent, carrying mutual benefit, we get larger results for effort expended than in the exercise of physical force, which attempts to exact advantage for one party at the expense of the other. I am not arguing over again the thesis of the first part of this book; but, as we shall see presently, the general principle of the diminishing factor of physical force in the affairs of the world carries with it a psychological change in human nature which modifies radically our impulses to sheer physical conflict. What it is important just now to keep in mind, is the incalculable intensification of this diminution of physical force by our mechanical development. The principle was obviously less true for Rome than it is for Great Britain or America: Rome, however imperfectly, lived largely by tribute. The sheer mechanical development of the modern world has rendered tribute in the Roman sense impossible. Rome did not have to create markets and find a field for the employment of her capital. We do. What result does this carry? Rome could afford to be relatively indifferent to the prosperity of her subject territory. We cannot. If the territory is not prosperous we have no market, and we have no field for our investments, and that is why we are checked at every point from doing what Rome was able to do. You can to some extent exact tribute by force; you cannot compel a man to buy your goods by force if he does not want them, and has not got the money to pay for them. Now, the difference which we see here has been brought about by the interaction of a whole series of mechanical changes--printing, gunpowder, steam, electricity, improved means of communication. It is the last-named which has mainly created the fact of credit. Now, credit is merely an extension of the use of money, and we can no more shake off the domination of the one than we can that of the other. We have seen that the bloodiest despot is himself the slave of money, in the sense that he is compelled to employ it. In the same way no physical force can, in the modern world, set at nought the force of credit.[93] It is no more possible for a great people of the modern world to live without credit than without money, of which it is a part. Do we not here get an illustration of the fact that intangible economic forces are setting at nought the force of arms?

One of the curiosities of this mechanical development, with its deep-seated psychological results, is the general failure to realize the real bearings of each step therein. Printing was regarded, in the first instance, as merely a new-fangled process which threw a great many copying scribes and monks out of employment. Who realized that in the simple invention of printing there was the liberation of a force greater than the power of kings? It is only here and there that we find an isolated thinker having a glimmering of the political bearing of such inventions of the conception of the great truth that the more man succeeds in his struggle with nature, the less must be the rôle of physical force between men, for the reason that human society has become, with each success in the struggle against nature, a completer organism. That is to say, that the interdependence of the parts has been increased, and that the possibility of one part injuring another without injury to itself, has been diminished. Each part is more dependent on the other parts, and the impulses to injury, therefore, must in the nature of things be diminished. And that fact must, and does, daily redirect human pugnacity. And it is noteworthy that perhaps the best service which the improvement of the instruments of man's struggle with nature performs is the improvement of human relations. Machinery and the steam-engine have done something more than make fortunes for manufacturers: they have abolished human slavery, as Aristotle foresaw they would. It was impossible for men in the mass to be other than superstitious and irrational until they had the printed book.[94] "Roads that are formed for the circulation of wealth become channels for the circulation of ideas, and render possible that simultaneous action upon which all liberty depends." Banking done by telegraphy concerns much more than the stockbroker: it demonstrates clearly and dramatically the real interdependence of nations, and is destined to transform the mind of the statesman. Our struggle is with our environment, not with one another; and those who talk as though struggle between the parts of the same organism must necessarily go on, and as though impulses which are redirected every day can never receive the particular redirection involved in abandoning the struggle between States, ignorantly adopt the formula of science, but leave half the facts out of consideration. And just as the direction of the impulses will be changed, so will the character of the struggle be changed; the force which we shall use for our needs will be the force of intelligence, of hard work, of character, of patience, self-control, and a developed brain, and pugnacity and combativeness which, instead of being used up and wasted in world conflicts of futile destructiveness, will be, and are being, diverted into the steady stream of rationally-directed effort. The virile impulses become, not the tyrant and master, but the tool and servant of the controlling brain.

The conception of abstract imponderable forces by the human mind is a very slow process. All man's history reveals this. The theologian has always felt this difficulty. For thousands of years men could only conceive of evil as an animal with horns and a tail, going about the world devouring folk; abstract conceptions had to be made understandable by a crude anthropomorphism. Perhaps it is better that humanity should have some glimmering of the great facts of the universe, even though interpreted by legends of demons, and goblins, and fairies, and the rest; but we cannot overlook the truth that the facts are distorted in the process, and our advance in the conception of morals is marked largely by the extent to which we can form an abstract conception of the fact of evil--none the less a fact because unembodied--without having to translate it into a non-existent person or animal with a forked tail.

As our advance in the understanding of morality is marked by our dropping these crude physical conceptions, is it not likely that our advance in the understanding of those social problems, which so nearly affect our general well-being, will be marked in like manner?

Is it not somewhat childish and elementary to conceive of force only as the firing off of guns and the launching of *Dreadnoughts*, of struggle as the physical struggle between men, instead of the application of man's energies to his contest with the planet? Is not the time coming when the real struggle will inspire us with the same respect and even the same thrill as that now inspired by a charge in battle; especially as the charges in battle are getting very out of date, and are shortly to disappear from our warfare? The mind which can only conceive of struggle as bombardment and charges is, of course, the Dervish mind. Not that Fuzzy-Wuzzy is not a fine fellow. He is manly, sturdy, hardy, with a courage, and warlike qualities generally, which no European can equal. But the frail and spectacled English official is his master, and a few score of such will make themselves the masters of teeming thousands of Sudanese; the relatively unwarlike Englishman is doing the same thing all over Asia, and he is doing it simply by virtue of superior brain and character, more thought, more rationalism, more steady and controlled hard work. The American is doing the same in the Philippines. It may be said that it is superior armament which does it. But what is the superior armament but the result of superior thought and work? And even without the superior armament the larger intelligence would still do it; for what the Englishman and American do, the Roman did of old, with the same arms as the inhabitants of his vassal worlds. Force is indeed the master, but it is the force of intelligence, character, and rationalism.

I can imagine the contempt with which the man of physical force greets the foregoing. To fight with words, to fight with talk! No, not words, but ideas. And something more than ideas. Their translation into practical effort, into organization, into the direction and administration of organization, into the strategy and tactics of human life.

What, indeed, is modern warfare in its highest phases but this? Is it not altogether out of date and ignorant to picture soldiering as riding about on horseback, bivouacking in forests, sleeping in tents, and dashing gallantly at the head of shining regiments in plumes and breastplates, and pounding in serried ranks against the equally serried ranks of the cruel foe, storming breaches as the "war," in short, of Mr. Henty's books for boys? How far does such a conception correspond to the reality--to the German conception? Even if the whole picture were not out of date, what proportion of the most military nation would ever be destined to witness it or to take part in it? Not one in ten thousand. What is the character even of military conflict but, for the most part, years of hard and steady work, somewhat mechanical, somewhat divorced from real life, but not a whit more exciting? That is true of all ranks; and in the higher ranks of the directing mind war has become an almost purely intellectual process. Was it not the late W. H. Steevens who painted Lord Kitchener as the sort of man who would have made an admirable manager of Harrod's Stores; who fought all his battles in his study, and regarded the actual fighting as the mere culminating incident in the whole process, the dirty and noisy part of it, which he would have been glad to get away from?

The real soldiers of our time--those who represent the brain of the armies--have a life not very different from that of men of any intellectual calling; much less of physical strife than is called for in many civil occupations; less than falls to the lot of engineers, ranchers, sailors, miners, and so on. Even with armies the pugnacity must be translated into intellectual and not into physical effort.[95]

The very fact that war was long an activity which was in some sense a change and relaxation from the more intellectual strife of peaceful life, in which work was replaced by danger, thought by adventure, accounted in no small part for its attraction for men. But, as we have seen, war is becoming as hopelessly intellectual and scientific as any other form of work: officers are scientists, the men are workmen, the army is a machine, battles are "tactical operations," the charge is becoming out of date; a little while and war will become the least romantic of all professions.

In this domain, as in all others, intellectual force is replacing sheer physical force, and we are being pushed by the necessities even of this struggle to be more rational in our attitude to war, to rationalize our study of it; and as our attitude generally becomes more scientific, so will the purely impulsive element lose its empire over us. That is one factor; but, of course, there is the greater one. Our respect and admiration goes in the long run, despite momentary setbacks, to those qualities which achieve the results at which we are all, in common, aiming. If those results are mainly intellectual, it is the intellectual qualities that will receive the tribute of our admiration. We do not make a man President because he holds the light-weight boxing championship, and nobody knows or cares whether Mr. Wilson or Mr. Taft would be the better man at golf. But in a condition of society in which physical force was still the determining factor it would matter all in the world, and even when other factors had obtained considerable weight, as during the Middle Ages, physical combat went for a great deal: the knight in his shining armor established his prestige by his prowess in arms, and the vestige of this still remains in those countries that retain the duel. To some small extent--a very small extent--a man's dexterity with sword and pistol will affect his political prestige in Paris, Rome, Budapest, or Berlin. But these are just interesting vestiges, which in the case of Anglo-Saxon societies have disappeared entirely. My commercial friend who declares that he works fifteen hours a day mainly for the purpose of going one better than his commercial rival across the street, must beat that rival in commerce, not in arms; it would satisfy no pride of either to "have it out" in the back garden in their shirt-sleeves. Nor is there the least danger that one will stick a knife into the other.

Are all these factors to leave the national relationship unaffected? Have they left it unaffected? Does the military prowess of Russia or of Turkey inspire any particular satisfaction in the minds of the individual Russian or of the individual Turk? Does it inspire Europe with any especial respect? Would not most of us just as soon be a non-military American as a military Turk? Do not, in short, all the factors show that sheer physical force is losing its prestige as much in the national as in the personal relationship?

I am not overlooking the case of Germany. Does the history of Germany, during the last half-century, show the blind instinctive pugnacity which is supposed to be so overpowering an element in international relationship as to outweigh all question of material interest? Does the commonly accepted history of the trickery and negotiation which preceded the 1870 conflict, the cool calculation of those who swayed Germany's policy during those years, show that subordination to the blind lust for battle which the militarist would persuade us is always to be an element in our international conflict? Does it not, on the contrary, show that German destinies were swayed by very cool and calculating motives of interest, though interest interpreted in terms of political and economic doctrines which the development of the last thirty years or so has demonstrated to be obsolete? Nor am I overlooking the "Prussian tradition," the fact of a firmly entrenched, aristocratic status, the intellectual legacy of pagan knighthood and Heaven knows what else. But even a Prussian Junker becomes less of an energumen as he becomes more of a scientist,[96] and although German science has of late spent its energies in somewhat arid specialization, the influence of more enlightened conceptions in sociology and statecraft must sooner or later emerge from any thoroughgoing study of political and economic problems. Of course, there are survivals of the old temper, but can it seriously be argued that, when the futility of physical force to accomplish those ends towards which we are all striving is fully demonstrated, we shall go on maintaining war as a sort of theatrical entertainment? Has such a thing ever happened in the past, when our impulses and "sporting" instincts came into conflict with our larger social and economic interests?

All this, in other words, involves a great deal more than the mere change in the character of warfare. It involves a fundamental change in our psychological attitude thereto. Not only does it show that on every side, even the military side, conflict must become less impulsive and instinctive, more rational and sustained, less the blind strife of mutually hating men, and more and more the calculated effort to a definite end; but it will affect the very well-springs of much of the present defense of war.

Why is it that the authorities I have quoted in the first chapter of this section--Mr. Roosevelt, Von Moltke, Renan, and the English clergymen--sing the praises of war as such a valuable school of morals?[97] Do these war advocates urge that war itself is desirable? Would they urge going to war unnecessarily or unjustly merely because it is good for us? Emphatically no. Their argument, in the last analysis, resolves itself into this: that war, though bad, has redeeming qualities, as teaching staunchness, courage, and the rest. Well, so has cutting our legs off, or an operation for appendicitis. Whoever composed epics on typhoid fever or cancer? Such advocates might object to the efficient policing of a town because, if it was full of cut-throats, the inhabitants would be taught courage. One can almost imagine this sort of teacher pouring scorn upon those weaklings who want to call upon the police for protection, and saying, "Police are for sentimentalists and cowards and men of slothful ease. What will become of the strenuous life if you introduce police?"[98]

The whole thing falls to the ground; and if we do not compose poems about typhoid it is because typhoid does not attract us and war does. That is the bottom of the whole matter, and it simplifies things a great deal to admit honestly that while no one is thrilled by the spectacle of disease, most of us are thrilled by the spectacle of war--that while none of us are fascinated by the spectacle of a man struggling with a disease, most of us are by the spectacle of men struggling with one another in war. There is something in warfare, in its story and in its paraphernalia, which profoundly stirs the emotions and sends the blood tingling through the veins of the most peaceable of us, and appeals to I know not what remote instincts, to say nothing of our natural admiration for courage, our love of adventure, of intense movement and action. But this romantic fascination resides to no small extent in that very spectacular quality of which modern conditions are depriving war.

As we become a little more educated, we realize that human psychology is a complex and not a simple thing; that because we yield ourselves to the thrill of the battle spectacle we are not bound to conclude that the processes behind it, and the nature behind it, are necessarily all admirable; that the readiness to die is not the only test of virility or a fine or noble nature.

In the book to which I have just referred (Mr. Steevens' "With Kitchener to Khartoum") one may read the following:

And the Dervishes? The honor of the fight must still go with the men who died. Our men were perfect, but the Dervishes were superb--beyond perfection. It was their largest, best, and bravest army that ever fought against us for Mahdism, and it died worthily for the huge empire that Mahdism won and kept so long. Their riflemen, mangled by every kind of death and torment that man can devise, clung round the black flag and the green, emptying their poor, rotten home-made cartridges dauntlessly. Their spearmen charged death every minute hopelessly. Their horsemen led each attack, riding into the bullets till nothing was left.... Not one rush, or two, or ten, but rush on rush, company on company, never stopping, though all their view that was not unshaken enemy was the bodies of the men who had rushed before them. A dusky line got up and stormed forward: it bent, broke up, fell apart, and disappeared. Before the smoke had cleared another line was bending and storming forward in the same track.... From the green army there now came only death-enamored desperadoes, strolling one by one towards the rifles, pausing to take a spear, turning aside to recognize a corpse, then, caught by a sudden jet of fury, bounding forward, checking, sinking limply to the ground. Now under the black flag in a ring of bodies stood only three men, facing the three thousand of the Third Brigade. They folded their arms about the staff and gazed steadily forward. Two fell. The last Dervish stood up and filled his chest; he shouted the name of his God and hurled his spear. Then he stood quite still, waiting. It took him full; he quivered, gave at the knees, and toppled with his head on his arms and his face towards the legions of his conquerors."

Let us be honest. Is there anything in European history--Cambronne, the Light Brigade, anything you like--more magnificent than this? If we are honest we shall say, No.

But note what follows in Mr. Steevens' narrative. What sort of nature should we expect those savage heroes to display? Cruel, perhaps; but at least loyal. They will stand by their chief. Men who can die like that will not betray him for gain. They are uncorrupted by commercialism. Well, a few chapters after the scene just described, one may read this:

As a ruler the Khalifa finished when he rode out of Omdurman. His own pampered Baggara horsemen killed his herdsmen and looted the cattle that were to feed them. Somebody betrayed the position of the reserve camels.... His followers took to killing one another.... The whole population of the Khalifa's capital was now racing to pilfer the Khalifa's grain.... Wonderful workings of the savage mind! Six hours before they were dying in regiments for their master; now they were looting his corn. Six hours before they were slashing our wounded to pieces; now they were asking us for coppers.

This difficulty with the soldier's psychology is not special to Dervishes or to savages. An able and cultivated British officer writes:

Soldiers as a class are men who have disregarded the civil standard of morality altogether. They simply ignore it. It is no doubt why civilians fight shy of them. In the game of life they do not play the same rules, and the consequence is a good deal of misunderstanding, until finally the civilian says he will not play with Tommy any more. In soldiers' eyes lying, theft, drunkenness, bad language, etc., are not evils at all. They steal like jackdaws. As to language, I used to think the language of a merchant ship's forecastle pretty bad, but the language of Tommies, in point of profanity and in point of obscenity, beats it hollow. This department is a specialty of his. Lying he treats with the same large charity. To lie like a trooper is quite a sound metaphor. He invents all sorts of elaborate lies for the mere pleasure of inventing them. Looting, again, is one of his preferred joys, not merely looting for profit, but looting for the sheer fun of the destruction.[99]

(Please, please, dear reader, do not say that I am slandering the British soldier. I am quoting a British officer, and a British officer, moreover,
who is keenly in sympathy with the person that he has just been describing.) He adds:

Are thieving, and lying, and looting, and bestial talk very bad things?
If they are, Tommy is a bad man. But for some reason or other, since I
got to know him, I have thought rather less of the iniquity of these things
than I did before.

I do not know which of the two passages that I have quoted is the more
striking commentary on the moral influence of military training; that
such training should have the effect which Captain March Phillips describes, or (as Mr. J.A. Hobson in his "Psychology of Jingoism" says) that
the second judgment should be given by a man of sterling character and
culture--the judgment, that thieving, and lying, and looting, and bestial
talk do not matter. Which fact constitutes the severer condemnation of
the ethical atmosphere of militarism and military training? Which is the
more convincing testimony to the corrupting influences of war?[100]

To do the soldiers justice, they very rarely raise this plea of war being
a moral training-school. "War itself," said an officer on one occasion, "is
an infernally dirty business. But somebody has got to do the dirty work
of the world, and I am glad to think that it is the business of the soldier
to prevent rather than to make war."

Not that I am concerned to deny that we owe a great deal to the soldier.
I do not know even why we should deny that we owe a great deal to the
Viking. Neither the one nor the other was in every aspect despicable.
Both have bequeathed a heritage of courage, sturdiness, hardihood, and
a spirit of ordered adventure; the capacity to take hard knocks and to
give them; comradeship and rough discipline--all this and much more. It
is not true to say of any emotion that it is wholly and absolutely good, or
wholly and absolutely bad. The same psychological force which made the
Vikings destructive and cruel pillagers made their descendants sturdy
and resolute pioneers and colonists; and the same emotional force which
turns so much of Africa into a sordid and bloody shambles would, with a
different direction and distribution, turn it into a garden. Is it for nothing
that the splendid Scandinavian race, who have converted their rugged
and rock-strewn peninsula into a group of prosperous and stable States,
which are an example to Europe, and have infused the great Anglo-Saxon stock with something of their sane but noble idealism, have the blood
of Vikings in their veins? Is there no place for the free play of all the best
qualities of the Viking and the soldier in a world still sadly in need of men
with courage enough, for instance, to face the truth, however difficult it
may seem, however unkind to our pet prejudices?

There is not the least necessity for the peace advocate to ignore facts in
this matter. The race of man loves a soldier just as boys love the pirate,
and many of us, perhaps to our great advantage, remain in part boys our
lives through. But as, growing out of boyhood, we regretfully discover the

sad fact that we cannot be pirates, that we cannot even hunt Indians, nor be scouts, nor even trappers, so surely the time has come to realize that we have grown out of soldiering. The romantic appeal of the ventures of the old Vikings, and even later of piracy,[101] was as great as that of war. Yet we superseded the Viking, and we hanged the pirate, though I doubt not we loved him while we hanged him; and I am not aware that those who urged the suppression of piracy were vilified, except by the pirates, as maudlin sentimentalists, who ignored human nature, or, in Homer Lea's phrase, as "half-educated, sick-brained visionaries, denying the inexorability of the primordial law of struggle." Piracy interfered seriously with the trade and industry of those who desired to earn for themselves as good a living as they could get, and to obtain from this imperfect world all that it had to offer. Piracy was magnificent, doubtless, but it was not business. We are prepared to sing about the Viking, but not to tolerate him on the high seas; and some of us who are quite prepared to give the soldier his due place in poetry and legend and romance, quite prepared to admit, with Mr. Roosevelt and Von Moltke and the rest, the qualities which perhaps we owe to him, and without which we should be poor folk indeed, are nevertheless inquiring whether the time has not come to place him (or a good portion of him) gently on the poetic shelf with the Viking; or at least to find other fields for those activities which, however much we may be attracted by them, have in their present form little place in a world in which, though, as Bacon has said, men like danger better than travail, travail is bound, alas!--despite ourselves--to be our lot.

CHAPTER VI

THE STATE AS A PERSON: A FALSE ANALOGY
AND ITS CONSEQUENCES

Why aggression upon a State does not correspond to aggression upon an individual--Our changing conception of collective responsibility--Psychological progress in this connection--Recent growth of factors breaking down the homogeneous personality of States.

Despite the common idea to the contrary, we dearly love an abstraction--especially, apparently, an abstraction which is based on half the facts. Whatever the foregoing chapters may have proved, they have at least proved this: that the character of the modern State, by virtue of a multitude of new factors which are special to our age, is essentially and fundamentally different from that of the ancient. Yet even those who have great and justified authority in this matter will still appeal to Aristotle's conception of the State as final, with the implication that everything which has happened since Aristotle's time should be calmly disregarded.

What some of those things are, the preceding chapters have indicated: First, there is the fact of the change in human nature itself, bound up with the general drift away from the use of physical force--a drift explained by the unromantic fact that physical force does not give so much response to expended effort as do other forms of energy. There is an interconnection of psychological and purely mechanical development in all this which it is not necessary to disentangle here. The results are evident enough. Very rarely, and to an infinitesimal extent, do we now employ force for the achievement of our ends. There is still a factor, however, which remains to be considered, and which has perhaps a more direct bearing on the question of continued conflict between nations than any of the other factors.

Conflicts between nations and international pugnacity generally imply a conception of a State as a homogeneous whole, having the same sort of responsibility that we attach to a person who, hitting us, provokes us to hit back. Now only to a very small and rapidly diminishing extent can a State be regarded as such a person. There may have been a time--Aristotle's time--when this was possible; but it is now impossible. Yet the fine-spun theories on which are based the necessity for the use of force, as between nations, and the proposition that the relationship of nations can only be determined by force, and that international pugnacity will always be expressed by a physical struggle between nations, all arise from this fatal analogy, which in truth corresponds to very few of the facts.

Thus Professor Spenser Wilkinson, whose contributions to this subject have such deserved weight, implies that what will permanently render the abandonment of force between nations impossible is the principle that "the employment of force for the maintenance of right is the foundation of all civilized human life, for it is the fundamental function of the State, and apart from the State there is no civilization, no life worth living.... The mark of the State is sovereignty, or the identification of force and right, and the measure of the perfection of the State is furnished by the completeness of this identification."

This, whether true or not, is irrelevant to the matter in hand. Professor Spenser Wilkinson attempts to illustrate his thesis by quoting a case which would seem to imply that those who take their stand against the necessity of armaments do so on the ground that the employment of force is wicked. There may be those who do this, but it is not necessary to introduce the question of right. If means other than force give the same result more easily, with less effort to ourselves, why discuss the abstract right? When Professor Spenser Wilkinson reinforces the appeal to this irrelevant abstract principle by a case which, while apparently relevant, is in truth irrelevant, he has successfully confused the whole issue. After quoting three verses from the fifth chapter of Matthew, he says:[102]

There are those who believe, or fancy they believe, that the words I have quoted involve the principle that the use of force or violence between man and man or between nation and nation is wicked. To the man who thinks it right to submit to any violence or be killed rather than use violence in resistance I have no reply to make; the world cannot conquer him, and fear has no hold upon him. But even he can carry out his doctrine only to the extent of allowing himself to be ill-treated, as I will now convince him. Many years ago the people of Lancashire were horrified by the facts reported in a trial for murder. In a village on the outskirts of Bolton lived a young woman, much liked and respected as a teacher in one of the Board-schools. On her way home from school she was accustomed to follow a footpath through a lonely wood, and here one evening her body was found. She had been strangled by a ruffian who had thought in this lonely place to have his wicked will of her. She had resisted successfully, and he had killed her in the struggle. Fortunately the murderer was caught, and the facts ascertained from circumstantial evidence were confirmed by his confession. Now the question I have to ask the man who takes his stand on the passage quoted from the Gospel is this: "What would have been your duty had you been walking through that wood and came upon the girl struggling with the man who killed her?" This is the crucial factor which, I submit, utterly destroys the doctrine that the use of violence is in itself wrong. The right or wrong is not in the employment of force, but simply in the purpose for which it is used. What the case establishes, I think, is that to use violence in resistance to violent wrong is not only right, but necessary.

The above presents, very cleverly, the utterly false analogy with which we are dealing. Professor Spenser Wilkinson's cleverness, indeed, is a little Machiavellian, because he approximates non-resisters of a very extreme type to those who advocate agreement among nations in the matter of armaments--a false approximation, for the proportion of those who advocate the reduction of armaments on such grounds is so small that they can be disregarded in this discussion. A movement which is identified with some of the acutest minds in European affairs cannot be disposed of by associating it with such a theory. But the basis of the fallacy is in the approximation of a State to a person. Now a State is not a person, and is becoming less so every day, and the difficulty, which Professor Spenser Wilkinson indicates, is a doctrinaire difficulty, not a real one. Professor Wilkinson would have us infer that a State can be injured or killed in the same simple way in which it is possible to kill or injure a person, and that because there must be physical force to restrain aggression upon persons, there must be physical force to restrain aggression upon States; and because there must be physical force to execute the judgment of a court of law in the case of individuals, there must be physical force to execute the judgment rendered by a decision as to differences between States. All of which is false, and arrived at by approximating a person to a State, and disregarding the numberless facts which render a person different from a State.

How do we know that these difficulties are doctrinaire ones? It is the British Empire which supplies the answer. The British Empire is made up in large part of practically independent States, and Great Britain not only exercises no control over their acts, but has surrendered in advance any intention of employing force concerning them.[103] The British States have disagreements among themselves. They may or may not refer their differences to the British Government, but if they do, is Great Britain going to send an army to Canada, say, to enforce her judgment? Everyone knows that that is impossible. Even when one State commits what is in reality a serious breach of international comity on another, not only does Great Britain refrain from using force herself, but so far as she interferes at all, it is to prevent the employment of physical force. For years now British Indians have been subjected to most cruel and unjust treatment in the State of Natal.[104] The British Government makes no secret of the fact that she regards this treatment as unjust and cruel; were Natal a foreign State, it is conceivable that she would employ force, but, following the principle laid down by Sir C. P. Lucas, "whether they are right or whether they are wrong, more perhaps when they are wrong than when they are right, they cannot be made amenable by force," the two States are left to adjust the difficulty as best they may, without resort to force. In the last resort the British Empire reposes upon the expectation that its Colonies will behave as civilized communities, and in the long run the expectation is, of course, a well-founded one, because, if they do not so behave, retribution will come more surely by the ordinary operation of social and economic forces than it could come by any force of arms.

The case of the British Empire is not an isolated one. The fact is that most of the States of the world maintain their relations one with another without any possibility of a resort to force; half the States of the world have no means of enforcing by arms such wrongs as they may suffer at the hands of other States. Thousands of Englishmen, for instance, make their homes in Switzerland, and it has happened that wrongs have been suffered by Englishmen at the hands of the Swiss Government. Would, however, the relations between the two States, or the practical standard of protection of British subjects in Switzerland, be any the better were Switzerland the whole time threatened by the might of Great Britain? Switzerland knows that she is practically free from the possibility of the exercise of that force, but this has not prevented her from behaving as a civilized community towards British subjects.

What is the real guarantee of the good behavior of one State to another? It is the elaborate interdependence which, not only in the economic sense, but in every sense, makes an unwarrantable aggression of one State upon another react upon the interests of the aggressor. Switzerland has every interest in affording an absolutely secure asylum to British subjects; that fact, and not the might of the British Empire, gives protection to British subjects in Switzerland. Where, indeed, the British subject has to depend upon the force of his Government for protection it is a very frail protection indeed, because in practice the use of that force is so cumbersome, so difficult, so costly, that any other means are to be preferred to it. When the traveler in Greece had to depend upon British arms, great as was relatively the force of those arms, it proved but a very frail protection. In the same way, when physical force was used to impose on the South American and Central American States the observance of their financial obligations, such efforts failed utterly and miserably--so miserably that Great Britain finally surrendered any attempt at such enforcement. What other means have succeeded? The bringing of those countries under the influence of the great economic currents of our time, so that now property is infinitely more secure in Argentina than it was when British gunboats were bombarding her ports. More and more in international relationship is the purely economic motive--and the economic motive is only one of several possible ones--being employed to replace the use of physical force. Austria, the other day, was untouched by any threat of the employment of the Turkish army when the annexation of Bosnia and Herzegovina was consummated, but when the Turkish population enforced a very successful commercial boycott of Austrian goods and Austrian ships, Austrian merchants and public opinion made it quickly plain to the Austrian Government that pressure of this nature could not be disregarded.

I anticipate the plea that while the elaborate interconnection of economic relations renders the employment of force as between nations unnecessary in so far as their material interests are concerned, those forces cannot cover a case of aggression upon what may be termed the moral property of nations. A critic of the first edition of this book[105] writes:

The State is the only complete form in which human society exists, and there are a multitude of phenomena which will be found only as manifestations of human life in the form of a society united by the political bond into a State. The products of such society are law, literature, art, and science, and it has yet to be shown that apart from that form of society known as the State, the family or education or development of character is possible. The State, in short, is an organism or living thing which can be wounded and can be killed, and like every other living thing requires protection against wounding and destruction.... Conscience and morals are products of social and not of individual life, and to say that the sole purpose of the State is to make possible a decent livelihood is as though a man should say that the sole object of human life is to satisfy the interests of existence. A man cannot live any kind of life without food, clothing, and shelter, but that condition does not abolish or diminish the value of the life industrial, the life intellectual, or the life artistic. The State is the condition of all these lives, and its purpose is to sustain them. That is why the State must defend itself. In the ideal, the State represents and embodies the whole people's conception of what is true, of what is beautiful, and of what is right, and it is the sublime quality of human nature that every great nation has produced citizens ready to sacrifice themselves rather than submit to an external force attempting to dictate to them a conception other than their own of what is right.

One is, of course, surprised to see the foregoing in the London *Morning Post*; the concluding phrase would justify the present agitation in India or in Egypt or Ireland against British rule. What is that agitation but an attempt on the part of the peoples of those provinces to resist "an external force attempting to dictate to them a conception other than their own of what is right"? Fortunately, however, for British Imperialism, a people's conception of "what is true, of what is beautiful, and of what is right," and their maintenance of that conception, need not necessarily have anything whatever to do with the particular administrative conditions under which they may live--the only thing that a conception of a "State" predicates. The fallacy which runs through the whole passage just quoted, and which makes it, in fact, nonsense, is the same fallacy which dominates the quotation that I have made from Professor Spenser Wilkinson's book, "Britain at Bay"--namely, the approximation of a State to a person, the assumption that the political delimitation coincides with the economic and moral delimitation, that in short a State is the embodiment of "the whole people's conception of what is true, etc." A State is nothing of the sort. Take the British Empire. This State embodies not a homogeneous conception, but a series of often absolutely contradictory conceptions of "what is true, etc."; it embodies the Mohammedan, the Buddhist, the Copt, the Catholic, the Protestant, the Pagan conceptions of right and truth. The fact which vitiates the whole of this conception of a State is that the frontiers which define the State do not coincide with the conception of any of those things which the London *Morning Post* critic has enumerated; there is no such thing as British morality as opposed to French or German morality, or art or industry. One may, indeed, talk of an English conception of life, because that is a conception of life peculiar to England, but it would be opposed to the conception of life in other parts of the same State, in Ireland, in Scotland, in India, in Egypt, in Jamaica. And what is true of England is true of all the great modern States. Every one of them includes conceptions absolutely opposed to other conceptions in the same State, but many of them absolutely agree with conceptions in foreign States. The British State includes, in Ireland, a Catholic conception in cordial agreement with the Catholic conception in Italy, but in cordial disagreement with the Protestant conception in Scotland, or the Mohammedan conception in Bengal. The real divisions of all those ideals, which the critic enumerates, cut right across State divisions, disregarding them entirely. Yet, again, it is only the State divisions which military conflict has in view.

What was one of the reasons leading to the cessation of religious wars between States? It was that religious conceptions cut across the State frontiers, so that the State ceased to coincide with the religious divisions of Europe, and a condition of things was brought about in which a Protestant Sweden was allied with a Catholic France. This rendered the conflict absurd, and religious wars became an anachronism.

Is not precisely the same thing taking place with reference to the conflicting conceptions of life which now separate men in Christendom? Have not we in America the same doctrinal struggle which is going on in France and Germany and Great Britain? To take one instance--social conflict. On the one side in each case are all the interests bound up with order, authority, individual freedom, without reference to the comfort of the weak, and on the other the reconstruction of human society along hitherto untried lines. These problems are for most men probably--are certainly coming to be, if they are not now--much more profound and fundamental than any conception which coincides with or can be identified with State divisions. Indeed, what are the conceptions of which the divisions coincide with the political frontiers of the British Empire, in view of the fact that that Empire includes nearly every race and nearly every religion under the sun? It may be said, of course, that in the case of Germany and Russia we have an autocratic conception of social organization as compared with a conception based on individual freedom in England and America. Both Mr. Hyndman and Mr. Blatchford seem to take this view. "To me," says the former, "it is quite evident that if we Socialists were to achieve success we should at once be liable to attack from without by the military Powers," an opinion which calmly overlooks the fact that Socialism and anti-militarism have gone much farther and are far better organized in the "military" States than they are in England, and that the military Governments have all their work cut out as it is to keep those tendencies in check within their own borders, without quixotically undertaking to perform the same service in other States.

This conception of the State as the political embodiment of homogeneous doctrine is due in large part not only to the distortion produced by false analogy, but to the survival of a terminology which has become obsolete, and, indeed, the whole of this subject is vitiated by those two things. The State in ancient times was much more a personality than it is to-day, and it is mainly quite modern tendencies which have broken up its doctrinal homogeneity, and that break-up has results which are of the very first importance in their bearing upon international pugnacity. The matter deserves careful examination. Professor William McDougal, in his fascinating work, "An Introduction to Social Psychology," says in the chapter on the instinct of pugnacity:

The replacement of individual by collective pugnacity is most clearly illustrated by barbarous peoples living in small, strongly organized communities. Within such communities individual combat and even expressions of personal anger may be almost completely suppressed, while the pugnacious instinct finds itself in perpetual warfare between communities whose relations remain subject to no law. As a rule no material benefit is gained, and often none is sought, in these tribal wars.... All are kept in constant fear of attack, whole villages are often exterminated, and the population is in this way kept down very far below the limit at which any pressure on the means of subsistence could arise. This perpetual warfare, like the squabbles of a roomful of quarrelsome children, seems to be almost wholly and directly due to the uncomplicated operation of the instinct of pugnacity. No material benefits are sought; a few heads and sometimes a slave or two are the only trophies gained, and if one asks an intelligent chief why he keeps up this senseless practice, the best reason he can give is that unless he does so his neighbors will not respect him and his people, and will fall upon them and exterminate them.

Now, how does such hostility as that indicated in this passage differ from the hostility which marks international differences in our day? In certain very evident respects. It does not suffice that the foreigner should be merely a foreigner for us to want to kill him: there must be some conflict of interest. The English are completely indifferent to the Scandinavian, the Belgian, the Dutchman, the Spaniard, the Austrian, and the Italian, and are supposed for the moment to be greatly in love with the French. The German is the enemy. But ten years ago it was the Frenchman who was the enemy, and Mr. Chamberlain was talking of an alliance with the Germans--England's natural allies, he called them--while it was for France that he reserved his attacks.[106] It cannot be, therefore, that there is any inherent racial hostility in English national character, because the Germans have not changed their nature in ten years, nor the French theirs. If to-day the French are England's quasi-allies and the Germans her enemies, it is simply because their respective interests or apparent interests have modified in the last ten years, and their political preferences have modified with them. In other words, national hostilities follow the exigencies of real or imagined political interests. Surely the point need not be labored, seeing that England has boxed the compass of the whole of Europe in her likes and dislikes, and poured her hatred upon the Spaniards, the Dutch, the Americans, the Danes, the Russians, the Germans, the French, and again the Germans, all in turn. The phenomenon is a commonplace of individual relationship: "I never noticed his collars were dirty till he got in my way," said someone of a rival.

The second point of difference with Professor McDougal's savage is that when we get to grips our conflict does not include the whole tribe; we do not, in the Biblical fashion, exterminate men, women, children, and cattle. Enough of the old Adam remains for us to detest the women and children, so that an English poet could write of the "whelps and dams of murderous foes"; but we no longer slaughter them.[107]

But there is a third fact which we must note--that Professor McDougal's nation was made up of a single tribe entirely homogeneous. Even the fact of living across a river was sufficient to turn another tribe into foreigners and to involve a desire to kill them. The development from that stage to the present has involved, in addition to the two factors just enumerated, this: we now include as fellow-countrymen many who would under the old conception necessarily be foreigners, and the process of our development, economic and otherwise, has made of foreigners, between whom, in Homer Lea's philosophy, there should exist this "primordial hostility leading inevitably to war," one State from which all conflict of interest has disappeared entirely. The modern State of France includes what were, even in historical times, eighty separate and warring States, since each of the old Gallic cities represented a different State. In England people have come to regard as fellow-citizens between whom there can be no sort of conflict of interest scores of tribes that spent their time mutually throat-cutting at no very distant period, as history goes. Anyone, particularly Americans, can recognize, indeed, that profound national differences like those which exist between the Welshman and the Englishman, or the Scotsman and the Irishman, need involve not only no conflict of interest, but even no separate political existence.

One has heard in recent times of the gradual revival of Nationalism, and it is commonly argued that the principle of Nationality must stand in the way of co-operation between States. But the facts do not justify that conclusion for a moment. The formation of States has disregarded national divisions altogether. If conflicts are to coincide with national divisions, Wales should co-operate with Brittany and Ireland against Normandy and England; Provence and Savoy with Sardinia against--I do not know what French province, because in the final rearrangement of European frontiers races and provinces have become so inextricably mixed, and have paid so little regard to "natural" and "inherent" divisions, that it is no longer possible to disentangle them.

In the beginning the State is a homogeneous tribe or family, and in the process of economic and social development these divisions so far break down that a State may include, as the British State does, not only half a dozen different races in the mother country, but a thousand different races scattered over various parts of the earth--white, black, yellow, brown, copper-colored. This, surely, is one of the great sweeping tendencies of history--a tendency which operates immediately any complicated economic life is set up. What justification have we, therefore, for saying dogmatically that a tendency to co-operation, which has swept before it profound ethnic differences, social and political divisions, which has been constant from the dawn of men's attempts to live and labor together, is to stop at the wall of modern State divisions, which represent none of the profound divisions of the human race, but mainly mere administrative convenience, and embody a conception which is being every day profoundly modified?

Some indication of the processes involved in this development has already been given in the outline sketch in Chapter II. of this section, to which the reader may be referred. I have there attempted to make plain that *pari passu* with the drift from physical force towards economic inducement goes a corresponding diminution of pugnacity, until the psychological factor which is the exact reverse of pugnacity comes to have more force even than the economic one. Quite apart from any economic question, it is no longer possible for any government to order the extermination of a whole population, of the women and children, in the old Biblical style. In the same way, the greater economic interdependence which improved means of communication have provoked must carry with it a greater moral interdependence, and a tendency which has broken down profound national divisions, like those which separated the Celt and the Saxon, will certainly break down on the psychological side divisions which are obviously more artificial.

Among the multiple factors which have entered into the great sweeping tendency just mentioned are one or two which stand out as most likely to have immediate effect on the breakdown of a purely psychological hostility embodied by merely State divisions. One is that lessening of the reciprocal sentiment of collective responsibility which the complex heterogeneity of the modern State involves. What do I mean by this sense of collective responsibility? To the Chinese Boxer all Europeans are "foreign devils"; between Germans, English, Russians, there is little distinction, just as to the black in Africa there is little differentiation between the various white races. Even the yokel in England talks of "them foreigners." If a Chinese Boxer is injured by a Frenchman, he kills a German, and feels himself avenged--they are all "foreign devils." When an African tribe suffers from the depredations of a Belgian trader, the next white man who comes into its territory, whether he happens to be an Englishman or a Frenchman, loses his life; the tribesmen also feel themselves avenged. But if the Chinese Boxer had our clear conception of the different European nations, he would feel no psychological satisfaction in killing a German because a Frenchman had injured him. There must be in the Boxer's mind some collective responsibility as between the two Europeans, or in the negro's mind between the two white men, in order to obtain this psychological satisfaction. If that collective responsibility does not exist, the hostility to the second white man, in each case, is not even raised.

Now, our international hostilities are largely based on the notion of a collective responsibility in each of the various States against which our hostility is directed, which does not, in fact, exist. There is at the present moment great ill-feeling in England against "the German." Now, "the German" is a non-existent abstraction. Englishmen are angry with the German because he is building warships, conceivably directed against them; but a great many Germans are as much opposed to that increase of armament as are the English, and the desire of the yokel to "have a go at them Germans" depends absolutely upon a confusion just as great as--indeed, greater than--that which exists in the mind of the Boxer, who cannot differentiate between the various European peoples. Mr. Blatchford commenced that series of articles which has done so much to accentuate this ill-feeling with this phrase:

Germany is deliberately preparing to destroy the British Empire; and later in the articles he added:

Britain is disunited; Germany is homogeneous. We are quarrelling about the Lords' Veto, Home Rule, and a dozen other questions of domestic politics. We have a Little Navy Party, an Anti-Militarist Party; Germany is unanimous upon the question of naval expansion.

It would be difficult to pack a more dangerous untruth into so few lines. What are the facts? If "Germany" means the bulk of the German people, Mr. Blatchford is perfectly aware that he is not telling the truth. It is not true to say of the bulk of the German people that they are deliberately preparing to destroy the British Empire. The bulk of the German people, if they are represented by any one party at all, are represented by the Social Democrats, who have stood from the first resolutely against any such intention. Now the facts have to be misstated in this way in order to produce that temper which makes for war. If the facts are correctly stated, no such temper arises.

What has a particularly competent German to say to Mr. Blatchford's generalization? Mr. Fried, the editor of *Die Friedenswarte*, writes:

There is no one German people, no single Germany.... There are more abrupt contrasts between Germans and Germans than between Germans and Indians. Nay, the contradistinctions within Germany are greater than those between Germans and the units of any other foreign nation whatever. It might be possible to make efforts to promote good understanding between Germans and Englishmen, between Germans and Frenchmen, to organize visits between nation and nation; but it will be forever impossible to set on foot any such efforts at an understanding between German Social Democrats and Prussian Junkers, between German Anti-Semites and German Jews.[108]

The disappearance of most international hostility depends upon nothing more intricate than the realization of facts which are little more com-plex than the geographical knowledge which enables us to see that the anger of the yokel is absurd when he pummels a Frenchman because an Italian has swindled him.

It may be argued that there never has existed in the past this identifi-cation between a people and the acts of its Government which rendered the hatred of one country for another logical, yet that hatred has arisen. That is true; but certain new factors have entered recently to modify this problem. One is that never in the history of the world have nations been so complex as they are to-day; and the second is that never before have the dominating interests of mankind so completely cut across State divi-sions as they do to-day. The third factor is that never before has it been possible, as it is possible by our means of communication to-day, to off-set a solidarity of classes and ideas against a presumed State solidarity.

Never at any stage of the world's development has there existed, as ex-ists to-day, the machinery for embodying these interests and class ideas and ideals which cut across frontiers. It is not generally understood how many of our activities have become international. Two great forces have become internationalized: Capital on the one hand, Labor and Socialism on the other.

The Labor and Socialist movements have always been international, and become more so every year. Few considerable strikes take place in any one country without the labor organizations of other countries fur-nishing help, and very large sums have been contributed by the labor organizations of various countries in this way.

With reference to capital, it may almost be said that it is organized so naturally internationally that formal organization is not necessary. When the Bank of England is in danger, it is the Bank of France which comes automatically to its aid, even in a time of acute political hostility. It has been my good fortune in the last ten years to discuss these matters with financiers on one side and labor leaders on the other, and I have always been particularly struck by the fact that I have found in these two class-es precisely the same attitude of internationalization. In no department of human activity is internationalization so complete as in finance. The capitalist has no country, and he knows, if he be of the modern type, that arms and conquests and jugglery with frontiers serve no ends of his, and may very well defeat them. But employers, as apart from capitalists, are also developing a strong international cohesive organization. Among the Berlin dispatches in the London *Times* of April 18, 1910, I find the following concerning a big strike in the building trade, in which nearly a quarter of a million men went out. Quoting a writer in the *North German Gazette*, the correspondent says:

The writer lays stress upon the efficiency of the employers' arrange-ments. He says, in particular, that it will probably be possible to ex-tend the lock-out to industries associated with the building industry, especially the cement industry, and that the employers are completing a ring of cartel treaties, which will prevent German workmen from finding employment in neighboring countries, and will insure for German employers all possible support from abroad. It is said that Switzerland and Austria were to conclude treaties yesterday on the same conditions as Sweden, Norway, Denmark, Holland, and France, and that Belgium and Italy would come in, so that there will be complete co-operation on the part of all Germany's neighbors except Russia. In the circumstances the men's organs rather overlabor the point when they produce elaborate evidence of premeditation. The *Vorwärts* proves that the employers have long been preparing for "a trial of strength," but that is admitted. The official organ of the employers says, in so many words, that any intervention is useless until "the forces have been measured in open battle."

Have not these forces begun already to affect the psychological domain with which we are now especially dealing? Do we place national vanity, for instance, on the same plane as individual vanity? Have we not already realized the absurdity involved?

I have quoted Admiral Mahan as follows:

That extension of national authority over alien communities, which is the dominant note in the world politics of to-day, dignifies and enlarges each State and each citizen that enters its fold.... Sentiment, imagination, aspiration, the satisfaction of the rational and moral faculties in some object better than bread alone, all must find a part in a worthy motive. Like individuals, nations and empires have souls as well as bodies. Great and beneficent achievement ministers to worthier contentment than the filling of the pocket.

Whatever we may think of the individuals who work disinterestedly for the benefit of backward and alien peoples, and however their lives may be "dignified and enlarged" by their activities, it is surely absurd to suppose that other individuals, who take no part in their work and who remain thousands of miles from the scene of action, can possibly be credited with "great and beneficent achievement."

A man who boasts of his possessions is not a very pleasant or admirable type, but at least his possessions are for his own use and do bring a tangible satisfaction, materially as well as sentimentally. His is the object of a certain social deference by reason of his wealth--a deference which has not a very high motive, if you will, but the outward and visible signs of which are pleasing to a vain man. But is the same in any sense true, despite Admiral Mahan, of the individual of a big State as compared to the individual of a small one? Does anyone think of paying deference to the Russian *mujik* because he happens to belong to one of the biggest empires territorially? Does anyone think of despising an Ibsen or a Björnsen, or any educated Scandinavian or Belgian or Hollander, because they happen to belong to the smallest nations in Europe? The thing is absurd, and the notion is simply due to inattention. Just as we commonly overlook the fact that the individual citizen is quite unaffected materially by the extent of his nation's territory, that the material position of the individual Dutchman as a citizen of a small State will not be improved by the mere fact of the absorption of his State by the German Empire, in which case he will become the citizen of a great nation, so in the same way his moral position remains unchanged; and the notion that an individual Russian is "dignified and enlarged" each time that Russia conquers some new Asiatic outpost, or Russifies a State like Finland, or that the Norwegian would be "dignified" were his State conquered by Russia and he became a Russian, is, of course, sheer sentimental fustian of a very mischievous order. This is the more emphasized when we remember that the best men of Russia are looking forward wistfully, not to the enlargement but to the dissolution, of the unwieldy giant "stupid with the stupidity of giants, ferocious with their ferocity" and the rise in its stead of a multiplicity of self-contained, self-knowing communities, "whose members will be united together by organic and vital sympathies, and not by their common submission to a common policeman."

How small and thin a pretense is all the talk of national prestige when the matter is tested by its relation to the individual is shown by the commonplaces of our everyday social intercourse. In social consideration everything else takes precedence of nationality, even in those circles where Chauvinism is a cult. British Royalty is so impressed with the dignity which attaches to membership of the British Empire that its Princes will marry into the royal houses of the smallest and meanest States in Europe, while they would regard marriage with a British commoner as an unheard-of *mésalliance*. This standard of social judgment so marks all the European royalties that at the present time not one ruler in Europe belongs, properly speaking, to the race which he rules. In all social associations an analogous rule is followed. In our "selectest" circles an Italian, Rumanian, Portuguese, or even Turkish noble, is received where an American tradesman would be taboo.

This tendency has struck almost all authorities who have investigated scientifically modern international relations. Thus Mr. T. Baty, the well-known authority on international law, writes as follows:

All over the world society is organizing itself by strata. The English merchant goes on business to Warsaw, Hamburg, or Leghorn; he finds in the merchants of Italy, Germany, and Russia the ideas, the standard of living, the sympathies, and the aversions which are familiar to him at home. Printing and the locomotive have enormously reduced the importance of locality. It is the mental atmosphere of its fellows, and not of its neighborhood, which the child of the younger generation is beginning to breathe. Whether he reads the *Revue des Deux Mondes* or *Tit-Bits*, the modern citizen is becoming at once cosmopolitan and class-centred. Let the process work for a few more years; we shall see the common interests of cosmopolitan classes revealing themselves as far more potent factors than the shadowy common interests of the subjects of States. The Argentine merchant and the British capitalist alike regard the Trade Union as a possible enemy--whether British or Argentine matters to them less than nothing. The Hamburg docker and his brother of London do not put national interests before the primary claims of caste. International class feeling is a reality, and not even a nebulous reality; the nebula has developed centres of condensation. Only the other day Sir W. Runciman, who is certainly not a Conservative, presided over a meeting at which there were laid the foundations of an International Shipping Union, which is intended to unite ship-owners of whatever country in a common organization. When it is once recognized that the real interests of modern people are not national, but social, the results may be surprising.[109]

As Mr. Baty points out, this tendency, which he calls "stratification," extends to all classes:

It is impossible to ignore the significance of the International Congresses, not only of Socialism, but of pacificism, of esperantism, of feminism, of every kind of art and science, that so conspicuously set their seal upon the holiday season. Nationality as a limiting force is breaking down before cosmopolitanism. In directing its forces into an international channel, Socialism will have no difficulty whatever[110].... We are, therefore, confronted with a coming condition of affairs in which the force of nationality will be distinctly inferior to the force of class-cohesion, and in which classes will be internationally organized so as to wield their force with effect. The prospect induces some curious reflections.

We have here, at present in merely embryonic form, a group of motives otherwise opposed, but meeting and agreeing upon one point: the organization of society on other than territorial and national divisions. When motives of such breadth as these give force to a tendency, it may be said that the very stars in their courses are working to the same end.

PART III

THE PRACTICAL OUTCOME

CHAPTER I

THE RELATION OF DEFENSE TO AGGRESSION

Necessity for defense arises from the existence of a motive for attack--Platitudes that everyone overlooks--To attenuate the motive for aggression is to undertake a work of defense.

The general proposition embodied in this book--that the world has passed out of that stage of development in which it is possible for one civilized group to advance its well-being by the military domination of another--is either broadly true or broadly false. If it is false, it can, of course, have no bearing upon the actual problems of our time, and can have no practical outcome; huge armaments tempered by warfare are the logical and natural condition.

But the commonest criticism this book has had to meet is that, though its central proposition is in essence sound, it has, nevertheless, no practical value, because--

1. Armaments are for defense, not for aggression.

2. However true these principles may be, the world does not recognize them and never will, because men are not guided by reason.

As to the first point. It is probable that, if we really understood truths which we are apt to dismiss as platitudes, many of our problems would disappear.

To say, "We must take measures for defense" is equivalent to saying, "Someone is likely to attack us," which is equivalent to saying, "Someone has a motive for attacking us." In other words, the basic fact from which arises the necessity for armaments, the ultimate explanation of European militarism, is *the force of the motive making for aggression*. (And in the word "aggression," of course, I include the imposition of superior force by the *threat*, or implied threat, of its use, as well as by its actual use.)

That motive may be material or moral; it may arise from real conflict of interest, or a purely imaginary one; but with the disappearance of prospective aggression disappears also the need for defense.

The reader deems these platitudes beside the mark?

I will take a few sample criticisms directed at this book. Here is the London *Daily Mail*:

The bigger nations are armed, not so much because they look for the spoils of war, as because they wish to prevent the horrors of it; arms are for defense.[111]

And here is the London *Times*:

No doubt the victor suffers, but who suffers most, he or the vanquished?"[112]

The criticism of the *Daily Mail* was made within three months of a "raging and tearing" big navy campaign, all of it based on the assumption that Germany *was* "looking for the spoils of war," the English naval increase being thus a direct outcome of such motives. Without it, the question of English increase would not have arisen.[113] The only justification for the clamor for increase was that England was liable to *attack*; every nation in Europe justifies its armaments in the same way; every nation consequently believes in the universal existence of this motive for attack.

The *Times* has been hardly less insistent than the *Mail* as to the danger from German aggression; but its criticism would imply that the motive behind that prospective aggression is not a desire for any political advantage or gain of any sort. Germany apparently recognizes aggression to be, not merely barren of any useful result whatsoever, but burdensome and costly into the bargain; she is, nevertheless, determined to enter upon it in order that though she suffer, someone else will suffer more![114]

In common with the London *Daily Mail* and the London *Times*, Admiral Mahan fails to understand this "platitude," which underlies the relation of defense to aggression.

Thus in his criticism of this book, he cites the position of Great Britain during the Napoleonic era as proof that commercial advantage goes with the possession of preponderant military power in the following passage:

Great Britain owed her commercial superiority then to the armed control of the sea, which had sheltered her commerce and industrial fabric from molestation by the enemy.

Ergo, military force has commercial value, a result which is arrived at by this method: in deciding a case made up of two parties you ignore one.

England's superiority was not due to the employment of military force, but to the fact that she was able to prevent the employment of military force against her; and the necessity for so doing arose from Napoleon's motive in threatening her. But for the existence of this motive to aggression--moral or material, just or mistaken--Great Britain, without any force whatsoever, would have been more secure and more prosperous than she was; she would not have been spending a third of her income in war, and her peasantry would not have been starving.

Of a like character to the remark of the *Times* is the criticism of the *Spectator*, as follows:

Mr. Angell's main point is that the advantages customarily associated with national independence and security have no existence outside the popular imagination.... He holds that Englishmen would be equally happy if they were under German rule, and that Germans would be equally

happy if they were under English rule. It is irrational, therefore, to take
any measures for perpetuating the existing European order, since only
a sentimentalist can set any value on its maintenance.... Probably in
private life Mr. Angell is less consistent and less inclined to preach the
burglar's gospel that to the wise man *meum* and *tuum* are but two names
for the same thing. If he is anxious to make converts, he will do well to
apply his reasoning to subjects that come nearer home, and convince the
average man that marriage and private property are as much illusions as
patriotism. If sentiment is to be banished from politics, it cannot reasonably be retained in morals.

As the reply to this somewhat extraordinary criticism is directly germane to what it is important to make clear, I may, perhaps, be excused
for reproducing my letter to the *Spectator*, which was in part as follows:

How far the foregoing is a correct description of the scope and character of the book under review may be gathered from the following statement of fact. My pamphlet does *not* attack the sentiment of patriotism
(unless a criticism of the duellist's conception of dignity be considered
as such); it simply does not deal with it, as being outside the limits of
the main thesis. I do *not* hold, and there is not one line to which your reviewer can point as justifying such a conclusion, that Englishmen would
be equally happy if they were under German rule. I do not conclude that
it is irrational to take measures for perpetuating the existing European
order. I do *not* "expose the folly of self-defense in nations." I do *not* object
to spending money on armaments at this juncture. On the contrary, I
am particularly emphatic in declaring that while the present philosophy
is what it is, we are bound to maintain our relative position with other
Powers. I admit that so long as there is danger, as I believe there is, from
German aggression, we must arm. I do *not* preach a burglar's gospel,
that *meum* and *tuum* are the same thing, and the whole tendency of my
book is the exact reverse: it is to show that the burglar's gospel--which
is the gospel of statecraft as it now stands--is no longer possible among
nations, and that the difference between *meum* and *tuum* must necessarily, as society gains in complication, be given a stricter observance than
it has ever heretofore been given in history. I do *not* urge that sentiment
should be banished from politics, if by sentiment is meant the common
morality that guides us in our treatment of marriage and of private property. The whole tone of my book is to urge with all possible emphasis the
exact reverse of such a doctrine; to urge that the morality which has been
by our necessities developed in the society of individuals must also be
applied to the society of nations as that society becomes by virtue of our
development more interdependent.

I have only taken a small portion of your reviewer's article (which runs
to a whole page), and I do not think I am exaggerating when I say that
nearly all of it is as untrue and as much a distortion of what I really say
as the passage from which I have quoted. What I do attempt to make
plain is that the necessity for defense measures (which I completely rec-

ognize and emphatically counsel) implies on the part of someone a motive for aggression, and that the motive arises from the (at present) universal belief in the social and economic advantages accruing from successful conquest.

I challenged this universal axiom of statecraft and attempted to show that the mechanical development of the last thirty or forty years, especially in the means of communication, had given rise to certain economic phenomena--of which re-acting bourses and the financial interdependence of the great economic centers of the world are perhaps the most characteristic--which render modern wealth and trade intangible in the sense that they cannot be seized or interfered with to the advantage of a military aggressor, the moral being, not that self-defense is out of date, but that aggression is, and that when aggression ceases, self-defense will be no longer necessary. I urged, therefore, that in these little-recognized truths might possibly be found a way out of the armament *impasse*; that if the accepted motive for aggression could be shown to have no solid basis, the tension in Europe would be immensely relieved, and the risk of attack become immeasurably less by reason of the slackening of the motive for aggression. I asked whether this series of economic facts--so little realized by the average politician in Europe, and yet so familiar to at least a few of the ablest financiers--did not go far to change the axioms of statecraft, and I urged re-consideration of such in the light of these facts.

Your reviewer, instead of dealing with the questions thus raised, accuses me of "attacking patriotism," of arguing that "Englishmen would be equally happy under German rule," and much nonsense of the same sort, for which there is not a shadow of justification. Is this serious criticism? Is it worthy of the *Spectator*?

To the foregoing letter the *Spectator* critic rejoins as follows:

If Mr. Angell's book had given me the same impression as that which I gain from his letter, I should have reviewed it in a different spirit. I can only plead that I wrote under the impression which the book actually made on me. In reply to his "statement of fact," I must ask your leave to make the following corrections: (1) Instead of saying that, on Mr. Angell's showing, Englishmen would be "equally happy" under German rule, I ought to have said that they would be equally well off. But on his doctrine that material well-being is "the very highest" aim of a politician, the two terms seem to be interchangeable. (2) The "existing European order" rests on the supposed economic value of political force. In opposition to this Mr. Angell maintains "the economic futility of political force." To take measures for perpetuating an order founded on a futility does seem to me "irrational." (3) I never said that Mr. Angell objects to spending money on armaments "while the present philosophy is what it is." (4) The stress laid in the book on the economic folly of patriotism, as commonly understood, does seem to me to suggest that "sentiment should be banished from politics." But I admit that this was only an inference, though, as I still think, a fair inference. (5) I apologize for the words "the burglar's gospel." They have the fault, incident to rhetorical phrases, of being more telling than exact.

This rejoinder, as a matter of fact, still reveals the confusion which prompted the first criticism. Because I urged that Germany could do England relatively little harm, since the harm which she inflicted would immediately react on German prosperity, my critic assumes that this is equivalent to saying that Englishmen would be as happy or as prosperous under German rule. He quite overlooks the fact that if Germans are convinced that they will obtain no benefit by the conquest of the English they will not attempt that conquest, and there will be no question of the English living under German rule either less or more happily or prosperously. It is not a question of Englishmen saying, "Let the German come," but of the German saying, "Why should we go?" As to the critic's second point, I have expressly explained that not the rival's real interest but what he deems to be his real interest must be the guide to conduct. Military force is certainly economically futile, but so long as German policy rests on the assumption of the supposed economic value of military force, England must meet that force by the only force that can reply to it.

Some years ago the bank in a Western mining town was frequently subjected to "hold-ups," because it was known that the great mining company owning the town kept large quantities of gold there for the payment of its workmen. The company, therefore, took to paying its wages mainly by check on a San Francisco bank, and by a simple system of clearances practically abolished the use of gold in considerable quantities in the mining town in question. The bank was never attacked again.

Now, the demonstration that gold had been replaced by books in that bank was as much a work of defense as though the bank had spent tens of thousands of dollars in constructing forts and earthworks, and mounting Gatling guns around the town. Of the two methods of defense, that of substituting checks for gold was infinitely cheaper, and more effective.

Even if the inferences which the *Spectator* reviewer draws were true ones, which for the most part they are not, he still overlooks one important element. If it were true that the book involves the "folly of patriotism," how is that in any way relevant to the discussion, since I also urge that nations are justified in protecting even their follies against the attack of other nations? I may regard the Christian Scientists, or the Seventh Day Adventists, or the Spiritualists, as very foolish people, and to some extent mischievous people; but were an Act of Parliament introduced for their suppression by physical force, I should resist such an act with all the energy of which I was capable. In what way are the two attitudes contradictory? They are the attitudes, I take it, of educated men the world over. The fact has no importance, and it hardly bears on this subject, but I regard certain English conceptions of life bearing on matters of law, and social habit, and political philosophy, as infinitely preferable to the German, and if I thought that such conceptions demanded defense indefinitely by great armaments this book would never have been written. But I take the view that the idea of such necessity is based on a complete illusion, not only because as a matter of present-day fact, and even in the present state of political philosophy, Germany has not the least intention of going to war with us to change our notions in law or literature, art or social organization, but also because if she had any such notion it would be founded upon illusions which she would be bound sooner or later to shed, because German policy could not indefinitely resist the influence of a general European attitude on such matters any more than it has been possible for any great and active European State to stand outside the European movement which has condemned the policy of attempting to impose religious belief by the physical force of the State. And I should regard it as an essential part of the work of defense to aid in the firm establishment of such a European doctrine, as much a part of the work of defense as it would be to go on building battleships until Germany had subscribed to it.

A great part of the misconception just dealt with arises from a hazily conceived fear that ideas like those embodied in this book must attenuate our energy of defense, and that we shall be in a weaker position relatively to our rivals than we were before. But this overlooks the fact that if the progress of ideas weakens our energies of defense, it also weakens our rival's energy of attack, and the strength of our relative positions is just what it was originally, with this exception: that we have taken a step towards peace instead of a step towards war, to which the mere piling up of armaments, unchecked by any other factor, must in the end inevitably lead.

But there is one aspect of this failure to realize the relation of defense to aggression, which brings us nearer to considering the bearing of these principles upon the question of practical policy.

CHAPTER II

ARMAMENT, BUT NOT ALONE ARMAMENT

Not the facts, but men's belief about facts, shapes their conduct--Solving a problem of two factors by ignoring one--The fatal outcome of such a method--The German Navy as a "luxury"--If both sides concentrate on armament alone.

"Not the facts, but men's opinions about the facts, are what matter," one thinker has remarked. And this is because men's conduct is determined, not necessarily by the right conclusion from facts, but the conclusion they believe to be right.

When men burned witches, their conduct was exactly what it would have been if what they believed to be true *had* been true. The truth made no difference to their behavior, so long as they could not see the truth. And so in politics. As long as Europe is dominated by the old beliefs, those beliefs will have virtually the same effect in politics as though they were intrinsically sound.

And just as in the matter of burning witches a change of behavior was the outcome of a change of opinion, in its turn the result of a more scientific investigation of the facts, so in the same way a change in the political conduct of Europe can only come about as the result of a change of thought; and that change of thought will not come about so long as the energies of men in this matter are centred only upon perfecting instruments of warfare. It is not merely that better ideas can only result from more attention being given to the real meaning of facts, but that the direct tendency of war preparation--with the suspicion it necessarily engenders and the ill-temper to which it almost always gives rise--is to create both mechanical and psychological checks to improvement of opinion and understanding. Here, for instance, is General von Bernhardi, who has just published his book in favor of war as the regenerator of nations, urging that Germany should attack certain of her enemies before they are ready to attack her. Suppose the others reply by increasing their military force? It suits Bernhardi entirely. For what is the effect of this increase on the minds of Germans possibly disposed to disagree with Bernhardi? It is to silence them and to strengthen Bernhardi's hands. His policy, originally wrong, has become relatively right, because his arguments have been answered by force. For the silence of his might-be critics will still further encourage those of other nations who deem themselves threatened by this kind of opinion in Germany to increase their armaments; and these increases will still further tend to strengthen Bernhardi's school, and still further silence his critics. The process by which force tends to crush reason is, unhappily, cumulative and progressive. The vicious circle can only be broken by the introduction somewhere of the factor of reason.

And this is precisely, my critics urge, why we need do nothing but concentrate on the instruments of force!

The all but invariable attitude adopted by the man in the street in this whole discussion is about as follows:

"What, as practical men, we have to do, is to be stronger than our enemy; the rest is theory, and does not matter."

Well, the inevitable outcome of such an attitude is catastrophe. It leads us not toward, but away from, solution.

In the first edition of this book I wrote:

Are we immediately to cease preparation for war, since our defeat cannot advantage our enemy nor do us in the long run much harm? No such conclusion results from a study of the considerations elaborated here. It is evident that so long as the misconception we are dealing with is all but universal in Europe, so long as the nations believe that in some way the military and political subjugation of others will bring with it a tangible material advantage to the conqueror, we all do, in fact, stand in danger from such aggression. Not his interest, but what he deems to be his interest, will furnish the real motive of our prospective enemy's action. And as the illusion with which we are dealing does, indeed, dominate all those minds most active in European politics, we (in England) must, while this remains the case, regard an aggression, even such as that which Mr. Harrison foresees, as within the bounds of practical politics. (What is not within the bounds of possibility is the extent of devastation which he foresees as the result of such attack, which, I think, the foregoing pages sufficiently demonstrate.)

On this ground alone I deem that England, or any other nation, is justified in taking means of self-defense to prevent such aggression. This is not, therefore, a plea for disarmament irrespective of the action of other nations. So long as current political philosophy in Europe remains what it is, I would not urge the reduction of the British war budget by a single sovereign.

I see no reason to alter a word of this. But if preparation of the machinery of war is to be the only form of energy in this matter--if national effort is to neglect all other factors whatsoever--more and more will sincere and patriotic men have doubts as to whether they are justified in co-operating in further piling up the armaments of any country. Of the two risks involved--the risk of attack arising from a possible superiority of armament on the part of a rival, and the risk of drifting into conflict because, concentrating all our energies on the mere instrument of combat, we have taken no adequate trouble to understand the facts of this case--it is at least an arguable proposition that the second risk is the greater. And I am prompted to this expression of opinion without surrendering one iota of a lifelong and passionate belief that a nation attacked should defend itself to the last penny and to the last man.

In this matter it seems fatally easy to secure either one of two kinds of action: that of the "practical man" who limits his energies to securing a policy which will perfect the machinery of war and disregard anything else; or that of the Pacifist, who, persuaded of the brutality or immorality of war, is apt to deprecate effort directed at self-defense. What is needed is the type of activity which will include both halves of the problem: provision for education, for a Political Reformation in this matter, *as well as* such means of defense as will meantime counterbalance the existing impulse to aggression. To concentrate on either half to the exclusion of the other half is to render the whole problem insoluble.

What must inevitably happen if the nations take the line of the "practical man," and limit their energies simply and purely to piling up armaments?

A British critic once put to me what he evidently deemed a poser: "Do you urge that we shall be stronger than our enemy, or weaker?"

To which I replied: "The last time that question was asked me was in Berlin, by Germans. What would you have had me reply to those Germans?"--a reply which, of course, meant this: In attempting to find the solution of this question in terms of one party, you are attempting the impossible. The outcome will be war, and war would not settle it. It would all have to be begun over again.

The British Navy League catechism says: "Defense consists in being so strong that it will be dangerous for your enemy to attack you."[115] Mr. Churchill, even, goes farther than the Navy League, and says: "The way to make war impossible is to make victory certain."

The Navy League definition is at least possible of application to practical politics, because rough equality of the two parties would make attack by either dangerous. Mr. Churchill's principle is impossible of application to practical politics, because it could only be applied by one party, and would, in the terms of the Navy League principle, deprive the other party of the right of defense. As a matter of simple fact, both the British Navy League, by its demand for two ships to one, and Mr. Churchill, by his demand for certain victory, deny in this matter Germany's right to defend herself; and such denial is bound, on the part of a people animated by like motives to themselves, to provoke a challenge. When the British Navy League says, as it does, that a self-respecting nation should not depend upon the goodwill of foreigners for its safety, but upon its own strength, it recommends Germany to maintain her efforts to arrive at some sort of equality with England. When Mr. Churchill goes farther, and says that a nation is entitled to be so strong as to make victory over its rivals certain, he knows that if Germany were to adopt his own doctrine, its certain outcome would be war.

In anticipation of such an objection, Mr. Churchill says that preponderant power at sea is a luxury to Germany, a necessity to Britain; that these efforts of Germany are, as it were, a mere whim in no way dictated by the real necessities of her people, and having behind them no impulse wrapped up with national needs.[116]

If that be the truth, then it is the strongest argument imaginable for the settlement of this Anglo-German rivalry by agreement: by bringing about that Political Reformation of Europe which it is the object of these pages to urge.

Here are those of the school of Mr. Churchill who say: The danger of aggression from Germany is so great that England must have an enormous preponderance of force--two to one; so great are the risks Germany is prepared to take, that unless victory on the English side is certain she will attack. And yet, explain this same school, the impulse which creates these immense burdens and involves these immense risks is a mere whim, a luxury; the whole thing is dissociated from any real national need.

If that really be the case, then, indeed, is it time for a campaign of Education in Europe; time that the sixty-five millions, more or less, of hard-working and not very rich people, whose money support alone makes this rivalry possible, learned what it is all about. This "whim" has cost the two nations, in the last ten years, a sum larger than the indemnity France paid to Germany. Does Mr. Churchill suppose that these millions know, or think, this struggle one for a mere luxury, or whim? And if they did know, would it be quite a simple matter for the German Government to keep up the game?

But those who, during the last decade in England, have in and out of season carried on this active campaign for the increase of British armaments, do *not* believe that Germany's action is the result of a mere whim. They, being part of the public opinion of Europe, subscribe to the general European doctrine that Germany is pushed to do these things by real national necessities, by her need for expansion, for finding food and livelihood for all these increasing millions. And if this is so, the English are asking Germany, in surrendering this contest, to betray future German generations--willfully to withhold from them those fields which the strength and fortitude of this generation might win. If this common doctrine is true, the English are asking Germany to commit national suicide.[117]

Why should it be assumed that Germany will do it? That she will be less persistent in protecting her national interest, her posterity, be less faithful than the British themselves to great national impulses? Has not the day gone by when educated men can calmly assume that any Englishman is worth three foreigners? And yet such an assumption, ignorant and provincial as we are bound to admit it to be, is the only one that can possibly justify this policy of concentrating upon armament alone.

Even Admiral Fisher can write:

The supremacy of the British Navy is the best security for the peace of the world.... If you rub it in, both at home and abroad, that you are ready for instant war, with every unit of your strength in the first line and waiting to be first in, and hit your enemy in the belly and kick him when he is down, and boil your prisoners in oil (if you take any), and torture his women and children, then people will keep clear of you.

Would Admiral Fisher refrain from taking a given line merely because, if he took it, someone would "hit him in the belly," etc.? He would repudiate the idea with the utmost scorn, and probably reply that the threat would give him an added incentive to take the line in question. But why should Admiral Fisher suppose that he has a monopoly of courage, and that a German Admiral would act otherwise than he? Is it not about time that each nation abandoned the somewhat childish assumption that it has a monopoly of the courage and the persistence in the world, and that things which would never frighten or deter it will frighten and deter its rivals?

Yet in this matter the English assume either that the Germans will be less persistent than they, or that in this contest their backs will break first. A coadjutor of Lord Roberts is calmly talking of a Naval Budget of 400 or 500 million dollars, and universal service as well, as a possibility of the all but immediate future.[118] If England can stand that now, why should not Germany, who is, we are told, growing industrially more rapidly than the English, be able to stand as much? But when she has arrived at that point, the English, at the same rate, must have a naval budget of anything from 750 to 1000 million dollars, a total armament budget of something in the region of 1250 millions. The longer it goes on, the worse will be England's relative position, because she has imposed on herself a progressive handicap.

The end can only be conflict, and already the policy of precipitating that conflict is raising its head.

Sir Edmund C. Cox writes in the premier English review, the *Nineteenth Century*, for April, 1910:

Is there no alternative to this endless yet futile competition in shipbuilding? Yes, there is. It is one which a Cromwell, a William Pitt, a Palmerston, a Disraeli, would have adopted long ago. This is that alternative--the only possible conclusion. It is to say to Germany: "All that you have been doing constitutes a series of unfriendly acts. Your fair words go for nothing. Once for all, you must put an end to your warlike preparations. If we are not satisfied that you do so, we shall forthwith sink every battleship and cruiser which you possess. The situation which you have created is intolerable. If you determine to fight us, if you insist upon war, war you shall have; but the time shall be of our choosing and not of yours, and that time shall be now." And that is where the present policy, the sheer bulldog piling up of armaments without reference to or effort towards a better political doctrine in Europe, inevitably leads.

CHAPTER III

IS THE POLITICAL REFORMATION POSSIBLE?

Men are little disposed to listen to reason, "therefore we should not talk reason"--Are men's ideas immutable?

We have seen, therefore--

1. That the need for defense arises from the existence of a motive for attack.

2. That that motive is, consequently, part of the problem of defense.

3. That, since as between the advanced peoples we are dealing with in this matter, one party is as able in the long run to pile up armaments as the other, we cannot get nearer to solution by armaments alone; we must get at the original provoking cause--the motive making for aggression.

4. That if that motive results from a true judgment of the facts; if the determining factor in a nation's well-being and progress is really its power to obtain by force advantage over others, the present situation of armament rivalry tempered by war is a natural and inevitable one.

5. That if, however, the view is a false one, our progress towards solution will be marked by the extent to which the error becomes generally recognized in international public opinion.

That brings me to the last entrenchment of those who actively or passively oppose propaganda looking towards reform in this matter.

As already pointed out, the last year or two has revealed a suggestive shifting of position on the part of such opposition. The original position of the defenders of the old political creeds was that the economic thesis here outlined was just simply wrong; then, that the principles themselves were sound enough, but that they were irrelevant, because not interests, but ideals, constituted the cause of conflict between nations. In reply to which, of course, came the query, What ideals, apart from questions of interest, lie at the bottom of the conflict which is the most typical of our time--what ideal motive is Germany, for instance, pursuing in its presumed aggression upon England? Consequently that position has generally been abandoned. Then we were told that men don't act by logic, but passion. Then the critics were asked how they explained the general character of *la haute politique*, its cold intrigues and expediency, the extraordinary rapid changes in alliances and *ententes*, all following exactly a line of passionless interest reasoned, though from false premises, with very great logic indeed; and were asked whether all experience does not show that, while passion may determine the energy with which a given line of conduct is pursued, the direction of that line of conduct is determined by processes of another kind: John, seeing James, his lifelong and long-sought enemy, in the distance, has his hatred passionately stirred, and harbors thoughts of murder. As he comes near he sees that it is not James at all, but a quiet and inoffensive neighbor, Peter. John's thoughts of murder are appeased, not because he has changed his nature, but because the recognition of a simple fact has changed the direction of his passion. What we in this matter hope to do is to show that the nations are mistaking Peter for James.

Well, the last entrenchment of those who oppose the work is the dogmatic assertion that though we are right as to the material fact, its demonstration can never be made; that this political reformation of Europe the political rationalists talk about is a hopeless matter; it implies a change of opinion so vast that it can only be looked for as the result of whole generations of educative processes.

Suppose this were true. What then? Will you leave everything severely alone, and leave wrong and dangerous ideas in undisturbed possession of the political field?

This conclusion is not a policy; it is Oriental fatalism--"Kismet," "the will of Allah."

Such an attitude is not possible among men dominated by the traditions and the impulses of the Western world. We do not let things slide in this way; we do not assume that as men are not guided by reason in politics, therefore we shall not reason about politics. The time of statesmen is absorbed in the discussion of these things. Our press and literature are deeply concerned in them. The talk and thought of men are about them. However little they may deem reason to affect the conduct of men, they go on reasoning. And progress in conduct is determined by the degree of understanding which results.

It is true that physical conflict marks the point at which the reason has failed; men fight when they have not been able to "come to an understanding" in the common phrase, which is for once correct. But is this a cause for deprecating the importance of clear understanding? Is it not, on the contrary, precisely why our energies should be devoted to improving our capacity for dealing with these things by reason, rather than by physical force?

Do we not inevitably arrive at the destination to which every road in this discussion leads? However we may start, with whatever plan, however elaborated or varied, the end is always the same--the progress of man in this matter depends upon the degree to which his ideas are just; man advances by the victories of his mind and character. Again we have arrived at the region of platitude. But also again it is one of those platitudes which most people deny. Thus the London *Spectator:*

For ourselves, as far as the main economic proposition goes, he preaches to the converted.... If nations were perfectly wise and held perfectly sound economic theories, they would recognize that exchange is the union of forces, and that it is very foolish to hate or be jealous of your co-operators.... Men are savage, bloodthirsty creatures ... and when their blood is up will fight for a word or a sign, or, as Mr. Angell would put it, for an illusion.

Criticism at the other end of the journalistic scale--that, for instance, from Mr. Blatchford--is of an exactly similar character. Mr. Blatchford says:

Mr. Angell may be right in his contention that modern war is unprofitable to both belligerents. I do not believe it, but he may be right. But he is wrong if he imagines that his theory will prevent European war. To prevent European wars it needs more than the truth of his theory: it needs that the war lords and diplomatists and financiers and workers of Europe shall believe the theory.... So long as the rulers of nations believe that war may be expedient (see Clausewitz), and so long as they believe they have the power, war will continue.... It will continue until these men are fully convinced that it will bring no advantage.

Therefore, argues Mr. Blatchford, the demonstration that war will not bring advantage is futile.

I am not here, for the purpose of controversy, putting an imaginary conclusion into Mr. Blatchford's mouth. It is the conclusion that he actually does draw. The article from which I have quoted was intended to demonstrate the futility of books like this. It was by way of reply to an early edition of this one. In common with the other critics, he must have known that this is not a plea for the impossibility of war (I have always urged with emphasis that our ignorance on this matter makes war not only possible, but extremely likely), but for its futility. And the demonstration of its futility is, I am now told, in itself futile!

I have expanded the arguments of this and others of my critics thus:

The war lords and diplomats are still wedded to the old false theories; *therefore* we shall leave those theories undisturbed, and generally deprecate discussion of them.

Nations do not realize the facts; *therefore* we should attach no importance to the work of making them known.

These facts profoundly affect the well-being of European peoples; *therefore* we shall not systematically encourage the efficient study of them.

If they were generally known, the practical outcome would be that most of our difficulties herein would disappear; *therefore* anyone who attempts to make them known is an amiable sentimentalist, a theorist, and so on, and so on.

"Things do not matter so much as people's opinions about things"[119]; *therefore* no effort shall be directed to a modification of opinion.

The only way for these truths to affect policy, to become operative in the conduct of nations, is to make them operative in the minds of men; *therefore* discussion of them is futile.

Our troubles arise from the wrong ideas of nations; *therefore* ideas do not count--they are "theories."

General conception and insight in this matter is vague and ill-defined, so that action is always in danger of being decided by sheer passion and irrationalism; *therefore* we shall do nothing to render insight clear and well-defined.

The empire of sheer impulse, of the non-rational, is strongest when associated with ignorance (*e.g.*, Mohammedan fanaticism, Chinese Box-erism), and only yields to the general progress of ideas (*e.g.*, sounder religious notions sweeping away the hate and horrors of religious perse-cution); *therefore* the best way to maintain peace is to pay no attention to the progress of political ideas.

The progress of ideas has completely transformed religious feeling in so far as it settles the policy of one religious group in relation to anoth-er; *therefore* the progress of ideas will never transform patriotic feeling, which settles the policy of one political group in relation to another.

What, in short, does the argument of my critics amount to? This: that so slow, so stupid is the world that, though the facts may be unassail-able, they will never be learned within any period that need concern us.

Without in the least desiring to score off my critics, and still less to be discourteous, I sometimes wonder it has never struck them that in the eyes of the profane this attitude of theirs must appear really as a most colossal vanity. "We" who write in newspapers and reviews understand these things; "we" can be guided by reason and wisdom, but the common clay will not see these truths for "thousands of years." I talk to the con-verted (so I am told) when my book is read by the editors and reviewers. *They*, of course, can understand; but the notion that mere diplomats and statesmen, the men who make up Governments and nations, should ever do so is, of course, quite too preposterous.

Personally, however flattering this notion might be, I have never been able to feel its soundness. I have always strongly felt the precise oppo-site--namely, that what is plain to me will very soon be equally plain to my neighbor. Possessing, presumably, as much vanity as most, I am, nevertheless, absolutely convinced that simple facts which stare an ordi-nary busy man of affairs in the face are not going to be forever hid from the multitude. Depend upon it, if "we" can see these things, so can the mere statesmen and diplomats and those who do the work of the world.

Moreover, if what "we" write in reviews and books does not touch men's reasons, does not affect their conduct, why do we write at all?

We do *not* believe it impossible to change or form men's ideas; such a plea would doom us all to silence, and would kill religious and political literature. "Public Opinion" is not external to men; it is made by men; by what they hear and read and have suggested to them by their daily tasks, and talk and contact.

If it *were* true, therefore, that the difficulties in the way of modifying political opinion were as vast as my critics would have us believe, that would not affect our conduct; the more they emphasize those difficulties, the more they emphasize the need for effort on our part.

But it is not true that a change such as that involved here necessarily "takes thousands of years." I have already dealt with the plea, but would recall only one incident that I have cited: a scene painted by a Spanish artist of the Court and nobles and populace in a great European city, gathered on a public holiday as for a festival to see a beautiful child burned to death for a faith that, as it plaintively said, it had sucked in with its mother's milk.

How long separates us from that scene? Why, not the lives of three ordinarily elderly people. And how long after that scene--which was not an isolated incident of uncommon kind, but a very everyday matter, typical of the ideas and feelings of the time at which it was enacted--was it before the renewal of such became a practical impossibility? It was not a hundred years. It was enacted in 1680, and within the space of a short lifetime the world knew that never again would a child be burned alive as the result of a legal condemnation by a duly constituted Court, and as a public festival, witnessed by the King and the nobles and the populace, in one of the great cities of Europe.

Or, do those who talk of "unchanging human nature" and "thousands of years" really plead that we are in danger of a repetition of such a scene? In that case our religious toleration is a mistake. Protestants stand in danger of such tortures, and should arm themselves with the old armory of religious combat--the rack, the thumbscrew, the iron maiden, and the rest--as a matter of sheer protection.

"Men are savage, bloodthirsty creatures, and will fight for a word or a sign," the *Spectator* tells us, when their patriotism is involved. Well, until yesterday, it was as true to say that of them when their religion was involved. Patriotism is the religion of politics. And as one of the greatest historians of religious ideas has pointed out, religion and patriotism are the chief moral influences moving great bodies of men, and "the separate modifications and mutual interaction of these two agents may almost be said to constitute the moral history of mankind."[120]

But is it likely that a general progress which has transformed religion is going to leave patriotism unaffected; that the rationalization and humanization which have taken place in the more complex domain of religious doctrine and belief will not also take place in the domain of politics? The problem of religious toleration was beset with difficulties incalculably greater than any which confront us in this problem. Then, as now, the old order was defended with real disinterestedness; then it was called religious fervor; now it is called patriotism. The best of the old inquisitors were as disinterested, as sincere, as single-minded, as are doubtless the best of the Prussian Junkers, the French Nationalists, the English militarists. Then, as now, the progress towards peace and security seemed to them a dangerous degeneration, the break-up of faiths, the undermining of most that holds society together. Then, as now, the old order pinned its faith to the tangible and visible instruments of protection--I mean the instruments of physical force. And the Catholic, in protecting himself by the Inquisition against what he regarded as the dangerous intrigues of the Protestant, was protecting what he regarded not merely as his own social and political security, but the eternal salvation, he believed, of un-born millions of men. Yet he surrendered such instruments of defense, and finally Catholic and Protestant alike came to see that the peace and security of both were far better assured by this intangible thing--the right thinking of men--than by all the mechanical ingenuity of prisons and tortures and burnings which it was possible to devise. In like manner will the patriot come finally to see that better than *Dreadnoughts* will be the recognition on his part and on the part of his prospective enemy, that there is no interest, material or moral, in conquest and military domina-tion?

And that hundred years which I have mentioned as representing an apparently impassable gulf in the progress of European ideas, a period which marked an evolution so great that the very mind and nature of men seemed to change, was a hundred years without newspapers--a time in which books were such a rarity that it took a generation for one to travel from Madrid to London; in which the steam printing-press did not exist, nor the railroad, nor the telegraph, nor any of those thousand contrivances which now make it possible for the words of an American statesman spoken to-day to be read by the millions of Europe to-morrow morning--to do, in short, more in the way of the dissemination of ideas in ten months than was possible then in a century.

When things moved so slowly, a generation or two sufficed to transform the mind of Europe on the religious side. Why should it be impossible to change that mind on the political side in a generation, or half a genera-tion, when things move so much more quickly? Are men less disposed to change their political than their religious opinions? We all know that *not* to be the case. In every country in Europe we find political parties advocating, or at least acquiescing in, policies which they strenuously opposed ten years ago. Does the evidence available go to show that the particular side of politics with which we are dealing is notably more im-pervious to change and development than the rest--less within the reach and influence of new ideas?

I must risk here the reproach of egotism and bad taste to call atten-tion to a fact which bears more directly on that point, perhaps, than any other that could be cited.

It is some fifteen years since it first struck me that certain economic facts of our civilization--facts of such visible and mechanical nature as reacting bourses and bank rate-movements, in all the economic capitals of the world, and so on--would soon force upon the attention of men a principle which, though existing for long past in some degree in human affairs, had not become operative to any extent. Was there any doubt as to the reality of the material facts involved? Circumstances of my occupa-tion happily furnished opportunities of discussing the matter thoroughly with bankers and statesmen of world-wide authority. There was no doubt on that score. Had we yet arrived at the point at which it was possible to make the matter plain to general opinion? Were politicians too ill-educated on the real facts of the world, too much absorbed in the rough-and-tumble of workaday politics to change old ideas? Were they, and the rank and file, still too enslaved by the hypnotism of an obsolete terminology to accept a new view? One could only put it to a practical test. A brief exposition of the cardinal principles was embodied in a brief pamphlet and published obscurely without advertisement, and bearing, necessarily, an unknown name. The result was, under the circumstances, startling, and certainly did not justify in the least the plea that there exists universal hostility to the advance of political rationalism. Encouragement came from most unlooked-for quarters: public men whose interests have been mainly military, alleged Jingoes, and even from soldiers. The more considerable edition has appeared in English, German, French, Dutch, Danish, Swedish, Spanish, Italian, Russian, Japanese, Erdu, Persian, and Hindustani, and nowhere has the Press completely ignored the book. Papers of Liberal tendencies have welcomed it everywhere. Those of more reactionary tendencies have been much less hostile than one could have expected.[121]

Does such an experience justify that universal rebelliousness to political rationalism on which my critics for the most part found their case? My object in calling attention to it is evident. If this is possible as the result of the effort of a single obscure person working without means and without leisure, what could not be accomplished by an organization adequately equipped and financed? Mr. Augustine Birrell says somewhere: "Some opinions, bold and erect as they may still stand, are in reality but empty shells. One shove would be fatal. Why is it not given?"

If little apparently has been done in the modification of ideas in this matter, it is because little relatively has been attempted. Millions of us are prepared to throw ourselves with energy into that part of national defense which, after all, is a makeshift, into agitation for the building of *Dreadnoughts* and the raising of armies, the things in fact which can be seen, where barely dozens will throw themselves with equal ardor into that other department of national defense, the only department which will really guarantee security, but by means which are invisible--the rationalization of ideas.

CHAPTER IV

METHODS

Relative failure of Hague Conferences and the cause--Public opinion the necessary motive force of national action--That opinion only stable if informed--"Friendship" between nations and its limitations--America's rôle in the coming "Political Reformation."

Much of the pessimism as to the possibility of any progress in this matter is based on the failure of such efforts as Hague Conferences. Never has the contest of armament been so keen as when Europe began to indulge in Peace Conferences. Speaking roughly and generally, the era of great armament expansion dates from the first Hague Conference.

Well, the reader who has appreciated the emphasis laid in the preceding pages on working through the reform of ideas will not feel much astonishment at the failure of efforts such as these. The Hague Conferences represented an attempt not to work through the reform of ideas, but to modify by mechanical means the political machinery of Europe, without reference to the ideas which had brought it into existence.

Arbitration treaties, Hague Conferences, International Federation involve a new conception of relationship between nations. But the ideals--political, economical, and social--on which the old conceptions are based, our terminology, our political literature, our old habits of thought, diplomatic inertia, which all combine to perpetuate the old notions, have been left serenely undisturbed. And surprise is expressed that such schemes do not succeed.

French politics have given us this proverb, "I am the leader, therefore I follow." This is not mere cynicism, but expresses in reality a profound truth. What is a leader or a ruler in a modern parliamentary sense? He is a man who holds office by virtue of the fact that he represents the mean of opinion in his party. Initiative, therefore, cannot come from him until he can be sure of the support of his party--that is, until the initiative in question represents the common opinion of his party. The author happened to discuss the views embodied in this book with a French parliamentary chief, who said in effect: "Of course you are talking to the converted, but I am helpless. Suppose that I attempted to embody these views before they were ready for acceptance by my party. I should simply lose my leadership in favor of a man less open to new ideas, and the prospect of their acceptance would not be increased, but diminished. Even if I were not already converted, it would be no good trying to convert me. Convert the body of the party and its leaders will not need conversion."

And this is the position of every civilized government, parliamentary or not. The struggle for religious freedom was not gained by agreements drawn up between Catholic States and Protestant States, or even between Catholic bodies and Protestant bodies. No such process was possible, for in the last resort there was no such thing as an absolutely Catholic State or an absolutely Protestant one. Our security from persecution is due simply to the general recognition of the futility of the employment of physical force in a matter of religious belief. Our progress towards political rationalism will take place in like manner.

There is no royal road of this kind to a better state. It seems decreed that we shall not permanently achieve improvement which we as individuals have not paid for in the coin of hard thinking.

Nothing is easier to achieve in international politics than academic declarations in favor of Peace. But governments being trustees have a first duty in the interests of their wards, or what they conceive to be such interests, and they disregard what is still looked upon as a conception having its origin in altruistic and self-sacrificing motives. "Self-sacrifice" is the last motive governments can allow themselves to consider. They are created to protect, not to sacrifice, the interests of which they are placed in charge.

It is impossible for governments to base their normal policies on conceptions which are in advance of the general standard of the political opinion of the people from whom they derive their power. The average man will, it is true, quite readily subscribe abstractly to a peace ideal, just as he will subscribe abstractly to certain religious ideals--to take no thought for the morrow, not to save up treasure upon earth--without the faintest notion of making them a guide of conduct, or, indeed, of seeing how they *can* be a guide of conduct. At peace meetings he will cheer lustily and sign petitions, because he believes Peace to be a great moral idea, and that armies, like the Police, are destined to disappear one day--on about the same day in his belief--when the nature of man shall have been altered.

One may be able fully to appreciate this attitude of the "average sensual man" without doubting the least in the world the sincerity, genuineness, wholeheartedness of these emotional movements in favor of peace, which from time to time sweep over a country (as on the occasion of the Taft-Grey exchange of views on arbitration). But what it is necessary to emphasize, what cannot be too often reiterated, is that these movements, however emotional and sincere, are not movements which can lead to breaking up the intellectual basis of the policy which produces armaments in the Western World. These movements embrace only one section of the factors making for peace--the moral and the emotional. And while those factors have immense power, they are uncertain and erratic in their operation, and when the shouting dies and there is a natural reaction from emotion, and it is a question once more of doing the humdrum week-day work of the world, of pushing our interests, of finding markets, of achieving the best possible generally for our nation as against other nations, of preparing for the future, of organizing one's efforts, the old code of compromise between the ideal and the necessary will be as operative as ever. So long as his notions of what war can accomplish in an economic or commercial sense remain what they are, the average man will not deem that his prospective enemy is likely to make the peace ideal a guide of conduct. Incidentally he would be right. At the bottom of his mind--and I say this not lightly and as a guess, but as an absolute conviction after very close observation--the ideal of peace is conceived as a demand that he weaken his own defenses on no better assurance than that his prospective rival or enemy will be well-behaved and not wicked enough to attack him.

It appeals to him as about equivalent to asking that he shall not lock his doors because to suppose people will rob him is to have a low view of human nature!

Though he believes his own position in the world (as a colonial Power, etc.) to be the result of the use of force by himself, of his readiness to seize what could be seized, he is asked to believe that foreigners will not do in the future what he himself has done in the past. He finds this difficult to swallow.

Save in his Sunday moods, the whole thing makes him angry. It appeals to him as "unfair," in that he is asked by his own countrymen to do something that they apparently do not ask of foreigners; it appears to him as unmanly, in that he is asked to surrender the advantage which his strength has secured him in favor of a somewhat emasculate ideal.

The patriot feels that his moral intention is every bit as sincere as that of the pacifist--that, indeed, patriotism is a finer moral ideal than pacifism. The difference between the pacifist and the advocate of *realpolitik* is an intellectual and not a moral one at all, and the assumption of superior morality which the former sometimes makes does the cause which he has at heart infinite harm. Until the pacifist can show that the employment of military force fails to secure material advantage, the common man will, in ordinary times, continue to believe that the militarist has a moral sanction as great as that underlying pacifism.

It may seem gratuitously ungracious to suggest that the very elevation which has marked peace propaganda in the past should have been the very thing that has sometimes stood in the way of its success. But such a phenomenon is not new in human development. There was as much good intention in the world of religious warfare and oppression as there is in ours. Indeed, the very earnestness of the men who burnt, tortured, and imprisoned and stamped out human thought with the very best motives, was precisely the factor which stood in the way of improvement.

Improvement came finally, not from better intention, but from an acuter use of the intelligence of men, from hard mental work.

So long as we assume that high motive, a better moral tone is all that is needed in international relations, and that an understanding of these problems will in some wonderful way come of itself, without hard and systematic intellectual effort, we shall make little headway.

Good feeling and kindliness and a ready emotion are among the most precious things in life, but they are qualities possessed by some of the most retrograde nations in the world, because in them they are not coupled with the homely quality of hard work, in which one may include hard thinking. This last is the real price of progress, and we shall make none of worth unless we pay it.

A word or two as to the rôle of "friendship" in international relations. Courtesy and a certain measure of good faith are essential elements wherever civilized men come in direct contact; without them organized society would go to pieces. But these invaluable elements never yet of themselves settled real differences; they merely render the other factors of adjustment possible. Why should one expect courtesy and good-fellowship to settle grave political differences between English and Germans when they altogether fail to settle such differences between English and English? What should we say of a statesman professing to be serious who suggested that all would be well between President Wilson and the lobbyists concerning the tariff, between the Democrats and Republicans on protection, between the millionaire and the day laborer on the question of the income tax, and a thousand and one other things--that all these knotty problems would disappear, if only the respective protagonists could be persuaded to take lunch together? Is it not a little childish?

Yet I am bound to admit that a whole school of persons who deal with international problems would have us believe that all international differences would disappear if only we could have enough junketings, dinner-parties, exchange visits of clergymen, and what not. These things have immense use in so far as they facilitate discussion and the elucidation of the policy in which the rivalry has its birth, and to that extent only. But if they are not vehicles of intellectual comprehension, if the parties go away with as little understanding of the factors and nature of international relationship as they had before such meetings took place, they have served no purpose whatsoever.

The work of the world does not get done merely by being good friends with everybody; the problems of international diplomacy are not to be solved merely by a sort of international picnic; that would make the world too easy a place to live in.

However ungracious it may seem, it is nevertheless dangerous to allow to go unchallenged the notion that the cultivation of "friendship and affection" between nations, irrespective of the other factors affecting their relationship, can ever seriously modify international politics. The matter is of grave importance, because so much good effort is spent in putting the cart before the horse, and attempting to create an operative factor out of a sentiment that can never be constant and positive one way or the other, since it must in the nature of things be largely artificial. It is a psychological impossibility in any ordinary workaday circumstances to have any special feeling of affection for a hundred or sixty or forty millions of people, composed of infinitely diverse elements, good, bad, and indifferent, noble and mean, pleasing and unpleasing, whom, moreover, we have never seen and never shall see. It is too large an order. We might as well be asked to entertain feelings of affection for the Tropic of Capricorn. As I have already hinted, we have no particular affection for the great mass of our own countrymen--your lobbyist enthusiast for Mr. Wilson, your railroad striker for the employer of labor, your Suffragette for your anti-Suffragette, and so on *ad infinitum.* Patriotism has nothing to do with it. The patriot is often the person who had the heartiest detestation for a large mass of his fellow-countrymen. Consider any anti-administration literature. As an English instance a glance at Mr. Leo Maxse's monthly masterpieces of epithet-making, or at what the pan-Germans have to say of their own Empire and Government ("poltroons in the pay of the English" is a choice tit-bit I select from one German newspaper), will soon convince one.

Why, therefore, should we be asked to entertain for foreigners a sentiment we do not give to our own people? And not only to entertain that sentiment, but to make (always in the terms of the present political beliefs) great sacrifices on behalf of it!

Need it be said that I have not the least desire to deprecate sincere emotion as a factor in progress? Emotion and enthusiasm form the divine stimulus without which no great things would be achieved; but emotion divorced from mental and moral discipline is not the kind on which wise men will place a very high value. Some of the intensest emotion of the world has been given to some of the worst possible objects. Just as in the physical world, the same forces--steam, gunpowder, what you will--which, controlled and directed may do an infinitely useful work--may, uncontrolled, cause accidents and catastrophes of the gravest kind.

Nor is it true that the better understanding of this matter is beyond the great mass of men, that sounder ideas depend upon the comprehension of complex and abstruse points, correct judgment in intricate matters of finance or economics. Things which seem in one stage of thought obscure and difficult are cleared up merely by setting one or two crooked facts straight. The rationalists, who a generation or two ago struggled with such things as the prevalent belief in witchcraft, may have deemed that the abolition of superstitions of this kind would take "thousands of years."

Lecky has pointed out that during the eighteenth century many judges in Europe--not ignorant men, but, on the contrary, exceedingly well-educated men, trained to sift evidence--were condemning people to death by hundreds for witchcraft. Acute and educated men still believed in it; its disproof demanded a large acquaintance with the forces and processes of physical nature, and it was generally thought that, while a few exceptional intelligences here and there would shake off these beliefs, they would remain indefinitely the possessions of the great mass of mankind.

What has happened? A schoolboy to-day would scout the evidence which, on the judgment of very learned men, sent thousands of poor wretches to their doom in the eighteenth century. Would the schoolboy necessarily be more learned or more acute than those judges? They probably knew a great deal about the science of witchcraft, were more familiar with its literature, with the arguments which supported it, and they would have hopelessly worsted any nineteenth-century schoolboy in any argument on the subject. The point is, however, that the schoolboy would have two or three essential facts straight, instead of getting them crooked.

All the fine theories about the advantages of conquest, of territorial aggrandizement, so learnedly advanced by the Mahans and the von Stengels; the immense value which the present-day politician attaches to foreign conquest, all these absurd rivalries aiming at "stealing" one another's territory, will be recognized as the preposterous illusions that they are by the younger mind, which really sees the quite plain fact that the citizen of a small State is just as well off as the citizen of a great. From that fact, which is not complex or difficult in the least, will emerge the truth that modern government is a matter of administration, and that it can no more profit a community to annex other communities, than it could profit London to annex Manchester. These things will not need argument to be clear to the schoolboy of the future--they will be self-evident, like the improbability of an old woman causing a storm at sea.

Of course, it is true that many of the factors bearing on this improvement will be indirect. As our education becomes more rational in other fields, it will make for understanding in this; as the visible factors of our civilization make plain--as they are making plainer every day--the unity and interdependence of the modern world, the attempt to separate those interdependent activities by irrelevant divisions must more and more break down. All improvement in human co-operation--and human co-operation is a synonym for civilization--must help the work of those laboring in the field of international relationship. But again I would re-iterate that the work of the world does not get itself done. It is done by men; ideas do not improve themselves, they are improved by the thought of men; and it is the efficiency of the conscious effort which will mainly determine progress.

When all nations realize that if England can no longer exert force towards her Colonies, others certainly could not; that if a great modern Empire cannot usefully employ force as against communities that it "owns," still less can we employ it usefully against communities that we do not "own"; when the world as a whole has learned the real lesson of British Imperial development, not only will that Empire have achieved greater security than it can achieve by battleships, but it will have played a part in human affairs incomparably greater and more useful than could be played by any military "leadership of the human race," that futile duplication of the Napoleonic rôle, which Imperialists of a certain school seem to dream for us.

It is to Anglo-Saxon practice, and to Anglo-Saxon experience, that the world will look as a guide in this matter. The extension of the dominating principle of the British Empire to European society as a whole is the solution of the international problem which this book urges. That extension cannot be made by military means. The English conquest of great military nations is a physical impossibility, and it would involve the collapse of the principle upon which the Empire is based if it were. The day for progress by force has passed; it will be progress by ideas or not at all.

Because these principles of free human co-operation between communities are, in a special sense, an Anglo-Saxon development, it is upon us that there falls the responsibility of giving a lead. If it does not come from us, who have developed these principles as between all the communities which have sprung from the Anglo-Saxon race, can we ask to have it given elsewhere? If we have not faith in our own principles, to whom shall we look?

English thought gave us the science of political economy; Anglo-Saxon thought and practice must give us another science, that of International Polity--the science of the political relationship of human groups. We have the beginnings of it, but it sadly needs systemization--recognition by those intellectually equipped to develop it and enlarge it.

The developments of such a work would be in keeping with the contributions which the practical genius and the positive spirit of the Anglo-Saxon race have already made to human progress.

I believe that, if the matter were put efficiently before them with the force of that sane, practical, disinterested labor and organization which have been so serviceable in the past in other forms of propaganda--not only would they prove particularly responsive to the labor, but Anglo-Saxon tradition would once more be associated with the leadership in one of those great moral and intellectual movements which would be so fitting a sequel to our leadership in such things as human freedom and parliamentary government. Failing such effort and such response, what are we to look for? Are we, in blind obedience to primitive instinct and old prejudices, enslaved by the old catchwords and that curious indolence which makes the revision of old ideas unpleasant, to duplicate indefinitely on the political and economic side a condition from which we have liberated ourselves on the religious side? Are we to continue to struggle, as so many good men struggled in the first dozen centuries of Christendom--spilling oceans of blood, wasting mountains of treasure--to achieve what is at bottom a logical absurdity; to accomplish something which, when accomplished, can avail us nothing, and which, if it could avail us anything, would condemn the nations of the world to never-ending bloodshed and the constant defeat of all those aims which men, in their sober hours, know to be alone worthy of sustained endeavor?

APPENDIX

ON RECENT EVENTS IN EUROPE

At the outbreak of the Balkan War "The Great Illusion" was subjected to much criticism, on the ground that the war tended to disprove its theses. The following quotations, one from Mr. Churchill, the First Lord of the Admiralty, and the other from the English *Review of Reviews*, are typical of many others.

Mr. Churchill said, in a speech at Sheffield:

Whether we blame the belligerents or criticize the powers, or sit in sackcloth and ashes ourselves is absolutely of no consequence at the present moment....

We have sometimes been assured by persons who profess to know that the danger of war has become an illusion.... Well, here is a war which has broken out in spite of all that rulers and diplomatists could do to prevent it, a war in which the Press has had no part, a war which the whole force of the money power has been subtly and steadfastly directed to prevent, which has come upon us, not through the ignorance or credulity of the people, but, on the contrary, through their knowledge of their history and their destiny, and through their intense realization of their wrongs and of their duties, as they conceived them, a war which from all these causes has burst upon us with all the force of a spontaneous explosion, and which in strife and destruction has carried all before it. Face to face with this manifestation, who is the man bold enough to say that force is never a remedy? Who is the man who is foolish enough to say that martial virtues do not play a vital part in the health and honor of every people? (Cheers.) Who is the man who is vain enough to suppose that the long antagonisms of history and of time can in all circumstances be adjusted by the smooth and superficial conventions of politicians and ambassadors?

The London *Review of Reviews* said in an article on "The Débâcle of Norman Angell":

Mr. Norman Angell's theory was one to enable the citizens of this country to sleep quietly, and to lull into false security the citizens of all great countries. That is undoubtedly the reason why he met with so much success.... It was a very comfortable theory for those nations which have grown rich and whose ideals and initiative have been sapped by over-much prosperity. But the great delusion of Norman Angell, which led to the writing of "The Great Illusion," has been dispelled forever by the Balkan League. In this connection it is of value to quote the words of Mr. Winston Churchill, which give very adequately the reality as opposed to theory.

In reply to these and similar criticisms I wrote several articles in the London Press, from which the following few pages are selected.

What has Pacifism, Old or New, to say now?

Is War impossible?

Is it unlikely?

Is it futile?

Is not force a remedy, and at times the only remedy?

Could any remedy have been devised on the whole as conclusive and complete as that used by the Balkan peoples?

Have not the Balkan peoples redeemed War from the charges too readily brought against it as simply an instrument of barbarism?

Have questions of profit and loss, economic considerations, anything whatever to do with this war?

Would the demonstration of its economic futility have kept the peace?

Are theories and logic of the slightest use, since force alone can determine the issue?

Is not war therefore inevitable and must we not prepare diligently for it?

I will answer all these quite simply and directly without casuistry or logic-chopping and honestly desiring to avoid paradox and "cleverness." Nor will these quite simple answers be in contradiction to anything that I have written, nor will they invalidate any of the principles I have attempted to explain.

My answers may be summarized thus:

(1) This war has justified both the Old Pacifism and the New. By universal admission events have proved that the Pacifists who opposed the Crimean War were right and their opponents wrong. Had public opinion given more consideration to those Pacifist principles, this country would not have "backed the wrong horse" and this war, two wars which have preceded it and many of the abominations of which the Balkan peninsula has been the scene during the last 60 years might have been avoided. In any case Great Britain would not now carry upon her shoulders the responsibility of having during half a century supported the Turk against the Christian and of having tried uselessly to prevent what has now taken place--the break-up of the Turk's rule in Europe.

(2) War is not impossible, and no responsible Pacifist ever said it was; it is not the likelihood of war which is the illusion, but its benefits.

(3) It is likely or unlikely according as the parties to a dispute are guided by wisdom or folly.

(4) It *is* futile and force is no remedy.

(5) Its futility is proven by the war waged daily by the Turks as conquerors, during the last 400 years. And if the Balkan peoples choose the less evil of two kinds of war and will use their victory to bring a system based on force and conquest to an end, we who do not believe in force and conquest will rejoice in their action and believe it will achieve immense

benefits. But if instead of using their victory to eliminate force, they in their turn pin their faith to it, continue to use it the one against the other and to exploit by its means the populations they rule; if they become not the organizers of social co-operation among the Balkan populations, but merely, like the Turks, their conquerors and "owners," then they in their turn will share the fate of the Turks.

(6) The fundamental causes of this war are economic in the narrower, as well as in the larger sense of the term; in the first because conquest was the Turk's only trade--he desired to live out of taxes wrung from a conquered people, to exploit them as a means of livelihood, and this conception was at the root of most of Turkish misgovernment. And in the larger sense its cause is economic because in the Balkans, remote geographically from the main drift of European economic development, there has not grown up that interdependent social life, the innumerable contacts which in the rest of Europe have done so much to attenuate primitive religious and racial hatreds.

(7) A better understanding by the Turk of the real nature of civilized government, of the economic futility of conquest, of the fact that a means of livelihood (an economic system) based upon having more force than someone else and using it ruthlessly against him is an impossible form of human relationship bound to break down, *would* have kept the peace.

(8) If European statecraft had not been animated by false conceptions, largely economic in origin, based upon a belief in the necessary rivalry of states, the advantages of preponderant force and conquest, the Western nations could have composed their quarrels and ended the abominations of the Balkan peninsula long ago--even in the opinion of the *Times*. And it is our own false statecraft--that of Great Britain--which has a large part of the responsibility for this failure of European civilization. It has caused us to sustain the Turk in Europe, to fight a great and popular war with that aim, and led us into treaties which, had they been kept, would have obliged us to fight to-day on the side of the Turk against the Balkan States.

(9) If by "theories" and "logic" is meant the discussion of and interest in principles, the ideas that govern human relationship, they are the only things that can prevent future wars, just as they were the only things that brought religious wars to an end--a preponderant power "imposing" peace playing no rôle therein. Just as it was false religious theories which made the religious wars, so it is false political theories which make the political wars.

(10) War is only inevitable in the sense that other forms of error and passion--religious persecution for instance--are inevitable; they cease with better understanding, as the attempt to impose religious belief by force has ceased in Europe.

(11) We should not prepare for war; we should prepare to prevent war; and though that preparation may include battleships and conscription, those elements will quite obviously make the tension and danger greater

unless there is also a better European opinion.

These summarized replies need a little expansion.

Had we thrashed out the question of war and peace as we must finally, it would hardly be necessary to explain that the apparent paradox in Answer No. 4 (that war is futile, and that this war will have immense benefits) is due to the inadequacy of our language, which compels us to use the same word for two opposed purposes, not to any real contradiction of fact.

We called the condition of the Balkan peninsula "Peace" until the attack was made on Turkey merely because the respective Ambassadors still happened to be resident in the capitals to which they were accredited.

Let us see what "Peace" under Turkish rule really meant and who is the real invader in this war. Here is a very friendly and impartial witness--Sir Charles Elliot--who paints for us the character of the Turk as an "administrator":

The Turk in Europe has an overweening sense of his superiority, and remains a nation apart, mixing little with the conquered populations, whose customs and ideas he tolerates, but makes little effort to understand. The expression, indeed, "Turkey in Europe" means indeed no more than "England in Asia," if used as a designation for India.... The Turks have done little to assimilate the people whom they have conquered, and still less, been assimilated by them. In the larger part of the Turkish dominions, the Turks themselves are in a minority.... The Turks certainly resent the dismemberment of their Empire, but not in the sense in which the French resent the conquest of Alsace-Lorraine by Germany. They would never use the word "Turkey" or even its oriental equivalent, "The High Country" in ordinary conversation. They would never say that Syria and Greece are parts of Turkey which have been detached, but merely that they are tributaries which have become independent, provinces once occupied by Turks where there are no Turks now. As soon as a province passes under another Government, the Turks find it the most natural thing in the world to leave it and go somewhere else. In the same spirit the Turk talks quite pleasantly of leaving Constantinople someday, he will go over to Asia and found another capital. One can hardly imagine Englishmen speaking like that of London, but they might conceivably speak so of Calcutta.... The Turk is a conqueror and nothing else. The history of the Turk is a catalogue of battles. His contributions to art, literature, science, and religion, are practically nil. Their desire has not been to instruct, to improve, hardly even to govern, but simply to conquer.... The Turk makes nothing at all; he takes whatever he can get, as plunder or pillage. He lives in the houses which he finds, or which he orders to be built for him. In unfavorable circumstances he is a marauder. In favorable, a *Grand Seigneur* who thinks it his right to enjoy with grace and dignity all that the world can hold, but who will not lower himself by engaging in art, literature, trade, or manufacture. Why should he, when there are other people to do these things for him. Indeed, it may be said that he takes from others even his religion, clothes, language, customs; there is hardly anything which is Turkish and not borrowed. The religion is Arabic; the language half Arabic and Persian; the literature almost entirely imitative; the art Persian or Byzantine; the costumes, in the Upper Classes and Army mostly European. There is nothing characteristic in manufacture or commerce, except an aversion to such pursuits. In fact, all occupations, except agriculture and military service are distasteful to the true Osmanli. He is not much of a merchant. He may keep a stall in a bazaar, but his operations are rarely undertaken on a scale which merits the name of commerce or finance. It is strange to observe how, when trade becomes active in any seaport, or upon the railway lines, the Osmanli retires and disappears, while Greeks, Armenians, and Levantines thrive in his place. Neither does he much affect law, medicine or the learned professions. Such callings are followed by Moslems but they are apt to be of non-Turkish race. But though he does none of these things ... the Turk is a soldier. The moment a sword or rifle is put into his hands, he instinctively knows how to use it with effect, and feels at home in the ranks or on a horse. The Turkish Army is not so much a profession or an institution necessitated by the fears and aims of the Government as the quite normal state of the Turkish nation.... Every Turk is a born soldier, and adopts other pursuits chiefly because times are bad. When there is a question of fighting, if only in a riot, the stolid peasant wakes up and shows surprising power of finding organization and expedients, and alas! a surprising ferocity. The ordinary Turk is an honest and good-humored soul, kind to children and animals, and very patient; but when the fighting spirit comes on him, he becomes like the terrible warriors of the Huns or Genghis Khan, and slays, burns, and ravages without mercy or discrimination.[122]

Such is the verdict of an instructed, travelled, and observant English author and diplomatist, who lived among these people for many years and who learned to like them, who studied them and their history. It does not differ, of course, appreciably, from what practically every student of the Turk has discovered: the Turk is the typical conqueror. His nation has lived by the sword and to-day he is dying by the sword, because the sword, the mere exercise of force by one man or group of men upon another, conquest in other words, is an impossible form of human relationship.

In order to maintain this evil form of relationship--its evil and futility constitute the whole basis of the principles I have attempted to illustrate--he has not even observed the rough chivalry of the brigand. The brigand, though he might knock men on the head, will refrain from having his force take the form of butchering women and disemboweling children. Not so the Turk. His attempt at Government will take the form of the obscene torture of children, of a bestial ferocity which is not a matter of dispute or exaggeration, but a thing to which scores, hundreds, thousands even of credible European witnesses have testified. "The finest gentleman, sir, that ever butchered a woman or burned a village," is the phrase that *Punch* most justly puts into the mouth of the defender of our traditional Turcophil policy.

This condition is "Peace" and the act which would put a stop to it is "War"! It is the inexactitude and inadequacy of our language which create much of the confusion of thought in this matter; we have the same term for action destined to achieve a given end and for counter-action destined to prevent it.

Yet we manage in other than the international field, in civil matters, to make the thing clear enough.

Once an American town was set on fire by incendiaries and was threatened with destruction. In order to save at least a part of it the authorities deliberately burned down a block of buildings in the pathway of the fire. Would those incendiaries be entitled to say that the town authorities were incendiaries also and "believed in setting fire to towns"? Yet this is precisely the point of view of those who tax Pacifists with approving war because they approve the measure aimed at bringing it to an end.

Put it another way. You do not believe that force should determine the transfer of property or conformity to a creed, and I say to you: "Hand me your purse and conform to my creed or I kill you." You say: "Because I do not believe that force should settle these matters, I shall try to prevent it settling them; therefore if you attack I shall resist; if I did not I should be allowing force to settle them." I attack; you resist and disarm me and say: "My force having neutralized yours and, the equilibrium being now established, I will hear any reasons you may have to urge for my paying you money or any argument in favor of your creed. Reason, understanding, adjustment shall settle it." You would be a Pacifist. Or, if you deem that that word connotes non-resistance, though to the immense bulk of Pacifists it does not, you would be an Anti-bellicist, to use a dreadful word coined by M. Emile Faguet in the discussion of this matter. If however you said: "Having disarmed you and established the equilibrium, I shall now upset it in my favor by taking your weapon and using it against you unless you hand me *your* purse and subscribe to *my* creed. I do this because force alone can determine issues and because it is a law of life that the strong should eat up the weak," you would then be a Bellicist.

In the same way, when we prevent the brigand from carrying on his trade--taking wealth by force--it is not because we believe in force as a means of livelihood, but precisely because we do not. And if, in preventing the brigand from knocking out brains, we are compelled to knock out his brains, is it because we believe in knocking out people's brains? Or would we urge that to do so is the way to carry on a trade or to govern a nation or that it could be the basis of human relationship?

In every civilized country, the basis of the relationship on which the community rests is this: no individual is allowed to settle his differences with another by force. But does this mean that if one threatens to take my purse, I am not allowed to use force to prevent it? That if he threatens to kill me, I am not to defend myself, because "the individual citizens are not allowed to settle their differences by force"? It is *because* of that, because the act of self-defense is an attempt to prevent the settlement of a difference by force, that the law justifies it.[123]

But the law would not justify me if, having disarmed my opponent, having neutralized his force by my own and re-established the social equilibrium, I immediately proceeded to upset it by asking him for his purse on pain of murder. I should then be settling the matter by force--I should then have ceased to be a Pacifist and have become a Bellicist.

For that is the difference between the two conceptions; the Bellicist says: "Force alone can settle these matters; it is the final appeal, therefore fight it out; let the best man win. When you have preponderant strength, impose your view; force the other man to your will; not because it is right, but because you are able to do so." It is the "excellent policy" which Lord Roberts attributes to Germany and approves.

We Anti-bellicists take an exactly contrary view. We say: "To fight it out settles nothing, since it is not a question of who is stronger, but of whose view is best and, as that is not always easy to establish, it is of the utmost importance in the interest of all parties, in the long run, to keep force out of it."

The former is the policy of the Turks. They have been obsessed with the idea that, if only they had enough of physical force ruthlessly exercised, they could solve the whole question of government, of existence for that matter, without troubling about social adjustment, understanding, equity, law, commerce; that "blood and iron" were all that was needed. The success of that policy can now be judged.

Good or evil will come of the present war according as the Balkan States are on the whole guided by the Bellicist or by the opposed principle. If, having now momentarily eliminated force as between themselves, they re-introduce it; if the strongest, presumably Bulgaria,[124] adopts Lord Roberts's "excellent policy" of striking because she has the preponderant force, enters upon a career of conquest of other members of the Balkan League and of the populations of the conquered territories and uses them for exploitation by military force--why then there will be no settlement and this war will have accomplished nothing save futile waste and slaughter. For they will have taken under a new flag, the pathway of the Turk to savagery, degeneration, death.

If on the other hand they are guided more by the Pacifist principle, if they believe that co-operation among States is better than conflict, if they believe that the common interest of all in good Government is greater than the special interest of anyone in conquest, that the understanding of human relationships, the capacity for the organization of society are the means by which men progress and not the imposition of force by one man or group upon another, why, they will have taken the pathway to better civilization. But then they will have disregarded Lord Roberts's advice.

This distinction between the two systems, far from being a matter of abstract theory of metaphysics or logic-chopping, is just the difference which distinguishes the Anglo-Saxon from the Turk, which distinguishes America from Turkey. The Turk has as much physical vigor as the American, is as virile, manly, and military. The Turk has the same raw materials of Nature, soil, and water. There is no difference in the capacity for the exercise of physical force--or if there is, the difference is in favor of the Turk. The real difference is a difference of ideas, of mind, outlook on the part of the individuals composing the respective societies; the Turk has one general conception of human society and the code and principles upon which it is founded, mainly a Militarist one; the American has another, mainly a Pacifist one. And whether the European society as a whole is to drift towards the Turkish ideal or towards the Anglo-Saxon ideal will depend upon whether it is animated mainly by the Pacifist or mainly by the Bellicist doctrine; if the former, it will stagger blindly like the Turk along the path to barbarism; if the latter, it will take a better road.

In dealing with answer No. 4 I have shown how the ambiguity of terms[125] used leads us so much astray in our notions of the real rôle of force in human relationships. But there is a curious phenomenon of thought which explains perhaps still more how misconceptions grow up on this subject and that is the habit of thinking of a war which, of course, must include two parties in terms solely of one party at a time. Thus one critic[126] is quite sure that because the Balkan peoples "recked nothing of financial disaster," economic considerations have had nothing to do with their war--a conclusion which seems to be arrived at by the process of judgment just indicated: to find the cause of conditions produced by two parties you shall rigorously ignore one. For there is a great deal of internal evidence for believing that the writer of the article in question would admit very readily that the efforts of the Turk to wring taxes out of the conquered peoples--not in return for a civilized administration, but simply as the means of livelihood, of turning conquest into a trade--had a very great deal to do in explaining the Turk's presence there at all and the Christian's desire to get rid of him; while the same article specifically states that the mutual jealousies of the great Powers, based on a desire to "grab" (an economic motive), had a great deal to do with preventing a peaceful settlement of the difficulties. Yet "economics" have nothing to do with it!

I have attempted elsewhere to make these two points--that it is on the one hand the false economics of the Turks and on the other hand the false economics of the Powers of Europe, coloring the policy and statecraft of both, which have played an enormous, in all human probability, a determining rôle in the immediate cause of the war; and, of course, a further and more remote cause of the whole difficulty is the fact that the Balkan peoples, never having been subjected to the discipline of that complex social life which arises from trade and commerce have not, or at least not so completely, outgrown those primitive racial and religious hostilities which at one time in Europe as a whole provoked conflicts like that now raging in the Balkans. The following article which appeared[127] at the outbreak of the war may summarize some of the points with which we have been dealing:--

"Polite and good-natured people think it rude to say 'Balkans' if a Pacifist be present. Yet I never understood why, and I understand now less than ever. It carries the implication that because war has broken out that fact disposes of all objection to it. The armies are at grips, therefore peace is a mistake. Passion reigns in the Balkans, therefore passion is preferable to reason.

"I suppose cannibalism and infanticide, polygamy, judicial torture, religious persecution, witchcraft, during all the years we did these 'inevitable' things, were defended in the same way, and those who resented all criticism of them pointed in triumph to the cannibal feast, the dead child, the maimed witness, the slain heretic, or the burned witch. But the fact did not prove the wisdom of those habits, still less their inevitability; for we have them no more.

"We are all agreed as to the fundamental cause of the Balkan trouble: the hate born of religious, racial, national, and linguistic differences; the attempt of an alien conqueror to live parasitically upon the conquered, and the desire of conqueror and conquered alike to satisfy in massacre and bloodshed the rancor of fanaticism and hatred.

"Well, in these islands, not so very long ago, those things were causes of bloodshed; indeed, they were a common feature of European life. But if they are inevitable in human relationship, how comes it that Adana is no longer duplicated by St. Bartholomew; the Bulgarian bands by the vendetta of the Highlander and the Lowlander; the struggle of the Slav and Turk, Serb and Bulgar, by that of Scots and English, and English and Welsh? The fanaticism of the Moslem to-day is no more intense than that of Catholic and heretic in Rome, Madrid, Paris, and Geneva at a time which is only separated from us by the lives of three or four elderly men. The heretic or infidel was then in Europe also a thing unclean and horrifying, exciting in the mind of the orthodox a sincere and honest hatred and a (very largely satisfied) desire to kill. The Catholic of the 16th century was apt to tell you that he could not sit at table with a heretic because the latter carried with him a distinctive and overpoweringly repulsive odor. If you would measure the distance Europe has travelled, think what this means: all the nations of Christendom united in a war lasting 200 years for the capture of the Holy Sepulcher; and yet, when in our day their representatives, seated round a table, could have had it for the asking, they did not deem it worth the asking, so little of the ancient passion was there left. The very nature of man seemed to be transformed. For, wonderful though it be that orthodox should cease killing heretic, infinitely more wonderful still is it that he should cease wanting to kill him.

"Just as most of us are certain that the underlying causes of this conflict are 'inevitable' and 'inherent in unchanging human nature,' so are we certain that so *un*-human a thing as economics can have no bearing on it.

"Well, I will suggest that the transformation of the heretic-hating and heretic-killing European is due mainly to economic forces; that it is because the drift of those forces has to so great a degree left the Balkans, where until yesterday the people lived a life little different from that which they lived in the time of Abraham, unaffected that war is now raging; that economic factors of a more immediate kind form a large part of the provoking cause of that war; and that a better comprehension by great nations of Europe of certain economic facts of their international relationship is essential before much progress towards solution can be made.

"But then by 'economics' of course I mean, not a merchant's profit or a money-lender's interest, but the method by which men earn their bread, which must also mean the kind of life they lead.

"We generally think of the primitive life of man--that of the herdsman or the tent liver--as something idyllic. The picture is as far as possible from the truth. Those into whose lives economics do not enter, or enter very little--that is to say, those who, like the Congo cannibal, or the Red Indian, or the Bedouin, do not cultivate, or divide their labor, or trade, or save, or look to the future, have shed little of the primitive passions of other animals of prey, the tigers and the wolves, who have no economics at all, and have no need to check an impulse or a hate. But industry, even of the more primitive kind, means that men must divide their labor, which means that they must put some sort of reliance upon one another; the thing of prey becomes a partner, and the attitude towards it changes. And as this life becomes more complex, as the daily needs and desires push men to trade and barter, that means building up a social organization, rules and codes and courts to enforce them; as the interdependence widens and deepens it necessarily means the cessation of certain hostilities. If the neighboring tribe wants to trade with you it must not kill you; if you want the services of the heretic you must not kill him, you must keep your obligation towards him, and mutual good faith is death to long-sustained hatreds.

"You cannot separate the moral from the social and economic development of a people. The great service of a complex social and industrial organization, which is built up by the desire of men for better material conditions, is not that it 'pays,' but that it makes a more interdependent human society, and that it leads men to recognize what is the best relationship among them. The fact of recognizing that some act of aggression is causing stocks to fall is not important because it may save Oppenheim's or Solomon's money but because it is a demonstration that we are dependent upon some community on the other side of the world, that their damage is our damage, and that we have an interest in preventing it. It teaches us, as only some such simple and mechanical means can teach, the lesson of human fellowship.

"It is by such means as this that Western Europe has in some measure, within its respective political frontiers, learned that lesson. Each nation has learned, within its own confines at least, that wealth is made by work, not robbery; that, indeed, general robbery is fatal to prosperity; that government consists not merely in having the power of the sword but in organizing society--in 'knowing how,' which means the development of ideas; in maintaining courts; in making it possible to run railways, post-offices, and all the contrivances of a complex society.

"Now rulers did not create these things; it was the daily activities of the people, born of their desires and made possible by the circumstances in which they lived, by the trading and the mining and the shipping which they carried on, that made them. But the Balkans have been geographically outside the influence of European industrial and commercial life. The Turk has hardly felt it at all. He has learned none of the social and moral lessons which interdependence and improved communications have taught the Western European, and it is because he had not learned these lessons, because he is a soldier and a conqueror to an extent and completeness that other nations of Europe lost a generation or two since, that the Balkanese are fighting and that war is raging.

"Not merely in this larger sense, but in the more immediate, narrower sense, are the fundamental causes of this war economic.

"This war arises, as the past wars against the Turkish conqueror have arisen, from the desire of the Christian peoples on whom he lives to shake off this burden. "To live upon their subjects is the Turks' only means of livelihood," says one authority. The Turk is an economic parasite and the healthy economic organism must end by rejecting him.

"The management of society, simple and primitive even as that of the Balkan mountains, needs some effort and work and capacity for administration; otherwise even rudimentary economic life cannot be carried on. The Turkish system, founded on the sword and nothing else ('the finest soldier in Europe'), cannot give that small modicum of energy or administrative capacity. The one thing he knows is brute force; but it is not by the strength of his muscles that an engineer runs a machine, but by knowing how. The Turk cannot build a road or make a bridge or administer a post-office or found a court of law. And these things are necessary. He will not let them be done by the Christian, who, because he did not belong to the conquering class, has had to work and has consequently come to possess whatever capacity for work and administration the country can show, because to do so would be to threaten the Turk's only trade. I the Turk granted the Christians equal political rights they would inevitably 'run the country.' And yet the Turk himself cannot do it; and he will not let others do it, because to do so would be to threaten his supremacy.

"The more the use of force fails, the more, of course, does he resort to it and that is why many of us who do not believe in force and desire to see it disappear from the relationship not merely of religious but of political groups, might conceivably welcome this war of the Balkan Christians, in so far as it is an attempt to resist the use of force in those relationships. Of course, I do not try to estimate the 'balance of criminality.' Right is not all on one side--it never is. But the broad issue is clear and plain. And only those concerned with the name rather than the thing, with nominal and verbal consistency rather than realities, will see anything paradoxical or contradictory in Pacifist approval of Christian resistance to the use of Turkish force.

"One fact stands out incontrovertibly from the whole weary muddle. It is quite clear that the inability to act in concert arises from the fact that in the international sphere the European is still dominated by illusions which he has dropped when he deals with home politics. The political faith of the Turk, which he would never think of applying at home as among the individuals of his nation, he applies pure and unalloyed when he comes to deal with foreigners as nations. The economic conception--using the term in that wider sense which I have indicated earlier in this article--which guides his individual conduct is the antithesis of that which guides his national conduct.

"While the Christian does not believe in robbery inside the frontier, he does without; while within the State he realizes that it is better for each to observe the general code, so that civilized society can exist, than for each to disregard it, so that society goes to pieces; while within the State he realizes that government is a matter of administration, not the seizure of property; that one town does not add to its wealth by 'capturing' another, that indeed one community cannot 'own' another--while, I say, he believes all these things in his daily life at home, he disregards them all when he comes to the field of international relationship, *la haute politique*. To annex some province by a cynical breach of treaty obligation (Austria in Bosnia, Italy in Tripoli) is regarded as better politics than to act loyally with the community of nations to enforce their common interest in order and good government. In fact, we do not believe that there can be a community of nations, because, in fact, we do not believe that their interests are common, but rival; like the Turk, we believe that if you do not exercise force upon your 'rival' he will exercise it upon you; that nations live upon one another, not by co-operation with one another--and it is for this reason presumably that you must 'own' as much of your neighbors as possible. It is the Turkish conception from beginning to end.

"It is because these false beliefs prevent the nations of Christendom acting loyally the one to the other, because each is playing for its own hand, that the Turk, with hint of some sordid bribe, has been able to play off each against the other.

"This is the crux of the matter. When Europe can honestly act in common on behalf of common interests some solution can be found. And the capacity of Europe to act in harmony will not be found as long as the accepted doctrines of European statecraft remain unchanged, as long as they are dominated by existing illusions."

FOOTNOTES

[1] "The True Way of Life" (Headley Brothers, London), p. 29. I am aware that many modern pacifists, even of the English school, to which these remarks mainly apply, are more objective in their advocacy than Mr. Grubb, but in the eyes of the "average sensual man" pacificism is still deeply tainted with this self-sacrificing altruism (see Chapter III, Part III), notwithstanding the admirable work of the French pacifist school.

[2] The *Matin* newspaper recently made a series of revelations, in which it was shown that the master of a French cod-fishing vessel had, for some trivial insubordinations, disemboweled his cabin-boy alive, and put salt into the intestines, and then thrown the quivering body into the hold with the cod-fish. So inured were the crew to brutality that they did not effectively protest, and the incident was only brought to light months later by wine-shop chatter. The *Matin* quotes this as the sort of brutality that marks the Newfoundland cod-fishing industry in French ships.

Again, the German Socialist papers have recently been dealing with what they term "The Casualties of the Industrial Battlefield," showing that the losses from industrial accidents since 1871--the loss of life during peace, that is--have been enormously greater than the losses due to the Franco-Prussian War.

[3] "The Interest of America in International Conditions." New York: Harper & Brothers.

[4] That is to say, all this was to have taken place before 1911 (the book appeared some years ago). This has its counterpart in the English newspaper feuilleton which appeared some years ago entitled, "The German Invasion of 1910."

[5] See letter to the *Matin*, August 22, 1908.

[6] In this self-seeking world, it is not reasonable to assume the existence of an inverted altruism of this kind.

[7] This is not the only basis of comparison, of course. Everyone who knows Europe at all is aware of the high standard of comfort in all the small countries--Scandinavia, Holland, Belgium, Switzerland. Mulhall, in "Industries and Wealth of Nations" (p. 391), puts the small States of Europe with France and England at the top of the list, Germany *sixth*, and Russia, territorially and militarily the greatest of all, at the very end. Dr. Bertillon, the French statistician, has made an elaborate calculation of the relative wealth of the individuals of each country. The middle-aged German possesses (on the established average) nine thousand francs ($1800); the Hollander *sixteen thousand* ($3200). (See *Journal*, Paris, August 1, 1910).

[8] The figures given in the "Statesman's Year-Book" show that, propor-

tionately to population, Norway has nearly three times the carrying trade of England.

⁹ See citation, pp. 14-15.

¹⁰ Major Stewart Murray, "Future Peace of the Anglo-Saxons." London: Watts and Co.

¹¹ *L'Information*, August 22, 1909.

¹² Very many times greater, because the bullion reserve in the Bank of England is relatively small.

¹³ Hartley Withers, "The Meaning of Money." Smith, Elder and Co., London.

¹⁴ See pp. 75-76.

¹⁵ See note concerning French colonial policy, pp. 122-124.

¹⁶ Summarizing an article in the *Oriental Economic Review*, the San Francisco *Bulletin* says: "Japan at this moment seems to be finding out that 'conquered' Korea in every real sense belongs to the Koreans, and that all that Japan is getting out of her war is an additional burden of statesmanship and an additional expense of administration, and an increased percentage of international complication due to the extension of the Japanese frontier dangerously close to her Continental rivals, China and Russia. Japan as 'owner' of Korea is in a worse position economically and politically than she was when she was compelled to treat with Korea as an independent nation." The *Oriental Economic Review* notes that "the Japanese hope to ameliorate the Korean situation through the general intermarriage of the two peoples; but this means a racial advance, and through it closer social and economic relations than were possible before annexation, and would probably have been easier of accomplishment had not the destruction of Korean independence embittered the people."

¹⁷ Spanish Four per Cents. were 42-1/2 during the war, and just prior to the Moroccan trouble, in 1911, had a free market at 90 per cent.

F. C. Penfold writes in the December (1910) *North American Review* as follows: "The new Spain, whose motive force springs not from the windmills of dreamy fiction, but from honest toil, is materially better off this year than it has been for generations. Since the war Spanish bonds have practically doubled in value, and exchange with foreign money markets has improved in corresponding ratio. Spanish seaports on the Atlantic and Mediterranean teem with shipping. Indeed, the nature of the people seems changing from a *dolce far niente* indolence to enterprising thrift."

¹⁸ London *Daily Mail*, December 15, 1910.

¹⁹ "Traité de Science des Finances," vol. ii., p. 682.

²⁰ "Die Wirtschafts Finanz und Sozialreform im Deutschen Reich." Leipzig, 1882.

²¹ "La Crise Économique," *Revue des Deux Mondes*, March 15, 1879.

²² Maurice Block, "La Crise Économique," *Revue des Deux Mondes*, March 15, 1879. See also "Les Conséquences Économiques de la Prochaine Guerre," Captaine Bernard Serrigny. Paris, 1909. The author says (p. 127): "It was evidently the disastrous financial position of Ger-

many, which had compelled Prussia at the outbreak of the war to borrow money at the unheard-of price of 11 per cent., that caused Bismarck to make the indemnity so large a one. He hoped thus to repair his country's financial situation. Events cruelly deceived him, however. A few months after the last payment of the indemnity the gold despatched by France had already returned to her territory, while Germany, poorer than ever, was at grips with a crisis which was to a large extent the direct result of her temporary wealth."

[23] "Das Deutsche Reich zur Zeit Bismarcks."

[24] The figures of German emigration are most suggestive in this connection. Although they show great fluctuation, indicating their reaction to many factors, they always appear to rise after the wars. Thus, after the wars of the Duchies they doubled, for the five years preceding the campaigns of 1865 they averaged 41,000, and after those campaigns rose suddenly to over 100,000. They had fallen to 70,000 in 1869, and then rose to 154,000 in 1872, and what is more remarkable still, the emigration did not come from the conquered provinces, from Schleswig-Holstein, Alsace or Lorraine, but from Prussia! While not for a moment claiming that the effect of the wars is the sole factor in this fluctuation, the fact of emigration as bearing on the general claim made for successful war demands the most careful examination. See particularly, "L'Émigration Allemande," *Revue des Deux Mondes*, January, 1874.

[25] The Montreal *Presse*, March 27, 1909.

[26] Speech, House of Commons, August 26, 1909. The New York papers of November 16, 1909, report the following from Sir Wilfrid Laurier in the Dominion Parliament during the debate on the Canadian Navy: "If now we have to organize a naval force, it is because we are growing as a nation--it is the penalty of being a nation. I know of no nation having a sea-coast of its own which has no navy, except Norway, but Norway will never tempt the invader. Canada has its coal-mines, its gold-mines, its wheat-fields, and its vast wealth may offer a temptation to the invader."

[27] The recent tariff negotiations between Canada and the United States were carried on directly between Ottawa and Washington, without the intervention of London. Canada regularly conducts her tariff negotiations, even with other members of the British Empire. South Africa takes a like attitude. The *Volkstein* of July 10, 1911, says: "The Union constitution is in full accord with the principle that neutrality is permissible in the case of a war in which England and other independent States of the Empire are involved.... England, as well as South Africa, would best be served by South Africa's neutrality" (quoted in *Times*, July 11, 1911). Note the phrase "independent States of the Empire."

[28] *Times*, November 7, 1911.

[29] The London *World*, an Imperialist organ, puts it thus: "The electoral process of reversing the results of the war is completed in South Africa. By the result of last week's contests Mr. Merriman has secured a strong working majority in both Houses. The triumph of the Bond at Cape Town

is no less sweeping than was that of Het Volk at Pretoria. The three territories upon which the future of the subcontinent depends are linked together under Boer supremacy ... the future federated or uniformed system will be raised upon a Dutch basis. If this was what we wanted, we might have bought it cheaper than with two hundred and fifty millions of money and twenty thousand lives."

[30] A Bill has been introduced into the Indian Legislative Council enabling the Government to prohibit emigration to any country where the treatment accorded to British Indian subjects was not such as met with the approval of the Governor-General. "As just treatment for free Indians has not been secured," says the London *Times*, "prohibition will undoubtedly be applied against Natal unless the position of free Indians there is ameliorated."

[31] Britain's total overseas trade for 1908 was $5,245,000,000, of which $3,920,000,000 was with foreigners, and $1,325,000,000 with her own possessions. And while it is true that with some of her Colonies Britain has as much as 52 per cent. of their trade--*e.g.*, Australia--it also happens that some absolutely foreign countries do a greater percentage even of their trade with Britain than do her Colonies. Britain possesses 38 per cent. of Argentina's foreign trade, but only 36 per cent. of Canada's, although Canada has recently given her a considerable preference.

[32] West Africa and Madagascar.

[33] It is a little encouraging, perhaps, for those of us who are doing what we may towards the dissemination of saner ideas, that an early edition of this book seems to have played some part in bringing about the change in French colonial policy here indicated. The French Colonial Ministry, for the purpose of emphasizing the point of view mentioned in *Le Temps* article, on two or three occasions called pointed attention to the first French edition of this book. In the official report of the Colonial Budget for 1911, a large part of this chapter is reprinted. In the Senate (see *Journal Officiel de la République Française*, July 2, 1911) the Rapporteur again quoted from this book at length, and devoted a great part of his speech towards emphasizing the thesis here set out.

[34] A financier to whom I showed the proofs of this chapter notes here: "If such a tax were imposed the output would be *nil.*"

[35] A correspondent sent me some interesting and significant details of the rapid strides made by Germany in Egypt. It had already been stated that a German newspaper would appear in October, 1910, and that the official notices of the mixed courts have been transferred from the local French newspapers to the German *Egyptischer Nachrichten*. During the years 1897-1907, German residents in Egypt increased by 44 per cent, while British residents increased by only 5 per cent. Germany's share of the Egyptian imports during the period 1900-1904 was $3,443,880, but by 1909 this figure reached $5,786,355. The latest German undertaking in Egypt was the foundation of the Egyptische Hypotheken Bank, in which all the principal joint-stock banks of Germany were interested. Its

capital was to be $2,500,000 and the six directors included three Germans, one Austrian, and two Italians.

Writing of "Home Sickness among the Emigrants" (the *London World*, July 19, 1910), Mr. F.. Aflalo said:

"The Germans are, of all nations, the least troubled with this weakness. Though far more warmly attached to the hearth than their neighbors across the Rhine, they feel exile less. Their one idea is to evade conscription, and this offers to all continental nations a compensation for exile, which to the Englishman means nothing. I remember a colony of German fishermen on Lake Tahoe, the loveliest water in California, where the pines of the Sierra Nevada must have vividly recalled their native Harz. Yet they rejoiced in the freedom of their adopted country, and never knew a moment's regret for the Fatherland."

[36] According to a recent estimate, the Germans in Brazil now number some four hundred thousand, the great majority being settled in the southern states of Rio Grande do Sul, Paraná, and Santa Catharina, while a small number are found in Sao Paulo and Espirito Santo in the north. This population is, for the most part, the result of natural increase, for of late years emigration thither has greatly declined.

In Near Asia, too, German colonization is by no means of recent origin. There are in Transcaucasia agricultural settlements established by Würtemberg farmers, whose descendants in the third generation live in their own villages and still speak their native language. In Palestine, there are the German Templar Colonies on the coast, which have prospered so well as to excite the resentment of the natives.

[37] London *Morning Post*, February 1, 1912.

[38] *North American Review*, March, 1912. See also citation, p. 15.

[39] April, 1912.

[40] "Germany and the Next War," by Gen. Friedrich von Bernhardi. London: Edwin Arnold, 1912.

[41] See, notably, the article from Admiral Mahan, "The Place of Power in International Relations," in the *North American Review* for January, 1912; and such books of Professor Wilkinson's as "The Great Alternative," "Britain at Bay," "War and Policy."

[42] "The Valor of Ignorance." Harpers.

[43] For an expression of these views in a more definite form, see Ratzenhofer's "Die Sociologische Erkenntniss," pp. 233, 234. Leipzig: Brockhaus, 1898.

[44] Speech at Stationer's Hall, London, June 6, 1910.

[45] "The Strenuous Life." Century Co.

[46] *McClure's Magazine*, August, 1910.

[47] Thomas Hughes, in his preface to the first English edition of "The Bigelow Papers," refers to the opponents of the Crimean War as a "vain and mischievous clique, who amongst us have raised the cry of peace." See also Mr. J. A. Hobson's "Psychology of Jingoism," p. 52. London: Grant Richards.

[48] *North American Review*, March, 1912.

[49] "The Interest of America in International Conditions." New York: Harper & Brothers.

[50] It is related by Critchfield, in his work on the South American Republics, that during all the welter of blood and disorder which for a century or more marked the history of those countries, the Roman Catholic priesthood on the whole maintained a high standard of life and character, and continued, against all discouragement, to preach consistently the beauties of peace and order. However much one may be touched by such a spectacle, and pay the tribute of one's admiration to these good men, one cannot but feel that the preaching of these high ideals did not have any very immediate effect on the social progress of South America. What has effected this change? It is that those countries have been brought into the economic current of the world; the bank and factory and railroad have introduced factors and motives of a quite different order from those urged by the priest, and are slowly winning those countries from military adventure to honest work, a thing which the preaching of high ideals failed to do.

[51] "To-day and To-morrow," p. 63. John Murray.

[52] Since the publication of the first edition of this book there has appeared in France an admirable work by M.J. Novikow, "Le Darwinisme Social" (Felix Alcan, Paris), in which this application of the Darwinian theory to sociology is discussed with great ability, and at great length and in full detail, and the biological presentation of the case, as just outlined, has been inspired in no small part by M. Novikow's work. M. Novikow has established in biological terms what, previous to the publication of his book, I attempted to establish in economic terms.

[53] Co-operation does not exclude competition. If a rival beats me in business, it is because he furnishes more efficient co-operation than I do; if a thief steals from me, he is not co-operating at all, and if he steals much will prevent my co-operation. The organism (society) has every interest in encouraging the competitor and suppressing the parasite.

[54] Without going to the somewhat obscure analogies of biological science, it is evident from the simple facts of the world that, if at any stage of human development warfare ever did make for the survival of the fit, we have long since passed out of that stage. When we conquer a nation in these days, we do not exterminate it: we leave it where it was. When we "overcome" the servile races, far from eliminating them, we give them added chances of life by introducing order, etc., so that the lower human quality tends to be perpetuated by conquest by the higher. If ever it happens that the Asiatic races challenge the white in the industrial or military field, it will be in large part thanks to the work of race conservation, which has been the result of England's conquest in India, Egypt, and Asia generally, and her action in China when she imposed commercial contact on the Chinese by virtue of military power. War between people of roughly equal development makes also for the survival of the unfit, since

we no longer exterminate and massacre a conquered race, but only their best elements (those carrying on the war), and because the conqueror uses up *his* best elements in the process, so that the less fit of both sides are left to perpetuate the species. Nor do the facts of the modern world lend any support to the theory that preparation for war under modern conditions tends to preserve virility, since those conditions involve an artificial barrack life, a highly mechanical training favorable to the destruction of initiative, and a mechanical uniformity and centralization tending to crush individuality, and to hasten the drift towards a centralized bureaucracy, already too great.

[55] One might doubt, indeed, whether the British patriot has really the feeling against the German that he has against his own countrymen of contrary views. Mr. Leo Maxse, in the *National Review* for February, 1911, indulges in the following expressions, applied, not to Germans, but to English statesmen elected by a majority of the English people: Mr. Lloyd George is a "fervid Celt animated by passionate hatred of all things English"; Mr. Churchill is simply a "Tammany Hall politician, without, however, a Tammany man's patriotism." Mr. Harcourt belongs to "that particular type of society demagogue who slangs Peers in public and fawns upon them in private." Mr. Leo Maxse suggests that some of the Ministers should be impeached and hanged. Mr. McKenna is Lord Fisher's "poll-parrot," and the House of Commons is the "poisonous Parliament of infamous memory," in which Ministers were supported by a vast *posse comitatus* of German jackals.

[56] Speech at Stationers' Hall, London, June 6, 1910.

[57] I have in mind here the ridiculous furore that was made by the British Jingo Press over some French cartoons that appeared at the outbreak of the Boer War. It will be remembered that at that time France was the "enemy," and Germany was, on the strength of a speech by Mr. Chamberlain, a quasi-ally. Britain was at that time as warlike towards France as she is now towards Germany. And this is only ten years ago!

[58] In his "History of the Rise and Influence of the Spirit of Rationalism in Europe," Lecky says: "It was no political anxiety about the balance of power, but an intense religious enthusiasm that impelled the inhabitants of Christendom towards the site which was at once the cradle and the symbol of their faith. All interests were then absorbed, all classes were governed, all passions subdued or colored, by religious fervor. National animosities that had raged for centuries were pacified by its power. The intrigues of statesmen and the jealousies of kings disappeared beneath its influence. Nearly two million lives are said to have been sacrificed in the cause. Neglected governments, exhausted finances, depopulated countries, were cheerfully accepted as the price of success. No wars the world had ever before seen were so popular as these, which were at the same time the most disastrous and the most unselfish."

[59] "Be assured," writes St. Augustine, "and doubt not that not only men who have obtained the use of their reason, but also little children

who have begun to live in their mother's womb and there died, or who, having been just born, have passed away from the world without the Sacrament of Holy Baptism, must be punished by the eternal torture of undying fire." To make the doctrine clearer, he illustrates it by the case of a mother who has two children. Each of these is but a lump of perdition. Neither has ever performed a moral or immoral act. The mother overlies one, and it perishes unbaptized. It goes to eternal torment. The other is baptized and saved.

[60] This appears sufficiently from the seasons in which, for instance, *autos da fé* in Spain took place. In the Gallery of Madrid there is a painting by Francisco Rizzi representing the execution, or rather the procession to the stake, of a number of heretics during the fêtes that followed the marriage of Charles II, and before the King, his bride, and the Court and clergy of Madrid. The great square was arranged like a theatre, and thronged with ladies in Court dress. The King sat on an elevated platform, surrounded by the chief members of the aristocracy.

Limborch, in his "History of the Inquisition," relates that among the victims of one *auto da fé* was a girl of sixteen, whose singular beauty struck all who saw her with admiration. As she passed to the stake she cried to the Queen: "Great Queen, is not your presence able to bring me some comfort under my misery? Consider my youth, and that I am condemned for a religion which I have sucked in with my mother's milk."

[61] *Spectator*, December 31, 1910.

[62] See quotations, pp. 161-162, from Homer Lea's book, "The Valor of Ignorance."

[63] Thus Captain d'Arbeux ("L'Officier Contemporaine," Grasset, Paris, 1911) laments "la disparition progressive de l'idéal de revanche," a military deterioration which is, he declares, working the country's ruin. The general truth of all this is not affected by the fact that 1911, owing to the Moroccan conflict and other matters, saw a revival of Chauvinism, which is already spending itself. The *Matin*, December, 1911, remarks: "The number of candidates at St. Cyr and St. Maixent is decreasing to a terrifying degree. It is hardly a fourth of what it was a few years ago.... The profession of arms has no longer the attraction that it had."

[64] "Germany and England," p. 19.

[65] See the first chapter of Mr. Harbutt Dawson's admirable work, "The Evolution of Modern Germany." T. Fisher Unwin, London.

[66] I have excluded the "operations" with the Allies in China. But they only lasted a few weeks. And were they war? This illustration appears in M. Novikow's "Le Darwinisme Social."

[67] The most recent opinion on evolution would go to show that environment plays an even larger rôle in the formation of character than selection (see Prince Kropotkin's article, *Nineteenth Century*, July, 1910, in which he shows that experiment reveals the direct action of surroundings as the main factor of evolution). How immensely, therefore, must our industrial environment modify the pugnacious impulse of our nature!

[68] See citations, pp. 161-166, notably Mr. Roosevelt's dictum: "In this world the nation that is trained to a career of unwarlike and isolated ease is bound to go down in the end before other nations which have not lost the manly and adventurous qualities." This view is even emphasized in the speech which Mr. Roosevelt recently delivered at the University of Berlin (see London *Times*, May 13, 1910). "The Roman civilization," declared Mr. Roosevelt--perhaps, as the *Times* remarks, to the surprise of those who have been taught to believe that *latifundia perditere Romam-*-"went down primarily because the Roman citizen would not fight, because Rome had lost the fighting edge." (See footnote, p. 237.)

[69] "The Valor of Ignorance." Harpers.

[70] See M. Messimy's Report on the War Budget for 1908 (annexe 3, p. 474). The importance of these figures is not generally realized. Astonishing as the assertion may sound, conscription in Germany is not universal, while it is in France. In the latter country every man of every class actually goes through the barracks, and is subjected to the real discipline of military training; the whole training of the nation is purely military. This is not the case in Germany. Very nearly half of the young men of the country are not soldiers. Another important point is that the part of the German nation which makes up the country's intellectual life escapes the barracks. To all practical purposes very nearly all young men of the better class enter the army as one year volunteers, by which they escape more than a few weeks of barracks, and even then escape its worst features. It cannot be too often pointed out that intellectual Germany has never been subjected to real barrack influence. As one critic says: "The German system does not put this class through the mill," and is deliberately designed to save them from the grind of the mill. France's military activities since 1870 have, of course, been much greater than those of Germany--Tonkin, Madagascar, Algeria, Morocco. As against these, Germany has had only the Hereros campaign. The percentages of population given above, in the text, require modification as the Army Laws are modified, but the relative positions in Germany and France remain about the same.

[71] *Vox de la Nación*, Caracas, April 22, 1897.

[72] Even Mr. Roosevelt calls South American history mean and bloody. It is noteworthy that, in his article published in the *Bachelor of Arts* for March, 1896, Mr. Roosevelt, who lectured Englishmen so vigorously on their duty at all costs not to be guided by sentimentalism in the government of Egypt, should write thus at the time of Mr. Cleveland's Venezuelan message to England: "Mean and bloody though the history of the South American republics has been, it is distinctly in the interest of civilization that ... they should be left to develop along their own lines.... Under the best of circumstances, a colony is in a false position; but if a colony is a region where the colonizing race has to do its work by means of other and inferior races, the condition is much worse. There is no chance for any tropical colony owned by a Northern race."

[73] June 2, 1910.

[74] See an article by Mr. Vernon Kellogg in the *Atlantic Monthly*, July, 1913. Seeley says: "The Roman Empire perished for want of men." One historian of Greece, discussing the end of the Peloponnesian wars, said: "Only cowards remain, and from their broods came the new generations."

Three million men--the élite of Europe--perished in the Napoleonic wars. It is said that after those wars the height standard of the French adult population fell abruptly 1 inch. However that may be, it is quite certain that the physical fitness of the French people was immensely worsened by the drain of the Napoleonic wars, since, as the result of a century of militarism, France is compelled every few years to reduce the standard of physical fitness in order to keep up her military strength, so that now even three-feet dwarfs are impressed.

[75] I think one may say fairly that it *was* Sydney Smith's wit rather than Bacon's or Bentham's wisdom which killed this curious illusion.

[76] See the distinction established at the beginning of the next chapter.

[77] M. Pierre Loti, who happened to be at Madrid when the troops were leaving to fight the Americans, wrote: "They are, indeed, still the solid and splendid Spanish troops, heroic in every epoch; one needs only to look at them to divine the woe that awaits the American shopkeepers when brought face to face with such soldiers." He prophesied *des surprises sanglantes*. M. Loti is a member of the French Academy.

[78] See also letter quoted, pp. 230-231.

[79] "Patriotism and Empire." Grant Richards.

[80] "For permanent work the soldier is worse than useless; his whole training tends to make him a weakling. He has the easiest of lives; he has no freedom and no responsibility. He is, politically and socially, a child, with rations instead of rights--treated like a child, punished like a child, dressed prettily and washed and combed like a child, excused for outbreaks of naughtiness like a child, forbidden to marry like a child, and called "Tommy" like a child. He has no real work to keep him from going mad except housemaid's work" ("John Bull's Other Island"). All those familiar with the large body of French literature, dealing with the evils of barrack-life, know how strongly that criticism confirms Mr. Bernard Shaw's generalization.

[81] September 11, 1899.

[82] Things must have reached a pretty pass in England when the owner of the *Daily Mail* and the patron of Mr. Blatchford can devote a column and a half over his own signature to reproaching in vigorous terms the hysteria and sensationalism, of his own readers.

[83] The *Berliner Tageblatt* of March 14, 1911, says: "One must admire the consistent fidelity and patriotism of the English race, as compared with the uncertain and erratic methods of the German people, their mistrust, and suspicion. In spite of numerous wars, bloodshed, and disaster, England always emerges smoothly and easily from her military crises and settles down to new conditions and surroundings in her usual cool

and deliberate manner.... Nor can one refrain from paying one's tribute
to the sound qualities and character of the English aristocracy, which
is always open to the ambitious and worthy of other classes, and thus
slowly but surely widens the sphere of the middle classes by whom they
are in consequence honored and respected--a state of affairs practically
unknown in Germany, but which would be to our immense advantage."

[84] "Der Kaiser und die Zukunft des Deutschen Volkes."

[85] See also the confirmatory verdict of Captain March Phillips, quoted
on p. 291.

86 "My Life in the Army," p. 119.

[87] I do not think this last generalization does any injustice to the essay,
"Latitude and Longitude among Reformers" ("Strenuous Life," pp. 41-61.
The Century Company).

[88] See for further illustration of the difference and its bearing in practical politics Chapter VIII, Part I, "The Fight for the Place in the Sun."

[89] See Chapter VII, Part I.

[90] Aristotle did, however, have a flash of the truth. He said: "If the ham-
mer and the shuttle could move themselves, slavery would be unnecessary."

[91] "Facts and Comments," p. 112.

[92] Buckle ("History of Civilization") points out that Philip II., who ruled
half the world and drew tribute from the whole of South America, was
so poor that he could not pay his personal servants or meet the daily
expenses of the Court!

[93] I mean by credit all the mechanism of exchange which replaces the
actual use or metal, or notes representing it.

[94] Lecky ("Rationalism in Europe," p. 76) says: "Protestantism could
not possibly have existed without a general diffusion of the Bible, and
that diffusion was impossible until after the two inventions of paper and
printing.... Before those inventions, pictures and material images were
the chief means of religious instruction." And thus religious belief became necessarily material, crude, anthropomorphic.

[95] "Battles are no longer the spectacular heroics of the past. The army
of to-day and to-morrow is a somber gigantic machine devoid of melo-
dramatic heroics ... a machine that it requires years to form in separate
parts, years to assemble them together, and other years to make them
work smoothly and irresistibly" (Homer Lea in "The Valor of Ignorance,"
p. 49).

[96] General von Bernhardi, in his work on cavalry, deals with this very
question of the bad influence on tactics of the "pomp of war," which he
admits must disappear, adding very wisely: "The spirit of tradition consists not in the retention of antiquated forms, but in acting in that spirit
which in the past led to such glorious success." The plea for the retention
of the soldier because of his "spirit" could not be more neatly disposed
of. See p. 111 of the English edition of Bernhardi's work (Hugh Rees,
London).

[97] See quotations, pp. 161-166.

[98] The following letter to the *Manchester Guardian*, which appeared at the time of the Boer War, is worth reproduction in this connection:

"SIR,--I see that 'The Church's Duty in regard to War' is to be discussed at the Church Congress. This is right. For a year the heads of our Church have been telling us what war is and does--that it is a school of character; that it sobers men, cleans them, strengthens them, knits their hearts; makes them brave, patient, humble, tender, prone to self-sacrifice. Watered by 'war's red rain,' one Bishop tells us, virtue grows; a cannonade, he points out, is an 'oratorio'--almost a form of worship. True; and to the Church men look for help to save their souls from starving for lack of this good school, this kindly rain, this sacred music. Congresses are apt to lose themselves in wastes of words. This one must not, surely cannot, so straight is the way to the goal. It has simply to draft and submit a new Collect for war in our time, and to call for the reverent but firm emendation, in the spirit of the best modern thought, of those passages in Bible and Prayer-Book by which even the truest of Christians and the best of men have at times been blinded to the duty of seeking war and ensuing it. Still, man's moral nature cannot, I admit, live by war alone; nor do I say with some that peace is wholly bad. Even amid the horrors of peace you will find little shoots of character fed by the gentle and timely rains of plague and famine, tempest and fire; simple lessons of patience and courage conned in the schools of typhus, gout, and stone; not oratorios, perhaps, but homely anthems and rude hymns played on knife and probe in the long winter nights. Far from me to 'sin our mercies,' or to call mere twilight dark. Yet dark it may become; for remember that even these poor makeshift schools of character, these second-bests, these halting substitutes for war--remember that the efficiency of every one of them, be it hunger, accident, ignorance, sickness, or pain, is menaced by the intolerable strain of its struggles with secular doctors, plumbers, inventors, schoolmasters, and policemen. Every year thousands who would once have been braced and steeled by manly tussles with small-pox or diphtheria are robbed of that blessing by the great changes made in our drains. Every year thousands of women and children must go their way bereft of the rich spiritual experience of the widow and the orphan."

[99] Captain March Phillips, "With Remington." Methuen. See pp. 259-60 for Mr. Blatchford's confirmation of this verdict.

[100] And here as to the officers--again not from me but from a very Imperialist and militarist quarter--the London *Spectator* (November 25, 1911), says: "Soldiers might be supposed to be free from pettiness because they are men of action. But we all know that there is no profession in which the leaders are more depreciated by one another than in the profession of arms."

[101] Professor William James says: "Greek history is a panorama of war for war's sake ... of the utter ruin of a civilization which in intellectual respects was perhaps the highest the earth has ever seen. The wars were

purely piratical. Pride, gold, women, slaves, excitement were their only motives."--*McClure's Magazine*, August, 1910.

[102] "Britain at Bay." Constable and Co.

[101] See quotation from Sir C. P. Lucas, p. 111-12.

[104] See details on this matter given in Chapter VII, Part I.

[105] London *Morning Post*, April 21, 1910. I pass over the fact that to cite all this as a reason for armaments is absurd. Does the *Morning Post* really suggest that the Germans are going to attack England because they don't like the English taste in art, or music, or cooking? The notion that preferences of this sort need the protection of *Dreadnoughts* is surely to bring the whole thing within the domain of the grotesque.

[106] I refer to the remarkable speech in which Mr. Chamberlain notified France that she must "mend her manners or take the consequences" (see London daily papers between November 28 and December 5, 1899).

[107] Not that a very great period separates us from such methods. Froude quotes Maltby's Report to Government as follows: "I burned all their corn and houses, and committed to the sword all that could be found. In like manner I assailed a castle. When the garrison surrendered, I put them to the misericordia of my soldiers. They were all slain. Thence I went on, sparing none which came in my way, which cruelty did so amaze their fellows that they could not tell where to bestow themselves." Of the commander of the English forces at Munster we read: "He diverted his forces into East Clanwilliam, and harassed the country; killed all mankind that were found therein ... not leaving behind us man or beast, corn or cattle ... sparing none of what quality, age, or sex soever. Beside many burned to death, we killed man, woman, child, horse, or beast or whatever we could find."

[108] In "The Evolution of Modern Germany" (Fisher Unwin, London) the same author says: "Germany implies not one people, but many peoples ... of different culture, different political and social institutions ... diversity of intellectual and economic life.... When the average Englishman speaks of Germany he really means Prussia, and consciously or not he ignores the fact that in but few things can Prussia be regarded as typical of the whole Empire."

[109] "International Law." John Murray, London.

[110] Lord Sanderson, dealing with the development of international intercourse in an address to the Royal Society of Arts (November 15, 1911), said: "The most notable feature of recent international intercourse, he thought, was the great increase in international exhibitions, associations, and conferences of every description and on every conceivable subject. When he first joined the Foreign Office, rather more than fifty years ago, conferences were confined almost entirely to formal diplomatic meetings to settle some urgent territorial or political question in which several States were interested. But as time had passed, not only were the number and frequency of political conferences increased, but a host of meetings of persons more or less official, termed indiscriminately confer-

ences and congresses, had come into being."

[111] January 8, 1910.

[112] March 10, 1910.

[113] "The German Government is straining every nerve, with the zealous support of its people, to get ready for a fight with this country" (*Morning Post*, March 1, 1912). "The unsatiated will of the armed State will, when an opportunity offers, attack most likely its most satiated neighbors without scruple, and despoil them without ruth" (Dr. Dillon, *Contemporary Review*, October, 1911).

[114] I have shown in a former chapter (Chapter VI., Part II) how these international hatreds are not the cause of conflict, but the outcome of conflicts or presumed conflicts of policy. If difference of national psychology--national "incompatibility of temper"--were the cause, how can we explain the fact that ten years since the English were still "hating all Frenchmen like the devil," and talking of alliance with the Germans? If diplomatic shuffling had pushed England into alliance with the Germans against the French, it would never have occurred to the people that they had to "detest the Germans."

[115] The German Navy Law in its preamble might have filched this from the British Navy League catechism.

[116] In an article published in 1897 (January 16) the London *Spectator* pointed out the hopeless position Germany would occupy if England cared to threaten her. The organ, which is now apt to resent the increased German Navy as implying aggression upon England, then wrote as follows: "Germany has a mercantile marine of vast proportions. The German flag is everywhere. But on the declaration of war the whole of Germany's trading ships would be at our mercy. Throughout the seas of the world our cruisers would seize and confiscate German ships. Within the first week of the declaration of war Germany would have suffered a loss of many million pounds by the capture of her ships. Nor is that all. Our Colonies are dotted with German trading-houses, who, in spite of a keen competition, do a great deal of business.... We should not, of course, want to treat them harshly; but war must mean for them the selling of their businesses for what they would fetch and going home to Germany. In this way Germany would lose a hold upon the trade of the world which it has taken her many years of toil to create.... Again, think of the effect upon Germany's trade of the closing of all her ports. Hamburg is one of the greatest ports of the world. What would be its condition if practically not a single ship could leave or enter it? Blockades are no doubt very difficult things to maintain strictly, but Hamburg is so placed that the operation would be comparatively easy. In truth the blockade of all the German ports on the Baltic or the North Sea would present little difficulty.... Consider the effect on Germany if her flag were swept from the high seas and her ports blockaded. She might not miss her colonies, for they are only a burden, but the loss of her sea-borne trade would be an equivalent to an immediate fine of at least a hundred million sterling.

In plain words, a war with Germany, even when conducted by her with the utmost wisdom and prudence, must mean for her a direct loss of a terribly heavy kind, and for us virtually no loss at all." This article is full of the fallacies which I have endeavored to expose in this book, but it logically develops the notions which are prevalent in both England and Germany; and yet Germans have to listen to an English Minister of Marine describing their Navy as a luxury!

[117] Here is the real English belief in this matter: "Why should Germany attack Britain? Because Germany and Britain are commercial and political rivals; because Germany covets the trade, the Colonies, and the Empire which Britain now possesses.... As to arbitration, limitation of armament, it does not require a very great effort of the imagination to enable us to see that proposal with German eyes. Were I a German, I should say: 'These islanders are cool customers. They have fenced in all the best parts of the globe, they have bought or captured fortresses and ports in five continents, they have gained the lead in commerce, they have a virtual monopoly of the carrying trade of the world, they hold command of the seas, and now they propose that we shall all be brothers, and that nobody shall fight or steal anymore,'" (Robert Blatchford, "Germany and England," pp. 4-13).

[118] "Facts and Fallacies." An answer to "Compulsory Service," by Field-Marshal Earl Roberts, V. C., K. G.

[119] Discussing the first edition of this book, Sir Edward Grey said: "True as the statement in that book may be, it does not become an operative motive in the minds and conduct of nations until they are convinced of its truth and it has become a commonplace to them" (Argentine Centenary Banquet, May 20, 1910).

[120] Lecky, "History of the Progress of Rationalism in Europe."

[121] I do not desire in the least, of course, to create the impression that I regard the truths here elaborated as my "discovery," as though no one had worked in this field before. Properly speaking, there is no such thing as priority in ideas. The interdependence of peoples was proclaimed by philosophers three thousand years ago. The French school of pacifists--Passy, Follin, Yves Guyot, de Molinari, and Estournelles de Constant--have done splendid work in this field; but no one of them, so far as I know, has undertaken the work of testing in detail the politico-economic orthodoxy by the principle of the economic futility of military force; by bringing that principle to bear on the everyday problems of European statecraft. If there is such an one--presenting the precise notes of interrogation which I have attempted to present here--I am not aware of it. This does not prevent, I trust, the very highest appreciation of earlier and better work done in the cause of peace generally. The work of Jean de Bloch, among others, though covering different ground from this, possesses an erudition and bulk of statistical evidence to which this can make no claim. The work of J. Novikow, to my mind the greatest of all, has already been touched upon.

[122] "Turkey in Europe," pp. 88-9 and 91-2.

It is significant, by the way, that the "born soldier" has now been crushed by a non-military race whom he has always despised as having no military tradition. Capt. F. W. von Herbert ("Bye Paths in the Balkans") wrote (some years before the present war): "The Bulgars, as Christian subjects of Turkey exempt from military service, have tilled the ground under stagnant and enfeebling peace conditions, and the profession of arms is new to them."

"Stagnant and enfeebling peace conditions" is, in view of subsequent events, distinctly good.

[123] I dislike to weary the reader with such damnable iteration, but when a British Cabinet Minister is unable in this discussion to distinguish between the folly of a thing and its possibility, one *must* make the fundamental point clear.

[124] This Appendix was written before the Balkan States fell to fighting one another. It is scarcely necessary to point out that the events of the last few days (early summer 1913) lend significance to the argument in the text.

[125] See p. 390.

[126] *Review of Reviews*, November, 1912.

[127] In the *Daily Mail*, to whose Editor I am indebted for permission to reprint it.

www.ingramcontent.com/pod-product-compliance
Lightning Source LLC
LaVergne TN
LVHW021053280126
830619LV00003BA/67